The Green Republic

CLASSICS OF IRISH HISTORY
General Editor: Tom Garvin

Original publication dates of reprinted titles are given in brackets

The Green Republic

A Visit to South Tyrone

A. P. A. O'GARA

UNIVERSITY COLLEGE DUBLIN PRESS
Preas Choláiste Ollscoile Bhaile Átha Cliath

First published by T. Fisher Unwin, London, 1902
This edition first published by University College Dublin Press 2005
Introduction © Edward A. Hagan 2005

ISBN 1-904558-23-2
ISBN 1393-6883

University College Dublin Press
Newman House, 86 St Stephen's Green
Dublin 2, Ireland
www.ucdpress.ie

Cataloguing in Publication data available from the British Library

Text design of preliminary matter by Lyn Davies, Frome, Somerset, England
Preliminary matter typeset in Ireland in Ehrhardt
by Elaine Burberry, Bantry, Co. Cork
Printed on acid-free paper in Ireland by ColourBooks, Dublin

CONTENTS

Note on the Text

The text of *The Green Republic* is reprinted as a facsimile of the T. Fisher Unwin edition of 1902.

Mr Frank Watters, a local historian in the village of Poyntzpass, County Armagh, has been instrumental in the preparation of this edition. Not only is he responsible for locating and providing the cover photographs, but he has also been an extremely knowledgeable source of background information on the life of W. R. MacDermott and the village of Poyntzpass itself.

INTRODUCTION
Edward A. Hagan

The title of William Robert MacDermott's 1902 'novel', *The Green Republic*, suggests a state of the twentieth-century Ireland-to-come. 'Green' and 'Republic' became words synonymous with Irish Nationalism, yet MacDermott (1839–1918) was more specifically prophetic than the current association of the words with nationalism usually suggests. MacDermott envisions the ascendancy of the new force in agriculture – the 'strong farmers', the former tenant farmers who were gaining title to their land via the Land Purchase Acts of the late nineteenth and early twentieth centuries. These new 'greens' would dominate the national consciousness, force emigration upon the mass of farm labourers, exact social welfare benefits from the non-landed mass, demand protection in their markets from competition, and, in general, utilise progress in agricultural technology, not to maximise production in the interests of the commonweal, but to reduce the amount of exertion necessary to produce enough wealth for the new owner to survive. Shifting from tillage to cattle and sheep grazing was the surest route to that new life of ease.

MacDermott's title has developed a deep irony that it may have lacked in 1902, but MacDermott saw that, as long as irresponsible power remained in the hands of either the old landlords or the new owner/occupiers, they would represent their own interests in governmental bodies. The inevitable result would be violence:

> the fraud and deception of the Green Republic must find its necessary complement in the untempered violence of the Red; the mass must retort on the agrarian, not in the light of reason, but under a sense of injury and under imperious necessity artificially induced by criminal legislation (p. 222).

We know now that the 'strong farmers' won this battle in the Irish Republic, and the Ireland of the graziers that MacDermott feared has come to pass. The threat of the Red Republic (broadly emblematic of agitation by the impoverished and unlanded mass) played a significant role in the 1916 rising and, while 'Red Republic' may now sound a bit too much like the 'Communist Red Menace', agitation by the impoverished and unlanded has continued to this day, particularly in the North. MacDermott may have worried that Irish-American interest in Irish problems might lead to uninformed support of either the 'greens' or the 'reds', and thus he casts *The Green Republic* as a work of non-fiction written by an Irish-American doctor, A. P. A. O'Gara – the pseudonym under which he first published the 'novel' in 1902.

O'Gara writes as a newly licensed doctor, educated in St Louis, on a visit to his uncle, Atty O'Gara, a dispensary doctor in South Tyrone but also a Confederate veteran of the American Civil War; thus MacDermott's sub-title for the book, *A Visit to South Tyrone*, portends a travelogue. Hardly. Instead O'Gara discovers the validity of MacDermott's underlying polemical purpose: the reorganisation of Irish agriculture into an industry run by joint stock companies like those that ran the railroads in England and Ireland. His discovery arises from developing a very sophisticated and deep understanding of the 'facts' of life among rural Ulster Protestants at the turn of the century. During his visit O'Gara is offered the opportunity to substitute for the dispensary doctor in a neighbouring district. His uncle encourages the young O'Gara to take on the temporary job and to use his time to develop an understanding of the problems of rural life in South Tyrone through 'noting the actual facts in the field of observation systematically and drawing inevitable conclusions' (p. 21). The young O'Gara accepts, dispensing with the Irish–American tourist role since he has already 'done Killarney and the Giants' Causeway' (p. 98).

MacDermott's choice of authorial and narratorial guise reflects both respect for and concern about American objectivity regarding Irish problems – the poles perhaps of Irish and English perceptions of Irish–American interest in Ireland. MacDermott's Irish–American O'Gara is no Fenian, but a modern social scientist, and O'Gara frequently uses the terms of social science as they have developed in the nineteenth century.

O'Gara and his uncle as well as other sophisticated characters such as Dr Capel, Count M'Qhan, and James Crowe all speak much as their creator, MacDermott, does in nine scholarly articles in the *New Ireland Review* between July 1897 and October 1908 and in almost weekly pieces in the *All Ireland Review* between 17 January 1903 and 3 February 1906. The first was edited by Fr. Thomas A. Finlay, SJ, a major force in the co-operative movement in agriculture and the Vice-President of Horace Plunkett's Irish Agricultural Organisation Society (IAOS); the second was edited by Standish James O'Grady, the so-called 'Father of the Irish Literary Renaissance', who in 1903 seems to have discovered[1] MacDermott after reading *The Green Republic*. Thereafter O'Grady printed excerpts from *The Green Republic* as well as MacDermott's short (but often weighty) commentaries. Before it was published as a book, O'Grady serialised MacDermott's novel/sociological study of the descendants of Ulster handloom weavers. *Foughilotra: A*

Forbye Story appeared in the *All Ireland Review* under the pseudonym 'Eustace Gildea' from 5 March 1904 to 17 December 1904. MacDermott's writing carried the *All Ireland Review* during its later years of existence[2] as O'Grady ceased weekly publication in 1905 (apparently due to illness) and then published it intermittently until its final issue in January 1907.

MacDermott, a medical doctor with a BA and a medical degree from Trinity College, Dublin, contributed highly sophisticated, statistically fortified articles not just on land and agriculture but on an assortment of topics such as the structure of local government, poor rates, tuberculosis, cotton growing in India, peasant proprietorship, Bishop Berkeley, and hygiene. MacDermott's writing reveals a man much under the influence of prominent nineteenth and early twentieth century thinkers. He clearly is much influenced by Herbert Spencer (1820–1903),[3] the English sociologist and philosopher, who led the way in examining social phenomena from a scientific point of view. MacDermott's journal articles also reveal his familiarity with the work of other notable thinkers such as Immanuel Kant (1724–1804), Arthur Schopenhauer (1788–1860), Nassau William Senior (1790–1864), Thomas Carlyle (1795–1881), Auguste Comte (1798–1857), John Stuart Mill (1806–1873), Thomas Henry Huxley (1825–95), Wilhelm Wundt (1832–1920), and Friedrich Wilhelm Nietzsche (1844–1900).

MacDermott is decidedly different in intellectual approach from his Irish contemporaries – a difference that the style of the Preface and the Conclusion to *The Green Republic* reflects. The opening and close of the book challenge the first-time reader and contrast sharply with the lively, reader-friendly chapters which introduce various South Tyrone characters. MacDermott frankly confesses to subordinating literary quality to science in the opening paragraph of the book. In fact he (speaking as the young Dr O'Gara) is worried that 'story' will overwhelm his purpose:

'not to give mere sketches of Irish agrarian life, but to call attention to the necessity for the study of agrarian industry by the method of induction, the accumulation of concrete instances in the actual field of observation' (p. 1).

MacDermott's method derives from that of Auguste Comte, inventor of the word 'sociology' and founder of the school of 'positivism'. Comte contended that a proper understanding of society could arise only from systematic observation guided by theoretical principles, and that theories must in turn be modified by observation; this kind of theoretical-empirical investigation could then lead to clear policy imperatives. But MacDermott more specifically follows Spencer in focusing on the individual (thus, the character studies in *The Green Republic*) and on farming *as an industry*. Spencer believed that science and philosophy led to increased individualism and progress. Before Charles Darwin and Alfred Russel Wallace propounded their theories of natural selection, Spencer had argued for evolution as the passing on of acquired traits. He derived his views of evolution by studying societies but held that social evolution (implicitly progressive) resulted in increasing individuation. In his studies of successful evolution of individuals, Spencer originated the phrase, 'the survival of the fittest'. MacDermott, as a very close observer of the differences in individuals, delineates two classes of individuals in much the same way that Nietzsche had done, especially in *The Genealogy of Morals* (1887). Nietzsche distinguished between those under the control of 'slave ethics' and those who spontaneously create 'aristocratic valuations' out of their own free will:

> Slave ethics requires for its inception a sphere different from and hostile to its own. Physiologically speaking, it requires an outside stimulus in order to act at all; all its action is reaction. The opposite is true of aristocratic valuations: such values grow and act spontaneously,

seeking out their contraries only in order to affirm themselves even more gratefully and delightedly.[4]

MacDermott, as a medical doctor familiar with the experimental psychology of the German physiologist and psychologist Wilhelm Wundt, was quite at home with a physiological basis for this kind of distinction in consciousness. In like manner, MacDermott dismisses the political economy of John Stuart Mill and Nassau William Senior. Implementing the principles of political economy is impossible because 'it gives no principle to put in the place of the arbitrary judgments of interested motives, and is fitly relegated to the planet Saturn when it stands in their way.' The problem is that it treats of 'the conditions of industry abstract from the human agency' (p. 9). A similar problem existed with theories of agriculture that were formulated by abstract thinking, not based on actual observation.

In his essay, 'Theories of agriculture', he argues:

The most valuable theorising is done off-hand and as nature's gift. The first thing we all do entering on life is to theorise and best do it then . . . mental life begins with an intent look, not all around – that would only lead to confusion – but at one object, say, the candle. An infant of average intelligence looks at the candle ten minutes after birth, essays a percept of it, that is, thinks of it as an outside object, makes the first step to the theory of objective existence . . .

Coleridge, in his Essay on Method, defines theory as description of what is in contradistinction to Law, which is possible only through our mental power of realising at once what *is* and *is not*. The infant in his first stage, is a pure theorist, defining what is and nothing more, but when he comes to wish, in particular, to wish for the moon, to like this and dislike that, factors enter his mental life which sadly vitiate his original fine power of theorising.[5]

Confusion, then, and political economy are the results of idle dreaming on what *is not*. The slave, MacDermott continues, 'begins to mix up what *is* with what *is not*, and soon gets that he cannot distinguish between the two, particularly when he does not want to'. MacDermott's 'infant formed a correct theory of the sun, earth, and stars as specific objects, but afterwards, in taking them as gods, did not form a theory of them, but gave occasion for the formation of a theory of himself'.[6] MacDermott, an iconoclast in his personal traits, who enjoyed being attacked as pro-landlord by the tenant farmers and as pro-tenant by the landlords, lays heavy and constant emphasis on the value of individualism throughout *The Green Republic*. His position on individualism, however, is tricky: he sharply criticises the outdated individualistic method of farming that is embodied in the family farm. He argues in 'Gorilla agriculture' that 'The individualistic system' is 'embodied mendacity in passing itself for what it is not – a form of industry'.[7] Following Spencer then, he calls for the organisation of farming into an industry. Spencer distinguished between military societies, which ensured loyalty by force, and industrial societies, which he viewed as voluntary and spontaneous. MacDermott saw the individualism of the tenant farmer as not true individualism but a slavish allegiance to custom. Real individualism results from what MacDermott's Uncle Atty advocates: the capability of 'true adaptation to the varying circumstances of individual life' or the freedom of the individual to 'accommodate himself to the circumstances of his own life' (p. 99).

In the twenty-first century we do not usually associate a value on individualism with corporations, and we may find it hard to see how their nineteenth-century version, joint stock companies, could facilitate Uncle Atty's 'true adaptation'. But MacDermott placed all of his hope in their modern systems of management and machinery, their public accountability, and their capability of offering employment and advancement for the labouring poor. MacDermott seems to have rather naively believed that the joint stock company organises society by securing the voluntary co-operation of its stockholders in order to maximise production, unlike traditional Irish agrarian society – the result of conquest, held together by force, and thus beset with constant terrorism. The joint stock company would structure the Irish economy and supplant the family as the economic structure of society: 'The failure of agriculture, as an industry, cannot be understood without a reference to the nature and conditions of family labour, to the inefficiency of the family institution as an industrial organisation' (p. 224). MacDermott could see that the political solutions on offer did not challenge the structure of family labour and kept various segments of society in competition with one another for dominance and privilege, not mutual assistance.

On the individual level this contention meant that the world was so constituted as to preclude the young from coming of age in any kind of healthy fashion. More specifically, it meant that the child, born with its ability to theorise about what is, was forced by an abstract religious code (like Law, one of the many forms of what is not) into slavery. *The Green Republic* offers the chilling episode of the forced marriage of Lucy Crowe. MacDermott situates her as an abused wife, torn between the common-sense need to escape from her husband and allegiance to a strict Presbyterian view of marriage as enforced by the narrowly conceived financial interests of her parents. One brother is 'Father' Crowe, the local Presbyterian minister; the other is James Crowe, an agnostic, who has broken away from the family and who 'never went by *hearsay*,[8] but took great pains to get at facts, and with all his quickness was slow and deliberate in forming his judgments' (p. 80). James is the model of the evolved self-creating person who lives according to his own inner lights, his own will. He owes much to MacDermott's awareness of the idea of 'will' in nineteenth-century thought.[9] He and his brother quarrel over emancipating their sister from the brutal control of the husband forced upon her by her parents. 'Father' Crowe, though keenly aware of his compromised position, is stuck with the Christian message that Nietzsche abhorred[10] and that MacDermott renders futile in the face of James's contempt for it. 'Father' Crowe (the 'honorific' title may be MacDermott's way of suggesting that 'popery'[11] is not limited to Catholics) moans, 'What is wrong is that I find myself preaching the Gospel of Love, of patience, forbearance and charity' (p. 71). His complaint resonates with Nietzschean condemnation of the asceticism that dominates Western Christian consciousness. He comes to recognise the fallacy of 'general law' – a term that places such law in the same realm as 'abstract theology' (p. 80) or abstract theory.

MacDermott's ideal Nietzschean character seems to be the ironic and insightful Count M'Qhan, a farmer, who recognises exactly how he is being benefited by the Land Purchase laws and openly advocates laziness (p. 103). He does not share any concept of asceticism and is thus willing to sound abhorrent. He knows he is no different from the landlords whom he is replacing, but he has no sense of shame about his position. He knows the farmers lie to themselves and claim virtue by abnegation: 'they represent themselves as hard-working men carrying on an industry under very difficult conditions' (p. 103). M'Qhan knows that there are a few altruists who value work in itself and for its service to others. He speaks of them with Nietzschean cynicism: 'The chief use of these few men is to serve as a cloak under cover of which the class [of "strong farmers"] may claim to be industrious, crazily bent on making money for other people. It is a pity our exceptions [to the norm of despising work] could not have a colony all to themselves to work out an awful example in degradation and extinction of the race' (p. 108).

The Green Republic

M'Qhan subverts the Christian idea of virtue and is presented as superior to an Episcopalian clergyman because his 'opinions had the value of worked-out problems of native thought, never marred by taking initial assumption for more than it was worth' (p. 119). In short, M'Qhan is a social scientist, an excellent observer of facts in the 'actual field.' He is not given to sentimentalities or pieties about human beings; he 'takes human beings as he would ants or bees. There are a few – a very few philosophers of the stamp, men who get out of the human mental plane, have no mental fellowship with men' (p. 115). Uncle Atty commends M'Qhan to his nephew with the dire recognition that Spencer's state of force or military society is really in place in South Tyrone. The uncle says, 'we are disowned by both landlord and farmer, not so much because we object to their system, but because we object to the terrorism which both equally rely on to maintain their interest, as they conceive it. Form any independent judgment of your own, and you shall find both your enemy' (p. 117–18).

MacDermott, in his articles in the *New Ireland Review* and in the *All Ireland Review*, carefully explains how he sees the land issue as a distraction from the real issue – the failure to organise farming as an industry (a Spencerian goal). His argument is that the mass of the people are being kept in slavery to the special interests of either the landlords or the new owners of the land, the former tenant farmers. Because the Land Purchase Acts[12] only serve the strong farmers and further marginalise the unlanded farm labouring class, he argues that further concessions to the strong farmers only set the stage for a Red revolution. O'Grady, sensing perhaps that MacDermott was edging too far to the right, warns him that 'there is another danger than that of the "Red Terror". It is the danger of "the White", viz., of the menaced interests flinging themselves into the arms of a brutal despotism, which promises to defend them and enslave the rest.'[13] MacDermott, nonetheless, judges that the joint stock company idea (which M'Qhan endorses, p. 176) will transform society by actually solving the real problem of the disability of the mass of the people. With Nietzsche, MacDermott understands full well that virtue will be defined by the selfish values of the new, dominant class of landowners to the suffocation of the individual wills of the mass:

> Taking a man as a single individual, we find him endowed with will by means of which to regulate his action and conduct. In reality he is in part automaton, in part an expression of will. Taking him as a member of society, however, his personal will is in great part abolished; he is subjected to a concourse of wills, or the representatives of such concourse: kings, parliaments, law, custom, convention, public opinion, so on. Now this force exerted on him is not truly of the nature of will; it is a mechanical resultant operating as a force, will itself being a physiological fact in the individual alone,[14] the evolution of which in him, beyond question, makes man what he is. With will is bound up the higher intelligence of man and his sense of right and wrong, since what he must do as forced or as matter of necessity, he cannot think of as right or wrong. Thus to think his obedience to law right, he must think of it as voluntary.[15]

MacDermott goes on to show how his view of the will derives from his study of Spencer. He sets Spencer up as the alternative to the Hobbesian notion that the individual receives freedom as 'a gift or grant from the social power over him'. MacDermott argues:

> Herbert Spencer was a biologist, what Hobbes was not, and opposed biological fact to the mere speculative thought of the last. Will is a physiological property in the individual, a fact even of anatomical structure in him, and was evolved through ages with its concomitants of intelligence and ethical concept in meeting any way and every way

force, even the brute forces of physical nature. Like the Satan of Milton, and the Prometheus of Æschylus, it had pitted itself from the first against apparently irresistible power – if Satanic in its art and modes, so, of necessity, through the brute nature of what it found opposed to it. For who did better for the race, the man who looked at the sun to worship it as a god, or he who looked at it to press it into our service?[16]

In so moving toward a position of praise for the active man, and not Spencer's adaptive man, MacDermott appears to be closer to Nietzsche:

The democratic bias against anything that dominates or wishes to dominate, our modern *misarchism* (to coin a bad word for a bad thing) has gradually so sublimated and disguised itself that nowadays it can invade the strictest, most objective sciences without anyone's raising a word of protest. In fact it seems to me that this prejudice now dominates all of physiology and the other life sciences, to their detriment, naturally, since it has conjured away one of their most fundamental concepts, that of *activity*, and put in its place the concept of *adaptation* – a kind of second-rate activity, mere reactivity. Quite in keeping with that bias, Herbert Spencer has defined life itself as an ever more purposeful inner adaptation to external circumstances. But such a view misjudges the very essence of life; it overlooks the intrinsic superiority of the spontaneous, aggressive, overreaching, reinterpreting and re-establishing forces, on whose action adaptation slowly supervenes. It denies, even in the organism itself, the dominant role of the higher functions in which the vital will appears active and shaping. The reader will recall that Huxley strongly objected to Spencer's 'administrative nihilism.' But here it is a question of much more than simply 'administration.'[17]

We can detect here in Nietzsche some of the eugenics 'on command' implicit in Yeats's injunction to poet and sculptor in

'Under Ben Bulben': 'Bring the soul of man to God,/Make him fill the cradles right'. It is hard to know how much of MacDermott Yeats read, but he was a subscriber to O'Grady's *All Ireland Review* and could find MacDermott inveighing in a letter against the marital practices that were causing genetic problems: 'Now in Ireland there are 90 per cent. young men between 20 and 25 unmarried, and 75 per cent. between 25 and 30; the raising [of] human stock being left to elderly men and women. Result, 22,000 admissions per annum into lunatic asylums as against 8,000 twenty-five years ago; meaning that half the families in Ireland are now tainted with insanity, a disease formerly unknown among the Catholics.'[18] Uncle Atty shares this point of view: because of the social dislocations of families, children are being born to physically unfit parents because of great disparities in age and the financial motives for marriage that ignore insanity (p. 86).

Yeats goes on in 'Under Ben Bulben' to urge Irish poets to 'Scorn the sort now growing up/All out of shape from toe to top'. MacDermott was fascinated by the idea of the physiological basis of will implicit in Yeats's poem. His notions about kinship become more clear when we turn to his remarkable 1904 novel, *Foughilotra: A Forbye Story*. The novel is a tale of the Oins family, descended from a line of weavers and thus heirs to a long heritage of living outside the 'Law.' Implicitly the Oins family is successful because it has managed to preserve its will against the outside world.

In *Foughilotra* MacDermott revises the nineteenth-century Dickensian tropes of the Angel in the House and the wayward childish adult and writes a kind of Ulster *Bleak House* in the dialect of the Montaighs area of North Armagh on the shores of Lough Neagh. The Esther Summerson of the piece is Jinnyann Oins, a teenage girl. Her parentage is unknown, and she is being raised by Wee Mon Oins, to whom she is related but she is not sure how, and by Pokeshins, who turns out to be her grandfather and who wants to raise her to be a lady. They live in a strange dwelling that seems to have been a castle at one time but has been in the Oins clan since at least 1700. In rooms worthy of Miss Havisham, we discover an idle handloom along with the artefacts of the witchcraft once practised by the clan. From Wee Mon Oins, Jinnyann receives a thorough education in the solidarity of the Oins family all over the world. She is brought up so that she achieves fluency in the dialect speech of Foughilotra[19] prior to learning 'standard English' and is therefore inoculated against the way of life that initial fluency in 'standard English' might inculcate. She also develops his preter-natural skills of observation that are apparently rooted in the Oins family's occult and alchemical past. Jinnyann is specifically schooled in avoidance of any kind of reliance upon the 'Law', and we can see in this training MacDermott's understanding of how will has operated among the Oins as a salvation against the outside pre-datory society. The unspoiled Jinnyann, like MacDermott's infant who correctly theorises, saves Wee Mon Oins from a terrible drinking problem by keeping him from committing murder and restoring him to a sense of will. Involvement with people outside the Oins family can only lead to disaster and entanglement. Much like involvement with the Court of Chancery in *Bleak House*, legal entanglements threaten the family in the form of Antonio D'Oyly, an aspiring legal clerk whose goal in life is to become the Lord Chancellor. (He resembles Jason Quirk in Maria Edgeworth's *Castle Rackrent*.) D'Oyly, whose name has been pretentiously re-styled from the common 'Doyle', has made it his sinister business to learn all of the legal secrets of the family. Jinnyann, armed secondarily with literacy and 'standard English' speech by the education of Pokeshins, saves the family from such entanglements while at the same time her 'highborn' parentage is discovered.

MacDermott's novel is extremely sophisticated, a sociological study of kinship and, in the case of the Oins family, a study of how

a successful family operates with a certain allegiance to and awareness of the Satanic. The Oins family resembles the anti-social
Snopes family in William Faulkner's fiction, and the novel offers
clear endorsement of the value of maintaining a family ethos that
does not acknowledge the legitimacy of state or societal control.
Kinship is an external bond that protects its members from the
enslaving power of society. In conferring redemptive power on the
Angel in the House, MacDermott is consistent in showing how a
girl brought up outside the socialising power of the mainstream
and who internalises the Oins clan's ethos keeps *will* fresh from
corruption. Wee Mon Oins, significantly, gets drunk *in town*
regularly and risks the family's fortune until he is dragged from the
precipice by the actions of his youthful charge, Jinnyann. She is
the antithesis of the children who are enslaved by their elders. As
Sergeant M'Coy points out in *The Green Republic*: 'the farmers
keep their children to work for them without wages and without
liberty, without fitting them and leaving them to take the chances
the world has for most. In my opinion make slaves or darned
runaway cusses of them' (p. 43).

The relationship between the young Dr O'Gara and his uncle,
the older Dr O'Gara, somewhat resembles what is happening in
Foughilotra. In the earlier book the education of the young is
reversed: the young O'Gara is formally educated first; the action of
the book is his guided, informal education into the necessary
inductive method of observation in the field – the great skill of
Wee Mon Oins. However, there is also the irony that the young
O'Gara may suffer from getting the formal education first. He may
be in no different position from other young adults: '"I am quite
disinterested in my inquiries," I said. "I am bound to go and live
with my father in St Louis, and have no intention of setting up as a
doctor in Ireland"' (p. 113). The kinship of the word 'bound' to
slavery does not seem accidental.

It also seems like no accident that while the places and their names in *The Green Republic* bear very close resemblance to the area around the village of Poyntzpass in Armagh[20] where MacDermott was the dispensary doctor, the imaginary South Tyrone was, in fact, the real district of T. W. Russell, the Liberal Unionist Protestant Home Rule MP for South Tyrone. MacDermott, then, is offering 'facts' with a very practical purpose in mind: to oppose the Liberal Unionist politics that Russell was advocating in South Tyrone in 1902. MacDermott appears to be writing in response to Russell without ever mentioning him. After offering keenly analytical descriptions of his characters, MacDermott becomes more openly political and topical about his purposes in the 'Conclusion' of *The Green Republic*. In being sharply critical of the proposal to have Parliament set aside £120,000,000 in loan guarantees for the purchase of land from landlords by the strong men (the Wyndham Act), he attacks an unnamed writer directly:

> If one thing could be more criminal than this legislation, it would be conduct in a writer claiming clear perception of the facts, and using language calculated to relieve the legislator of responsibility, to allow him without rebuke to pose as the representative of the artificially induced mental impotence of the mass, only to betray it to its own ignorance. This is the only apology I can make for attaching the note of criminality to the long series of legislative measures in the conceived interest of the agrarian (p. 223).

The 'facts' seem to have been of recent vintage, for Russell, writing in 1902, had insisted:

> We must get back to SINGLE OWNERSHIP OF THE LAND. Fortunately the method and the machinery for securing this end are both at work in Ireland. We have only to amend the one and quicken

the pace of the other to secure a complete and final solution of what I
again venture to call the real Irish difficulty.'[21]

Russell goes on to claim that land purchase is a panacea: 'that
wherever it has been carried out peace has prevailed, prosperity
has ensued, men have taken to minding their business and the
natural Toryism of the Irish peasant has asserted itself'.[22] In his
1901 book, *Ireland and the Empire: A Review 1800–1900*, Russell had
written in the same romantic fashion that touched off MacDermott's
charge of criminality against this 'new Toryism': 'the safety of the
State is perhaps better secured by the passionate attachment of the
peasant to the soil. He has clung to it for centuries; he clings to it
still. Wherever the operation of purchase has been carried through,
it has succeeded. Arthur Young's assertion that "ownership turns
sand into gold" has once again been proved true.'[23]

MacDermott could only be indignant in the face of such
rhetoric; Russell termed the £120,000,000 fund a 'loan' –
from MacDermott's point of view, a lie. Russell may be answering MacDermott when he says, 'People talk of England finding
£120,000,000 to buy out Irish landlords'.[24] To give Russell his due,
his argument arises from a sense that Ulster, because of its loyalty
to British rule, has not benefited as it should have from previous
land purchase legislation. Land purchase was embraced to a much
greater degree in the other three provinces; in those provinces the
tenant farmers used 'methods of their own to compel their
landlords in large numbers to sell. In Ulster these methods are
unknown'.[25] In short, Russell claims that violence was used to
intimidate landlords in the other provinces into selling their land.
We can see however the implied demagogic threat that Ulster will
soon discover the value of violence.

For MacDermott, demagoguery is an unforgivable abuse of
power, and, from his point of view, Russell, in advocating policies

that would benefit his new men of property, was manipulating the new Presbyterian oligarchy in South Tyrone. The case of Andy M'Queen in *The Green Republic* seems particularly directed at Russell who was supporting the candidacy of the new owner farmers for local offices. M'Queen is insane but left to run a farm and is an example of disability through insanity. The manipulative M'Indoo convinces M'Queen to think of himself as a candidate for Parliament. Uncle Atty says: 'M'Queen is a sample of our local governing element. You may note him also as a sample of the men the gulled community are about to give one hundred and twenty millions to' (p. 59). MacDermott goes on to describe the new Presbyterian oligarchy: 'These men elect themselves to informal control; then elect the member of Parliament [Russell], the Presbyterian clergy, local boards and officials, and aspire to appoint the magistrates and control the police; perhaps in time the nomination of the judges and the Privy Council may become the object of their ambition' (p. 91).

MacDermott could hardly have been more offensive to the majority of the people he worked among. The young Dr O'Gara perceives that Dr Capel believes that the Ulster Protestants he serves are intolerant of 'anything but a rigid conventional life'. They tyrannise one another by demanding 'servile deference to non-essential forms and formulas and stultifying individual character and conduct' (p. 99). This attack is specific in nature: he is attacking as 'non-essential' the founding document of the Presbyterian Church – The Westminster Confession of Faith. In the concluding 'L'Envoi' to *Foughilotra*, MacDermott speaks at length in praise of the 'Non-Subscribing Presbyterians', i.e., the Presbyterians who do not subscribe to the Westminster Confession. He writes: 'The Confession of Westminster is perhaps the grossest piece of impertinence to God as Absolute and Unconditioned Being the wit of man ever devised'.[26] The Non-Subscribing

Presbyterians were accused of Arianism, or of doubting the doctrine of the Trinity. In the novel, Pogue says of the Oins clan, 'we were as well known as Non-Subscribing Presbyterians as ye are as a Catholic. They fastened Arians on us, the long an' short of it bein' all the time that we was positive no one way.'[27] MacDermott would like the agnosticism of this view of the Trinity; Pogue is saying they weren't sure they were Trinitarians or Unitarians.

For a man who could see the value in not being sure, MacDermott could be quite outspoken and doctrinaire about his point of view. Russell was not alone in opposing MacDermott's dismissal of land purchase as a cure for failing agriculture. In supporting the stock company option, MacDermott was implicitly attacking the work of Horace Plunkett and Fr Thomas Finlay (who was publishing his articles in the *New Ireland Review*). Plunkett and Finlay believed in the value of technical instruction in the latest advances in agriculture. MacDermott believed such attempts were doomed to failure and could not reverse the slide towards grazing and away from tillage. MacDermott certainly valued advanced farming techniques, but he saw Plunkett and Finlay as only delaying the inevitable because they were not addressing the essential issue. Plunkett and Finlay were trying to promote farming co-operatives as well as occupier ownership, and MacDermott did not like to oppose them. Writing as O'Gara, however, he says: 'It is painful to me to find myself in diametric opposition to Mr Horace Plunkett's views as to the value of peasant proprietorship; but the farmers know so well the defects of their own system that they are, at bottom, profoundly distrustful of their own political leaders.'[28]

Plunkett did read *The Green Republic* but relegated comment on it to a dismissive footnote in his 1904 book, *Ireland in the New Century*:

Yet another view which seems to uproot most agrarian ideas in Ireland has been put forward by Dr O'Gara in *The Green Republic* (Fisher

Unwin, 1902). His main conclusion is that the present disastrous state of our rural economy is due to our treating land as an object of property and not of industry. He advocates the cultivation of the land by syndicates holding farms of 20,000 acres and tilling them by the lavish application of modern machinery as the only way to meet American competition. His book is able and suggestive, but it is perhaps, a work of supererogation to discuss a theory the whole moral of which is the expediency of absolutely divorcing the functions of the proprietor and the manager of the land at a time when the consensus of opinion in Ireland is in favour of uniting them, and in view of the fact that under the new Land Act the future of the country seems inevitably to lie for a long time in the hands of a peasant proprietary.[29]

MacDermott's reaction to such commentary may be easily guessed: he had little use for the 'consensus of opinion' and would argue that Plunkett was insisting on just accepting things as they are, no matter how bad they are.

At the suggestion of Yeats, Plunkett had placed AE [George Russell] in the editorship of the newspaper of the IAOS. AE, a mystic, combined advice columns on how to grow turnips with poems by Yeats on the pages of *The Irish Homestead*. (Joyce called it the 'Pigs' Paper'.) His editorial policy must have amused MacDermott, a social scientist with a great sense of humour. In any event we can infer some scepticism about the value of what he saw as the aestheticism of the literary revival. Dr John Devine, for example, disparages the artist's preference for the picturesque at the expense of the functional (pp. 149–50 below). Writing about a visit to 'Dr O'Gara', O'Grady echoes this suspicion of the benefits of a renewed political and literary culture: 'I found this doctor, who has directed such a blazing stream of satire upon the rural population, a man of a most tender heart and affectionate temper, deeply attached to and nobly sympathetic with all these poor

BIBLIOGRAPHY OF WORKS (1897–1918*)
by W. R. MacDermott

'Jenner's inquiry: a memorial review', *Medical Press and Circular* 113, 16 (14 Oct. 1896), pp. 383–7.

'The administrative unity of Ireland', *New Ireland Review* 7 (1897), pp. 257–64.

'The increase of insanity in England', *Medical Press and Circular* 114, 18 (5 May 1897), pp. 454–6.

'Governmental anarchy', *New Ireland Review* 8 (1897), pp. 72–82.

'The abolition of poor-rate', *New Ireland Review* 8 (1898), pp. 264–75.

'The local government bargain', *New Ireland Review* 9 (1898), pp. 114–19.

'The teaching of synthetic anatomy', *Medical Press and Circular* 116, 19 (11 May 1898), pp. 484–5.

'The report on old age pensions', *Medical Press and Circular* 117, 20 (16 Nov. 1898), 505–8.

'The basis for old age pensions in Ireland', *New Ireland Review* 10 (1899), pp. 371–8.

'Insanity and education', *Medical Press and Circular* 118, 21 (24 May 1899), pp. 532–4.

'Monistic physiology', *Medical Press and Circular* 119, 12 (20 Sept. 1899), pp. 295–7.

[O'Gara, A. P. A.] *The Green Republic: A Visit to South Tyrone*. London: T. Fisher Unwin, 1902.

* Frank Watters reports that MacDermott was a fairly regular letter writer to *The Newry Reporter* during these years.

[O'Gara, A. P. A.] 'From *The Green Republic*', *All Ireland Review* 17 Jan.
   1903, p. 33; 24 Jan. 1903, p. 41; 14 Mar. 1903, pp. 66–7.

[O'Gara, A.] 'From the author of *The Green Republic*', letter to the Editor,
   All Ireland Review 14 Mar. 1903, p. 68.

'Insanity and morality', *Westminster Review* 159 (1903), pp. 291–7.

'The suicide of the race', *Westminster Review* 159 (1903), pp. 695–703.

'The problem of insanity in Ireland', *Edinburgh Medical Journal* N.S. 14,
   3 (Sept. 1903), pp. 223–3.

'Agriculture ideal and real', letter to the Editor, *All Ireland Review* 17 Oct.
   1903, p. 323.

'Gorilla agriculture', letter to the Editor, *All Ireland Review* 17 Oct. 1903,
   p. 325.

'The interest of labour and the interest of the labourer', *All Ireland
   Review* 31 Oct. 1903, p. 347.

'Where every prospect pleases and only man is vile', *All Ireland Review*
   7 Nov. 1903, p. 364.

'Reaping with the sickle', *All Ireland Review* 21 Nov. 1903, p. 383.

'Homeopathic protection', *All Ireland Review* 5 Dec. 1903, p. 408.

'The minority of one', *All Ireland Review* 19 Dec. 1903, pp. 435–6.

'Whose bread I eat, his song I sing', *All Ireland Review* 16 Jan. 1904,
   pp. 27–8.

'Theories of agriculture', *All Ireland Review* 20 Feb. 1904, pp. 89–90.

Untitled response to Ard-Righ. *All Ireland Review* 27 Feb. 1904, p. 100.

'Agrarian panmixia', *Westminster Review* 161 (1904), pp. 327–44.

[Gildea, Eustace.] *Foughilotra: A Forbye Story. All Ireland Review*
   5 Mar. 1904, pp. 112–14; 12 Mar. 1904, p. 123; 26 Mar. 1904, pp. 150–2;
   2 Apr. 1904, pp. 162–4; Apr. 1904, pp. 174–5; 16 Apr. 1904, pp. 186–8;
   23 Apr. 1904, pp. 198–200; 30 Apr. 1904, pp. 210–11; 7 May 1904,
   pp. 222–4; 14 May 1904, pp. 234–5; 21 May 1904, pp. 246–8; 28 May
   1904, pp. 258–9; 4 June 1904, pp. 270–1; 11 June 1904, pp. 282–3;
   18 June 1904, pp. 294–6; 25 June 1904, pp. 306–8; 2 July 1904, pp.
   318–20; 9 July 1904, pp. 330–2; 16 July 1904, pp. 342–4; 23 July 1904,
   pp. 354–6; 30 July 1904, pp. 366–8; 6 Aug. 1904, pp. 378–80; 13 Aug.
   1904, pp. 390–2; 20 Aug. 1904, pp. 402–4; 27 Aug. 1904, pp. 414–16;
   3 Sept. 1904, pp. 426–8; 10 Sept. 1904, pp. 438–40; 17 Sept. 1904,

pp. 450–2; 24 Sept. 1904, pp. 462–4; 1 Oct. 1904, pp. 474–6; 8 Oct. 1904, pp. 486–8; 15 Oct. 1904, pp. 498–500; 22 Oct. 1904, pp. 510–12; 29 Oct. 1904, pp. 522–4; 5 Nov. 1904, pp. 534–6; 12 Nov. 1904, pp. 546–8; 19 Nov. 1904, pp. 558–60; 26 Nov. 1904, pp. 570–2; 3 Dec. 1904, pp. 582–4; 10 Dec. 1904, pp. 594–6; 17 Dec. 1904, pp. 606–7.

'Cotton growing in India', *All Ireland Review* 12 Mar. 1904, pp. 123–4.

'Taxation of ground rents', *All Ireland Review* 12 Mar. 1904, p. 125.

'Wanted: a constitution', *All Ireland Review* 26 Mar. 1904, pp. 148–9.

'Irish pauperism', *All Ireland Review* 11 June 1904, pp. 279–80.

[O'Gara, A.P.A.] 'Individualistic agrarianism', *All Ireland Review* 18 June 1904, pp. 291–2.

'The study of bionomics in relation to the diminishing birth-rate', *Medical Press and Circular* 124, 7 (17 Aug. 1904), pp. 163–5.

'Mr. Balfour's address', *All Ireland Review* 27 Aug. 1904, pp. 416–17.

[O'Gara, A. P. A.]. 'What the Agricultural Department does? – nothing. What it can do? – nothing', *All Ireland Review* 1 Oct. 1904, pp. 472–3.

'The Irish in America', *All Ireland Review* 3 Dec. 1904, pp. 580–1.

'The Ulster Party and Ireland', *All Ireland Review* 10 Dec. 1904, p. 592–.

'On the value of the official reports on insanity', *Medical Press and Circular* 124, 26 (28 Dec. 1904), pp. 677–9.

Foughilotra: A Forbye Story. Dublin: Sealy, Bryers & Walker, [1906].

'Peasant proprietorship in France and England', *All Ireland Review* 18 Mar. 1905, pp. 125–6.

'Soldiers and labourers', *All Ireland Review* 25 Mar. 1905, pp. 137–8.

'Race or system?' *All Ireland Review* 1 Apr. 1905, pp. 147–48.

'Labour from Connaught', Letter to the Editor. *All Ireland Review* 1 Apr. 1905, p. 149.

'Sir Horace Plunkett's epilogue', *All Ireland Review* 29 Apr. 1905, pp. 197–8.

'The Irish village under its new masters', *New Ireland Review* 24 (1905), pp. 129–38.

'Bishop Berkeley', *All Ireland Review* 5 Aug. 1905, p. 303.

'Irish vital statistics', *New Ireland Review* 28 (1907), pp. 129–42.

'The nationalisation of labour', *New Ireland Review* 29 (1908), pp. 196–209.

'The relation of pathology to mechanics and chemistry', *Medical Press and Circular* 136, 13 (25 Mar. 1908), pp. 342–4.

'The Prevention of Tuberculosis Bill', *New Ireland Review* 30 (1908), pp. 85–98.

'The inheritance of insanity and tuberculosis', *Medical Press and Circular* 137, 3 (15 July 1908), pp. 60–2.

'The science of life', *Medical Press and Circular* 140, 7 (16 Feb. 1910), pp. 167–70.

'Notes on vision – I', *Medical Press and Circular* 141, 16 (19 Oct. 1910), pp. 406–8.

'Notes on vision – II', *Medical Press and Circular* 141, 20 (16 Nov. 1910), pp. 507–9.

'Notes on vision – III', *Medical Press and Circular* 142, 4 (25 Jan. 1911), pp. 87–9.

'Notes on vision. – IV', *Medical Press and Circular* 142, 11 (15 Mar. 1911), pp. 276–7.

Letter to the Editor, *Medical Press and Circular* 144, 1 (3 Jan. 1912), pp. 21–2.

'The term personality', letter to the Editor, *Medical Press and Circular* 146, 21 (21 May 1913), p. 561.

'A note on the stains used in bacteriological research', *Medical Press and Circular* 151, 4 (28 July 1915), pp. 77–9.

[MacDermott, *et al.*]. 'Re Graded scale of salaries for dispensary medical officers', letter to the Editor, *Medical Press and Circular* 156, 10 (6 Mar. 1918), p. 184.

THE GREEN REPUBLIC

A VISIT TO SOUTH TYRONE

" Sub patribus duris, tironum."—*Hor. Sat. lib.* i. 2. 17.

BY

A. P. A. O'GARA, M.D.

London

T. Fisher Unwin

MDCCCCII

PREFACE

THIS work is meant not to give mere sketches of Irish agrarian life, but to call attention to the necessity for the study of agrarian industry by the method of induction, the accumulation of concrete instances in the actual field of observation. The personal humanity of the sketches shall serve their purpose if it rivets the attention of readers unversed in economic argument on the method.

A method which starts on facts not open to question. It is fact unquestioned that the mass of mankind is under disability, made up of women, children, aged, sick, and infirm. Again, the term disability covers much more than this physical fact. A large section of physically capable persons is under disability because they do not produce but have to purchase the necessities of life. The care of families and households, domestic service, the education of children, and so on, lessen immensely the number available for the production of the means of existence. Farther, a vast growth of industries, which, however important in themselves, do not produce these means, places the burden of meeting their wants on those engaged in essentially productive industry. This growth is the leading feature of modern civilised communities, and is placing ever more and more a heavier charge on the fraction devoted to the production of the absolute necessities of life.

It may thus be seen that those capable of industry make up a small minority of mankind, and that of this minority only a fraction is engaged in necessary production.

A fact of the utmost importance follows from this. The

human individual in general is under disability both from the circumstances of life and from inclination. Individuals are found who work from habit, or even apparently for the sake of working, but in the general case they work to meet disability and provide against it, and the case being met their efforts relax. The worker or member of the industrial minority has as his nearer interest the contingency of personal disability, to which he sacrifices the interest of his industry; he favours old-age pensions, free education, free everything, regardless of the fact that these things place an immense burden on his industry, mainly in the interest of the non-industrial majority, his share in the benefits being in proportion to his numbers and not to what he contributes to their cost.

The interest of the majority, that is, of numbers, under the general conditions of individual life is the interest of disability, an interest representing not intelligence but immediate and imperious necessities, and is thus uncorrected by any view of the interest of industry on the part of the industrial minority.

Some philosophers tell us that the modern tendency of government to meet the case of disability is due to the growth of a spirit of humanity and Christian altruism, that is, of an ethical sense. The view, I conceive, is not a mere unimportant error of no practical effect. The influence of numbers on the regulation of society and government, always considerable, has always been in the interest of disability, and as the influence obtains increased weight, that interest comes to be served, though not necessarily well served, in proportion. Every interest, however, that really determines human conduct is at bottom an expression of necessity arising under the conditions of individual life, a common expression only as far as these conditions are common; conditions peculiar to the individual, compelling him to act for himself and often to take up an attitude of defence or offence against the community. A pack of wolves act together to meet common necessity, but the individual wolf under disability is abandoned to Fate, or even said to be devoured by his fellows. This may be applied to mankind, with a variation making it to some extent respectful. If a man under the influence of an altruistic ideal places himself under self-imposed and exceptional disability by willingness to give his life and means up to his fellows, it is certain that he shall be robbed to his last shilling. The attitude of self-defence in the individual as against the community expresses a fact of necessity; the altruistic concept is for him not only a one-sided but an impossible base for conduct under the sanction of rational judgment. If a man gives away his life and means, it can only be to serve a few, and not necessarily to serve them well; the gift cannot reach the community and cannot serve it as an example.

It is the altruism of the community, the fact that the many exist for the few, that seeks correction in modern times, an altruism non-ethical, non-intelligent, mechanical and therefore, though apparently in the interest of the individual, compatible with unlimited trespass on him.

This gives the observer his first and necessary instruction in entering on the field of actual observation. If he enters the field under the impression that the phenomena under view express action, the outcome of intelligence, of ethical ideas and rational judgment, he can arrive at no conclusion; his labour will be wasted, or, worse, he will be betrayed to the current jargon of conflicting interests. He must, of course, form ethical and rational judgments of what he observes, consider it as right or wrong, but if he transfers these judgments to the things observed, supposes them actuated and decided by them, he will end as one more actor on a noisy over-crowded stage.

He may conceive numbers, *i.e.*, the community, acting in an interest not its own, in the interest of a few individuals, as acting in an altruistic sense only as he transfers a concept of his own mind to it. The action of numbers is to meet the primary necessities of life common to all, and these met, they may be said to become indifferent to material interests. The action of the individual, *quâ* individual, is determined by inclinations, opportunities, and abilities not common to the mass, and which the mass, not sharing in, passively allows him to indulge or make use of. A man who spends his time and money in collecting pictures raises thereby no issue with the community for which no such object exists, and the pursuit does not touch. We hear incessant complaints of the improvidence and thriftlessness of the mass, but these complaints take for granted desires which do not actuate it, opportunities and abilities which do not exist for it. The ability to accumulate and use, not abuse, wealth is rare, even in individuals ; in general, when wealth falls to the average man, the representative of numbers, he wastes and abuses it. The idea that the mass could meet its disability by accumulation of wealth in it is an economic error; the accumulation would need to be of impossible magnitude financially, and, if possible, would not attain its object, would make bread dearer than gold. The mass tolerates the accumulation of wealth by individuals, not indeed through any perception of this fact, but as it tolerates the collection of pictures, because it is an individual not the common mode under the conditions of human life. The mass has to meet its necessities under these conditions by current income, and leaves meeting them by accumulation of wealth to the individual. What passes as its opposition to this is in reality a fact of competition in the individual sphere.

The true issue between numbers and the individual expresses the fact that the majority is dependent on the minority capable of work and engaged in essential production for current income. It is the industrial minority, virtually a class of individuals, that the mass under disability presses on as its only effective and adequate means of support. Thus it is the amount of food raised from year to year from the soil that determines the attitude of the mass dependent on it to the class engaged in its production. If the supply is adequate to the mass needs the mass treats the individual agriculturalist as a man who knows his own business and does not interfere with him no matter what his methods may be. If, however, the supply failed, and the mass had to go to Egypt to buy bread, it would fall on the money fund in the hand of individuals, only to find that it would not go far or last long. A case of necessity would arise to be met only by pressure on the landed interest; the essentially non-agrarian community would have to revert by a violent revolution to the agrarian form.

When, free from preconception, we enter the actual field of observation, we cannot fail to see at once that this, whether accomplished violently under the stress of circumstances or imperceptibly, would mean a reversion to barbarism. All important as the production of food from the soil is, when we compare it with the developed and developing non-agrarian industry, we find it under conditions which stamp it and its ideas and ideals as an unmodified inheritance from barbaric times. All modern non-agrarian industry developed and is developing by accommodation to the organic conditions of human life, by which the mass is under disability and dependent for the means of existence on a small industrial minority. This accommodation is effected by the industry being worked for a maximum production by a minimum of efficient labour, by a staff of managers and workers as nearly as possible in measured proportion to the work to be done, and therefore producing for the mass and not for those actually engaged in it. What nowadays would we think of a railroad managed so as to support an indefinitely large crowd of persons on it without reference to the work to be done and without discrimination as to their ability to do the work? Can we imagine what it would be under the supposition that it is worked by its owners irrespective of their age, sex, physical and mental ability. But this is exactly the system under which the industry on which the existence of the community depends is carried on, a system dating from the times when the community was almost wholly agrarian. In the actual field of observation the inquirer will find the occupation of land at the mercy of chance, determined by every accident of human life without reference to fundamental use and purpose. He will find some few of the occupiers actual lunatics, and many of them from the economic point of view the equivalents of lunatics, as incapable as lunatics of labour and the management of labour. He will find the land subdivided in such a way as to totally preclude its economic working in the interest even of those on it. The cultivation of the soil should aim at its improvement, the development and maintenance of its potential capabilities. He will find that such cultivation as there is, as a rule, takes whatever nature may give unaided, and often represents gross trespass on the natural fund of fertility. At every turn instances will occur to him where what industry achieves in one generation is wasted and worn out in the next; he must note the system as failing to give continuous and sustained cultivation from generation to generation, and because the holdings pass from individual to individual under no provision for ability. By far the larger and best part of the land he will find in the hands of large holders—cattle runs in a state of nature, giving no employment, supporting no population on it, and making but a meagre contribution to the support of the general population. He will be told that this is because cultivation does not pay, but if he accepts the statement instead of looking at and considering the personal conditions of life to which the holders subordinate as matter of necessity their possession of the land, he may close his inquiry and add his voice to the political choir. Considering the conditions of life of the holder he will note him as the average representative of numbers, and therefore under disability, accommodating his work to his life. This will fix for him the position that the agrarian system, the system of individual occupation and management of the land, vests the great instrument of production without correction in the hands of disability to the injury of disability.

Passing to a relatively small and barren area in the hands of a mass of small holders, he will find that its cultivation must pay, since, like all petty traders, these holders, to live at all, must have enormous profits on a small turnover and business. But the very magnitude of the return from cultivation renders the income of the holder precarious, places it at the mercy of the seasons, of flux of prices and ability for labour—a necessarily variable factor. Enormous profits, however, he must see, under the most uneconomical form of working the land accrue from its cultivation, the cultivation of the poorest part of it, only to be wasted in a vain attempt to meet the excess and waste of unorganised labour under his view.

In Ireland one person out of every eight who comes to die, dies as the pauper inmate of a workhouse, and in addition to this a large number die on out-door relief and are buried at the public expense. In the actual field of observation our inquirer can satisfy himself that the common statement that the agricultural labourer is better off in the workhouse where he comes to die than as he lives outside is, in general, true. With a little pains he can satisfy himself further that the poor laws, building labourers' cottages, and so forth, however meritorious in intention, are cruel mockeries for the agricultural labourer. To live the man must have adequate and constant wages, and in the long run what is done for him at the public expense cheapens and disadvantages his labour, is taken out of him in his wage and constancy of employment. The employer aims at commanding labour when he wants it and dispensing with it when he does not want it, and as serving this aim the public provision is a subsidy in favour, not indeed of the employer's true interest, but of a system vitiated by dependence on pauperism.

In short, by the simple plan of making an inventory of the owners and occupiers of the land, and of the labourers on it, the inquirer brings into view a system under which labour and the land, its instrument of production, are subordinated without correction to the personal conditions of individual life. The meaning of this is that everything that would favour increased production from the soil—good land, high prices for its produce, cheapened food for the labourer, the benefits of machinery, the growth of great markets on the spot, even protective duties and other illicit subsidies—must necessarily tend to diminish production. The widespread impression, a delusion mischievous in the extreme, that the opposite must be the case rests on the false assumption that the majority of us are capable of industry and of responding to its incentives. The merit of inquiry in the actual field of observation is that it shows us the land in the hands of men under the general condition of disability in an exaggerated degree. Thus the aged are owners and occupiers of land, and therefore in charge of its cultivation out of all proportion to their numbers relative to population, following the rule that property and wealth in every form tends to accumulate in the hands of those who have had the opportunities of time. But wealth, like every other advantage that falls to the aged and those otherwise under disability, is used to minimise exertion, and thereby meet the case of disability. On the small and barren area in the hands of the small holders we find the human mass at its worst; on the vast area of rich land in the hands of large and relatively wealthy holders we see in waste and abuse the great instrument of production at its worst.

The inquiry indicated is one of the conditions of human

life under which industry has to be effected, conditions which the great non-agrarian industries have met by a method of correction and elimination of disability, a method undergoing continuous development in the interest of mankind, while the so-called industry of agriculture remains stationary under an antiquated and savage system.

Political economy, in treating the conditions of industry abstract from the human agency, supplies no corrective for this; failing to grasp the conditions of human life under which industry occurs, it gives no principle to put in the place of the arbitrary judgments of interested motives, and is fitly relegated to the planet Saturn when it stands in their way. This is peculiarly so in the case of the agrarian system.

"There are," an able exponent of the science states, "thirty-seven millions of acres in England and Wales. Of these it has been calculated that not eighty-five thousand, less in fact than one four-hundredth part, are in a state of high cultivation, and that five millions are waste. All that is not waste is productively employed; but how small is its produce compared to the amount to which unlimited labour and abstinence might raise it!" [1]

It should be noted that production, the return from land left in the natural state, is so small relatively to the potential capability of the same land, that by far the larger area of England may properly be described as waste. Natural pastures, land cropped to give what its natural fund of fertility allows, game preserves and mountain sheep-walks produce something. Our position is that actual observation shows that the landholder, whether owner or occupier, contents himself with this limited production, not because the development of the potential capabilities of his land would be unremunerative, but because the personal conditions of life in sum place that development beyond him. This may be seen by supposing the same persons set to work a rail-

[1] *Political Economy.* N. W. Senior, London, 1858, p. 82.

road in the same way as they work the land. Under the supposition the road would be worked by minimum exertion for a return infinitely less than that which organised management and labour shows it can yield.

"But although the land in England is capable of producing ten times, or more than ten times, as much as it now produces, it is probable that its present produce will never be quadrupled, and almost certain that it will never be decupled." [1]

This statement is rested on the abstract position that "agricultural skill remaining the same, additional labour employed on the land within a given district produces in general a less proportionate return."

By reference to the field of concrete fact it may be seen that the grand characteristic of the agriculture of the United Kingdom, and, indeed, of every country with few and doubtful exceptions, under the system of individual occupation and management of the land is that the great areas of good soil are virtually waste while the mass of agrarian population is crowded on small and barren patches on which its labour is spent under the most uneconomical conditions for a return large indeed but inadequate for its secure support. In the light of this fact it cannot be allowed that the application of labour to the land is determined by its remunerativeness, much less that increment of the application can be in proportion to a case of virtual non-application, a case undetermined by remunerativeness.

Since John Stuart Mill and Senior wrote, the area under cultivation in England has decreased instead of increased, a fact mainly of decrease of labour applied to the great area of superior soil, and indicating that it is worked not for possible remuneration but under a condition to be fulfilled by a minimum of industrial exertion. The base of the idle abstraction, the taking agricultural skill as remaining the same, is the reverse of concrete fact. The development and

[1] *Political Economy.* N. W. Senior, London, 1858, p. 83.

improvement of mechanical appliances enable one man now to do as much work as five did formerly, but this potentiality, like that of the soil itself, virtually lies dormant and without its natural effect.   To a limited extent it has operated in the larger and better area, but only to answer the condition of minimum exertion under which the land is worked ; as it cheapens and facilitates production it enables a lessened production to meet the general conditions of life of the landholders.   The small holders it has not reached at all, and is altogether inapplicable under their system.

The development of the business of transportation does not necessarily follow on the mechanical inventions it utilises.   These inventions called for specific abilities in those that worked them ; their working was not a thing to be left to everybody, to the man who possessed capital and to the man merely capable of physical labour.   The inventions would have remained useless for the purposes of mankind if left in the hands of the unorganised crowd of average individuals to work and manage.

The essential concrete fact I direct attention to is that the agrarian system, the system of leaving agriculture, or rather its necessary instrument, the land, to an unorganised crowd of individuals—this system remaining the same, production is and must always be under a condition in sum of minimum exertion, that condition being incidental to any sum of individuals taken at random.   In the agrarian crowd operating discretely the rich man uses his capital, the poor man his labour, to meet the personal conditions of life, with the result that production is determined without correction by these conditions, and not only Political Economy but every enunciation of principle is lost on a sphere dominated by the necessities and untempered impulses of disability.

This system is found everywhere in a historic attitude of aggression on the non-agrarian industries and the great communities their organisation has built up.   Going back to the times when Britain was almost entirely an agrarian community, we find it a scene of perennial disorder and distress, the mass on the land steeped in poverty and misery, and its masters engaged in an incessant struggle for the land with no industrial object in view. When by development of the means of transportation, and the opening up of new areas uncharged with the support of local population, a great non-agrarian industrial population came into existence, the factions of the old agrarian society united to prey on it and meet without curing the disability of its internal economy from a new source. If anything could have drawn out the latent fund of potential ability in the soil, of potential ability in its holders, it would have been this growth of population able to buy food. The actual fact, the decay of such agricultural industry there was, poor as it ever was, and of the population engaged in it, miserable as it ever was, is met with an attitude of mental paralysis as if an inscrutable problem. Trading on this mental attitude in the community, the outcome of taking the efficiency of the human agency engaged in the production of food for granted, the agrarian makes incessant demands on the community for protective duties, for exceptional taxation in his favour, for loans of immense sums of public money to carry on by novel means the never-ending struggle for the possession of the land. If the mental attitude was not there, it would have been seen long ago that these boons, in common with every other advantage that falls to the holders of land—good soil, large areas of it, ready and enlarging markets, mechanical inventions—go not to promote production but to minimise exertion. Thus, as far as these boons have been granted, they have invariably falsified the pretences advanced to cover their demand, but the campaign still goes on, its fraud and deception cloaked by sincerity and stupidity.

In the actual field of observation it can be seen at once that the cultivation of any single farm turns, not on what it might produce or might pay, but on the conditions of life of the holder as an individual. Thus the holder being, as he may be, a lunatic, or the economic equivalent of a lunatic, the fact will determine the state of his holding. What applies to a single farm applies to the sum of them ; they are not worked for a maximum production or a maximum profit, but to meet conditions of life in sum. In the common mind, and indeed in Political Economy, however, the sum of individual holders is taken as aiming at, and capable of aiming at, maximum production and profit, that is, doing what for a host of reasons not one of them is found in a position to do. To repeat, as the importance of the point may justify me in doing, the sum of individual farmers, like any other sum of individuals taken at random, represents both industrial disability and the necessary pressure of such disability on the minority capable of industrial exertion, and indeed on every source available for its needs or exposed to it—the community at large, for instance—a pressure regulated by necessity, not discretion and intelligence. The typical farm in the concrete field is itself an expression of disability and of undue pressure on labour. So far from additional labour on it being barred by unremunerativeness, the actual labour spent on it must be either in excess or overtaxed. For suppose 5000 acres are held by 100 farmers, taken for the sake of argument as fully competent men, we have one manager for every two or three labourers when one could manage the labour necessary to work the whole area. Again, the labour necessary to work the whole area as one farm up to a given standard would not suffice to work it as a hundred 50-acre farms up to the same standard ; in the latter case either the standard must be lowered or labour be overtaxed, and have to do much more than if the area was worked as a whole. The mass of wheat production of the Western States exported is mainly drawn from areas of from 2000 to 5000 acres under a single manager, and with an economy of labour impossible in small holdings. This reasoning, of course, does not apply in Britain where the vast crowd of managers is under the general condition of disability, but it at once obtains weight as thought is turned towards reform of the agrarian system on economic principles.

A reform urgently called for wherever the system of individual occupation of the land prevails. The Eastern States of the American Union, with a greater area and a lesser population than the United Kingdom, are, perhaps, as much dependent on foreign food production as the last. Their political identity, with their source of supply, is only a sentimental qualification of the fact of economic dependence, a fact which, as it means waste and non-cultivation of their own land, is an injury, no matter how and from what quarter necessary food is drawn. In the same way, the idea that the United Kingdom should turn for her food supply from foreign countries to her colonies only diverts attention from the waste and non-cultivation of her own land. It is about on a par with the proposal to adopt the policy of Pharaoh and accumulate great reserves of grain in the country. Both serve to confirm the delusion that the land of Britain is not able to support its people, a delusion that finds its answer in every patch of fairly well-cultivated ground by calculating what the volume of production of the whole area would be, making every allowance, if at anything near the same rate.

I direct attention here to the true method of studying the agrarian system, by observation and induction in the concrete field, confident that it will lead to economic principles on which to base reform of the system. It will be said, however, that the system must die of its own internal distress and disorder, can never be saved by the enunciation of principles out of the reach of its mind, a mind determined through time immemorial to confusion and conflict—*inter arma silent leges.* It will be said that if the life of purely agricultural communities like Ireland

and India depends on apprehension by their people of economic principles, there is nothing to save them from a miserable existence and extinction by famine. That such is the case may appear when we find England, a great non-agrarian community, and therefore under the influence of mind in varied directions as no purely agrarian society can be, standing in mental confusion before the abuse and non-cultivation of her land and dependence on food raised abroad, before a state of things ever inflicting incalculable injury on her people and exposing them to extinction by famine.

But economic principle may have some chance of being understood and applied when it clearly serves interests in themselves merely selfish or expression of necessity. A case of the kind appears to exist in Ireland as the result of legislation which has placed individual ownership of land not only in immediate abeyance but permanent insecurity. The old landowners have been turned into rent-chargers, and in presence of a machinery operating to extinguish their charge without compensation. The new owners, *in esse* and *posse* under land purchase, in respect of three-fourths of the soil in large and medium-sized holdings, inherit and would inherit from their predecessors a position, the insecurity of which would be increased by the precedent of expropriation. The true motive impulse against the old Irish land holders comes from the great mass of small occupiers which holds a mere fraction of the area of the country, and the impulse would remain to operate against the small class which occupies three-fourths of the land and would receive three-fourths of the benefits of land purchase. The ownership of the old landlords being irretrievably gone, their remaining interest would be best served by basing ownership on the joint-stock principle, and working the land as the railroads are worked. The plan would restore prospective value to their interest, and make it secure and in command of a market. It is plain that the same reasoning applies to the class of large occupiers whether in its present position or as taking the place of the landlord class. This is so obvious that it would be blindness to their immediate interest in these powerful classes not to promote any movement which would seek to apply to the cultivation of the land the principles and methods under which the great non-agrarian industries have thriven. It is their one way of meeting the political agitation which is ruining them, and of obviating the dangers of continued trespass on an injured and long-suffering community.

The reader would go in vain to South Tyrone or any other district in Ireland to identify the personalities and circumstances given in these sketches, but the lessons the sketches convey are all the stronger, because, not only in South Tyrone and every other part of Ireland, but wherever individual occupation of the land prevails, he has only to observe to accumulate instances from actual life, many far stranger than my fictions, but all of the same purport. If he makes his induction systematic and wide enough, he will be amazed not so much at the total industrial incompetence of the agrarian community as at the way that inherent incompetence, a purely economic fact remediable only by economic means, has been charged on government, on form of tenure, on Free Trade, on anything and everything but its true and natural cause, the disability of any sum of individuals taken at random and operating without correction under the condition. He will conclude that until that cause is recognised, and the correction which other industries have adopted is applied the agrarian sphere must remain, as it always has been in the past, a scene of disorder and distress.

THE GREEN REPUBLIC

A VISIT TO SOUTH TYRONE

I

INTRODUCTION

" THE Problem of To-day—Preformation or Epigenesis ? " my
uncle said, taking a German work on biology out of my hand.
" Well, if you must have mental exercise, though on a holi-
day, cannot you take up our problem of to-day here by way
of relaxation ? "

" What is your problem here ? "

" Compulsory sale—tenant *versus* landlord."

" That seems to me no problem, sir, but two opposed
statements incapable of any common conclusion. It is a
case of political forces to be decided like mechanical forces
in opposition as such."

I had just taken my medical degrees and come on a visit
to my uncle and namesake, Atty O'Gara, dispensary doctor
of the Jigglestreet district in South Tyrone, with the
secondary object of supplementing my hitherto theoretical
studies by practice or field work. With that object in view
it took me to be self-reliant, for my uncle, not being a dog-
matic man, was a poor teacher. He was playfully loose
about opinions, his own as well as those of others. He
made up his mind only when action called for decision of
judgment, quickly and easily enough, but never without *ex
post facto* questioning. In the practice of his profession he
so constantly found the human mechanism at fault that
necessarily the observation covered also the mental form.

In this there was no indifference, no cynicism which is so often an affectation and no charity, the outcome of contempt for humanity.

"Well," he said, "if our great problem is of that nature there is ample room for stating it as such. Our farmers state the transfer of the ownership of the land as the solution of a problem, but do not state the problem."

"And, of course, state in the form of a solution, simply because it is a transfer of valuable property to themselves. It would be absurd to expect correct reasoning from them under such temptation to reason backwards."

"Reasoning!" my uncle said, with a curious smile. "The prize is so valuable to them that they do not discredit their case by allowing it to be supposed that it is one open to be reasoned about. Their reasoning begins and ends with the means whereby their solution may take practical form."

"Then, uncle, why should I take up a question from which reason is as much banished as from a fight between thieves for their spoil? The more fully I might satisfy my own mind the more dissatisfied I would be with discreet silence. I was a sound Money Democrat in Missouri when the Bimetallists put free speech and golden silence in the ratio of one to sixteen. It was a relief to come to Europe and exchange free silver for free thought and its free expression."

A smile again lit my uncle's face. I sometimes wondered whether my rather saturnine countenance ever became so intelligent.

"My first thoughts of life," he said, "came to me in the Southern States in the slavery times, and remain with me as conceptions of the free community. The lions and tigers, bears and foxes took being caught, caged and made to lead the life of a menagerie as spoiling their dream of freedom; and it would just as much have offended freedom to have forbidden those having the power to catch and cage the beasts to use it."

"You mean that freedom in human affairs is only power in sets of men to follow their natural bent and interest. The slave-owners meant by freedom their power as masters, and their opponents, equally as power in themselves, to be exercised as power against power."

I knew my uncle would go back on his own proposition to qualify it, and more, meant to interest me in a question by the easy operation of committing me to an argument.

"I mean," he said, "that our farmers here, as a body, mean by freedom their power to act according to their natural bent and interest. Stripped of disguise they want their landlord's place, position and property to enable them to act towards their dependents and the community in perfect freedom. Put any power over them in place of the landlord, demand responsibility in the exercise of the powers they have or seek and, if you were serious, their agitation would at once collapse. They want freedom from the landlord and freedom to use or abuse the land, use or abuse their dependants at their own sweet will. You are right in saying that no problem is stated. State the problem in any terms allowing discussion and you are a landlord's man. You might go back to America for freedom of speech or thought. The slave owner or bimetallist would as soon have allowed his interest, as conceived by himself, to be treated as an open question as would the Irish farmer."

"Why then take the pains to conceive and state the problem?"

"Because the conception and statement of the problem would necessarily bring into the field and appeal to all the interests concerned in the question. There are forty-one and a half millions of persons in the British Islands deeply interested in the cultivation of the land, and as all the landlords and all the farmers having an appreciable interest in Irish land barely number 100,000, a great interest and power exists which may be brought to consider itself and intervene in the dispute."

"I hate politics," I said, to break the thread of argument, "and am taken up with the biological problem. Why do you concern yourself with the land? you do not own or occupy an acre?"

"Your pretty cousin in St. Louis, Adarose M'Gillivray, says she loves politics, particularly presidential elections, because they make her clean mad. When you come under American female autocracy can you hope to escape politics?"

"Adarose," I answered rather coldly, "means that she loves excitement. I don't. For the life of me I could not get excited as she did about bimetallism without knowing anything about it."

"Nor again if you knew all that could be known about it."

My uncle smiled and continued,—

"You give me your qualification for considering our land question, which in its most important aspect is not a political or even an economical one, but one touching the vital status of the whole people, their health, their terms and conditions of life as dependent on the supply of food from the soil. If that supply is not as cheap, abundant and certain as it can possibly be made, then a grievous injury is inflicted on them. I take an interest as a medical man in the land question because I am quite sure the agrarian system has killed far more in the century than war, far more than all other evil agencies put together, shortened length of life, made life miserable, precarious, not worth living. The keynote of the system is that it does not provide against the untoward but inevitable conditions of human life, leaves those under it at the mercy of circumstance. The Irish farmers would have a fine case if the case depended on the amount of lunacy, disease, and dipsomania among them traceable to the habitual uncertainties of their position."

"The popular idea is that rural is much healthier and more conducive to longevity than city life or the life of manufacturing districts."

"The popular idea is that a green Christmas makes a fat churchyard, and that one notion would prove the vast superiority of medical observation and experience. Take facts one by one. There is far more insanity and increase of insanity in Ireland than in England. In England there is far more insanity in the purely agricultural districts than in the city and manufacturing centres. The same thing applies to Ireland ; our most thinly peopled county, Meath, the model farmer's county, takes the palm for lunacy. We are to read along with this that the state of the city is greatly determined by the continuous rural migration into it. The rustic, broken down in health or fortune, betakes himself to the town, and his break down in both respects is a huge item."

"You are," I observed, "bringing into view now the

terms of a problem. The political farmer, reasoning from his desire for possession of the land, admits, perhaps exaggerates, the evils his class labours under with the intention to get us to jump headlong to the conclusion that the possession he covets is the cure for them. You simply note the evils you observe without any preconception, depending on their accurate description to give their causes and remedies."

"It is you," my uncle said with some emphasis, "I wish to take that method. I have been longer in the world than you, and have not yet made up my mind that I have a call to better the lot of humanity. Every year about the same number of cases of disease pass through my hands, excess in one being balanced by defect in another, and I expect the same thing to go on during my time. The Irish dispensary doctor, with no hope for himself, cannot be enthusiastic about those he serves. You are young, not damped by my experience, and it is certain that the agrarian position calls for scientific study if only to meet the tissue of interested misrepresentation which perplexes and deceives the public mind."

But I was not inclined to give up the studies I was pursuing, and my uncle observing my hesitation to adopt his suggestion went on in a different tone.

"Well, well, in driving round the country visiting farmers and labourers you cannot help but have what they are, what they do and can do, forced on your mind, and you must form judgments about them. By-and-by you may naturally and easily fall into the way of noting the actual facts in the field of observation systematically and drawing inevitable conclusions. When you learn what the question actually is you may perhaps think it as well worth studying and writing about as bimetallism or the great issue between Epigenesis and Preformation."

I was glad to dismiss the subject on these terms, which committed me to nothing, but still as I wished to be committed to nothing I said,—

" I suppose I cannot but pick up information in the way you say, and learn the nature of the question where only it can be learned—in the field. But much more is required. The farmers evidently have the advantage of a constructed and constructive position, and mere destructive criticism, no matter how unanswerable it may be, can have little weight. Their system exists, and from their point of view needs to be strengthened and developed, and no matter what fault may be found with it, only by proposing something better to put in its place can it be practically challenged. From what I know at present I could not take sides with the landlords or indeed against them, with the tenants or against them. I can see plenty of faults in their system as it is and was, but have no system to put in its place."

My uncle answered, with his usual pleasant and intelligent smile, in contrast, I am sure, to my unsmiling gravity,—

"You are proving, as you have been doing throughout, your competence to deal with the question. Suppose you simply, in the first instance, observe facts in the actual field, you may trust the process in the end to suggest the best means for the cultivation of the soil, or means better than those now in practice. You are right in seeing that the determination of these means is necessary to justify the question as a practical one, but at the outset you can only have faith in the determination as possible, and faith that force shall be forthcoming to secure their adoption."

"What change," I asked, "would you make in the agrarian system, and who would you look to for power to effect the change? You would not, I am sure, appeal to either landlord or tenant."

My uncle answered rather gravely,—

"If I was prepared with an answer to that question, I certainly would not be prepared to give it. I suggest a problem to you under the condition that you shall solve it yourself, and of course with confidence in your ability to solve it. I hear landlords sometimes, tenants every day, at the thing, and want to see how a fresh young man with scientific training and no personal interest to consult would handle it. I have done when I suggest the subject to you, under the condition that you shall copy from Nature, not from other men's work, observe in the actual field, use your own methods and form your own judgments. Never mind what an old man reared in a slave-owning family may think or say ; I have my own views, of course, but I do not wish to impose them on you. Keep to downright fact—fact in your range—and trust to it. If you paint a black sky and flashes of lightning, you may be sure the thunder will be taken for granted—an old saying."

This was final as far as my uncle was concerned, but final for myself only so far as to give me willingness to pursue facts of observation if they easily suggested or carried with them plain conclusions. I had travelled through the greater part of Ireland, gone to political and land meetings, observed the condition of the people and land, but if I had acquired any knowledge it went along with the conviction that knowledge was not power or influence, but, like bitter medicine, a thing to be rejected or taken in very unwillingly. The knowledge that had power was knowledge of the passions, prejudices, and party feelings which bound individuals into a reckless, mindless mass, lost to even the instinct of self-preservation and to rational motives of self-interest. Just because that knowledge was power, it held the field, and could easily rout not poor human thinkers of our times alone on it, but all the angels and prophets of Jewish story.

This is as true of the mass in America as in Ireland, but the cases otherwise are not parallel. Ireland cannot afford to put political passions and prejudices above plain economical principles and sound views of self-interest, while the long bill America has paid, and is paying, for economical heresies and political follies, for even a gigantic civil war, her people have so far been able to meet without being ruined or tempted to greater excesses.

In Ireland no break in the cloud of adversity which has so long covered the island is visible. The population steadily diminishes from decade to decade without diminishing pauperism and emigration ; the birth-rate is fallen to an abnormal figure ; the area under tillage—a tenth of the surface in extent and quality—is a miserable pretence at the cultivation and improvement of the soil, and, even so, is a sixth less than what it was twenty years ago. This evidences increasing impoverishment of the diminishing mass for which increasing wealth in the monied class is no compensation.

When I heard this unpromising condition of the country imputed to the British Government and the landlords, I felt that the Irish people might as well throw the blame on their climate or on the small size of their island. Any possible Irish Government would be much the same at

bottom as the British, with the same nature, the same disposition and methods, and would be as much open to blame,
deserved and undeserved.   An Irish Parliament would be
neither more nor less wise than the Westminster body, and
as far as the Irish people are ignorant of their own affairs
it would reflect that state of mind.   There would indeed be
one material difference.   Ireland is so much an agrarian
country that an Irish Parliament would be practically a
body of farmers ; the interests which mitigate agrarian rule
in Westminster would be absent.   For this reason it might
be a more untrustworthy and incompetent body.

The agrarian system is the key to the position in Ireland
and the United Kingdom.   The British Parliament is to an
undue extent the creature of that system, and an Irish
Legislature would be wholly its tool and instrument.

In the slavery times the State Legislatures in the South
were entirely in the interest of the slave owners, relatively
a smaller body than the landowners of the United Kingdom.
So was for long years the Congress of the United States.
Would any rational man blame these bodies for the manner
in which they governed, or propose to mend the state of
the country by tinkering with them ?   Would he not go to
the system in the country of which they were the mere
mouthpieces, and consider it in the first place, and whether
it should or could be changed ?

In the same way the British Parliament is the creature
of a system which must be held responsible for both the
condition of the country and the spirit of its government,
and the craze of the Irish people for a Local Government
which would be even more its creature, seemed to me a
proof that they utterly failed to see the real cause of the
evils they have so long suffered, and which threaten their
extinction as a nation.

In travelling through the British Islands, long before
South Tyrone and my uncle had suggested the agrarian
question to me, I had noted that the greater part of the
country was uncultivated, though quite capable of cultivation, and that apart from this the state of the cultivated
area was a travesty on industry, had no right to be looked
on as exhibiting an organised industry.   With this impression on my mind I cared little to consider how it came that
the food producer in America with worse land, more un-

certain conditions of climate, costlier labour and thousands of miles of land and sea carriage to pay for, could undersell the producer on the spot. It was clear to me that the competition was not between producer and producer, but a one-sided affair between producer and non-producer. British agriculture was not an industry organised for systematic production, but conformed to the traditional purpose of supporting those actually on the land in their traditional manner. It is absurd to say that it is exposed to and ruined by foreign competition. The industry which produces a ton where ten tons are required, may complain that the price of its ton is lowered, but it cannot complain of being excluded from a market which admittedly it cannot supply. The foreigner, heavily handicapped by transport charges and other adverse factors, created the market for food in Britain which he supplies; he did not oust and does not exclude any home producer from it. If it is admitted that the demand of the market can be met by home production, the real question that arises is the competence of the mechanism of that production to satisfy the demand of the market, its ability better to support a large population which must be fed somehow. The home producer has already in his favour the necessity of that population, which compels it to pay a price for food enhanced by transport and other charges, which in nothing like the same degree fall on him. When under this condition by the growth of population an immense market is created at his door, and it is found that he not only does not respond to the demand, but lessens his already insignificant contribution towards it, an incentive and encouragement to his industry, than which no greater could be supplied, is proved an utter failure.

At the time I was indifferent to the questions that occurred to me, having no intention of studying them, but still they had the precious quality of strongly impressing themselves; they could not present themselves and be forgotten. The man who dominated in the agrarian system wherever I met him did not need deep study; to speak to him was enough to make him speak for himself in the plainest terms; a mighty self and Ego he impressed himself indelibly on the understanding and memory. In England the non-agrarian element is the people, though not the

State; the agrarian is the State, and as the State calls himself, and really thinks himself the people. It would be wrong to say that the agrarian element is the State, or as a whole pretends to the power of the State, except as under deception and manipulation, as wrong as to say that the slave as well as his master in slavery times in America was the State. The agrarian element, including landlords, farmers and labourers, is but a tenth of the population of the British Islands, and only a tenth in the element itself has any appreciable interest in the land and any political initiative; the nine-tenths has force indeed, but only the force of a dead, mindless mass under direction from without. The owners of the land and the small section of occupiers having an appreciable interest in the land, call them a 100,000 or even 200,000 persons, are practically the agrarian power, and that power is wholly a traditional one, a heritage from ancient times, not a power conformed to the management of an industry all important in the interest of the whole people. Again, these 100,000 or 200,000 persons are so far above the average range of circumstance that their range of interest is relatively a wide one; they are free to act under motives not falling under the head of pecuniary interest. Secure of the means of support, usually with a surplus over what is necessary, naturally the first call on them is not to better a position of superiority, but to maintain and use it in the traditional manner. This gives the personal characteristic of the agrarian whether he is a landlord or farmer. He lives for himself alone, as no other man in the industrial world does. He is not the manager of an organised industry nor yet a sharer in its profits. Ownership and occupation of the land begins and ends with himself and his own purposes. His position is that of a king whose title to the throne is not invalidated by his being a lunatic or a child. He may or may not cultivate the land; he may be blind, lame, half insane; his title remains unaffected. If he has to support himself on his land under the condition of disability, when he does so as he best can, he discharges his duty to himself, and he is conscious of no other. He is not managing a business for others, he does not dream that he is called on to produce food for forty millions of persons; the forty millions might starve, and he would be quite unconscious of any wrong done them by his inability or un-willingness to cultivate the land. The foolish forty millions depend on the pressure of necessity forcing him to cultivate, but that pressure is met when he supports himself, which he may do otherwise than by the land. Since the land is not cultivated he does not cultivate it, or, to be accurate, the extent to which he cultivates it is to be ascertained by direct observation in the field, and not deduced from a theoretical assumption.

The agrarian who holds the land of the country to cultivate it or not at his arbitrary discretion, regardless of the interest of forty millions of people, is with reason a mighty self and Ego. The man who can do so must be in possession of inordinate power, a power which should be allowed to no man, to no set of men. But because he has the power his chief interest is to maintain it, to maintain the vast power which possession of the land gives him, not merely to preserve it, but to preserve it under the condition of considering no interest but his own, to use it to make himself the State under no condition of responsibility.

I was familiar with the position which the slave-owner had held in the United States, and which he might hold still had not his power intoxicated him. Under the forms of democracy the small slave-owning oligarchy had been able to keep up a system which violated all ethical and economical principles, and therefore degraded and de-moralised the white as well as the black. I had no faith in the forms of government under which the Southern whites lived and died for the slave-owner.

True democracy is fixed by expression of principle, not by leaving arbitrary choice of government to the mass. The Southern whites lived and died for a vile oligarchy. The French unanimously voted absolute power to a despot with a bad record against him. But we would search history in vain for a stronger case of the inability of the democracy to assert democratic principles, popular rights and interests, than that presented to us in the United Kingdom at the present day. We have there over forty millions of persons nearly entirely in dangerous depend-ence on foreign-raised food, their own land uncultivated, entrusting without question their government to the small body of persons responsible for that state of things. We

see them do so when the question for them is not whether
their land could or could not support them, but, taking the
actual fact of non-cultivation, whether that fact is a necessary one or due to gross defects in the agrarian system.
The defects are gross and glaringly obvious, but, nevertheless, we see them at the bidding of the agrarian oligarchs
bolstering up the system, by grants of public money, and
respectfully entertaining demands in its favour which all
the other interests in the country put together dare not
advance.   Stupendous as was the act of folly of the
Southern whites in going to war for their oligarchs, it is
quite outdone by the submission of the British people to an
interest which, neither cultivating the land nor capable of
cultivating it, would yet, if allowed, exclude or tax foreign-
raised food, raise prices and expose the millions which trust
it to misery and famine.

The man who would go to the Sultan to make a Christian
of him, to the Pope to convert him to Protestantism, to the
Archbishop of Canterbury to convince him of the superiority of the Presbyterian Confession of Westminster over the
Thirty-nine Articles, would justly be thought a lunatic.
These personages would be traitors if they sacrificed to their
personality the great trust placed in them—their position
effaces their individuality—and every reasonable man would
respect the position.   The representative agrarian in the
same way is outside and beyond the reach of argument;
he is committed to the system, to live or die with it.   Indications of reform and openings for attack must be sought
in the system itself and not from the point of view that its
personality is open to reason.   These indications and openings I could not fail to see existed to justify study.   The
system was a house divided against itself, covering interests
united only by a common policy of aggression on the great
non-agrarian majority.   To awaken a spirit of resistance to
that policy in the last would, if successful, be enough to
bring down a house depending not on its own internal
strength, but on support from without, and on power of
commanding that support.

I had formed these views almost unconsciously, and with
no purpose of elaborating them; when residence in South
Tyrone and my uncle's suggestion recalled them formally
to me I was not at all bound to them; they were not pre-

conceptions which I set about confirming and developing, but tentative views, resting, I fully admitted to myself, on imperfect observation. I knew that that observation would need to be enlarged and systematised before valid conclusions could be drawn from it. One point, a starting-point, however, I was in no doubt about. I held that agriculture, the production of food from the soil, should above and beyond all other industries be an industry organised in the interest of the whole people, since their very existence depended on it. The question for me then was the actual organisation of the industry, whether it served that interest and had the intention and ability of serving it. When it is proposed to give the Irish occupiers of land the use of from one to two hundred millions of the public money, the money almost entirely of the non-agrarian element, badly needing it for its own purposes, even if we do not look any farther, it is important to determine by actual observation whether these occupiers cultivate the land, or, adhering to their system, can under any circumstances cultivate it, and whether the gift would serve or injure the industry. To say—and it is constantly both said and thought—that the personal interest of the industrial is the interest of the industry, is a vicious assumption. If every industrial in the country was given £100 a year to live on, every industry in it would be ruined. The necessary aim of the Irish owner and occupier of land is to meet the general case of disability—a case he meets by becoming as far as possible independent of actual industry. The effect of the older legislation, dictated by the landowner, was to assure him in the position of a non-industrial; that of recent legislation goes only to secure the same position to the occupier, with even greater injury to the agricultural industry. What is no question calling for interminable discussion, but a fact staring one in the face, is that the agrarian lives and can live on the land in a position of disability. The question is why he should be allowed to make his disability a pretext for endless offence against the sense, means and interest of the community. It is quite true that disability, the common lot not only of the agrarian element but of all mankind, has to be met one way or another : but the confused and endless land question is only an expression of the futile and nugatory manner in which the agrarian has ever met it. The question is solved at once by setting aside the futile attempt to make the possession of the land meet the case of each individual under the inevitable conditions of human life, and organising agricultural industry on the base of obtaining a maximum production with a minimum of labour, that is, in the interest of the community. But I did not take up this solution as a preconception. The reader who follows or repeats for himself the method given here must, I believe, be forced to the conclusion I arrived at.

II

MRS M'KIBBIN

THE day after the conversation I have given, I drove with my uncle to an out-dispensary some four miles from Jiggle-street. The journey, however, was not there and back; a number of visits to patients made it one of sixteen miles.

My uncle's servant, who used his whip and tongue as he liked, was an old friend. Pat M'Coy rhymed himself a droll boy, but the drollery was like a champagne unloved by ladies—dry, austere, suggestive of crab juice. He always called my uncle Colonel, and received the title of Sergeant in return. My uncle never gave me an account of his experiences in America during, and previous to, the Civil War, but I knew that M'Coy's connection with him dated from childhood, and that the latter had saved his life in some skirmish in Missouri. As a thing not to be kept a secret, my uncle told this and, moreover, that it was M'Coy who had induced him to cut the infernal nonsense, as he called the military service of the Confederate States. Farther than this he never went, except to say that if he wrote his personal history it would be under the title, *Memoirs of an Idiot*. M'Coy was always impenetrable as to details, but still, with his help, I read this to mean that his master had placed intelligence, courage and daring at the service of what, in the end, he felt was a bad cause. Yes, M'Coy was impenetrable for a rather talkative man; the only fact of historical interest he was free with was that, when the M'Coys he belonged to got located in Georgia, with Indians to talk to, the Misses M'Coy learned to give an answer without giving any information, and set the example in the use of speech to their male connections.

It was a favourite position with him, possibly through his experience of war, and on this occasion he pressed on

me to tell the people in these parts " plenty," as the best
means of avoiding enlarging their stock of information.

" But, M'Coy," I objected, " Irishmen have not to go to
America to learn to do that. They do it quite naturally."

" Naturally, yes, sir. It is, I allow, natural in them to
talk enough, telling nothing. They do get that length
correct as a judge in court, only to spoil all by letting you
see that what they tell you is nothing to what they know.
They could pass themselves as rale ignorant, that easy, but
their consate 'ill not let them."

Coming to a farmhouse of the better class, a grave-look-
ing elderly woman stopped the car in order to speak to my
uncle.

" Well, Mrs M'Kibbin, I hope there is nothing wrong
with you to-day?"

" No, doctor, nothing, the Lord be thankit, that calls for
the healer of bodily ills. I just want——"

But M'Coy, considering his lesson of importance, went
on with it while my uncle spoke to the woman, merely
dropping his voice. Mrs M'Kibbin, however, interrupted
herself suddenly to listen, looking intently critical, to what
he was saying.

" Consate! Yes, sir. In America, in general, we just
tell you what you know, and that leaves us free to tell you
no more. Confine yourself here, sir, to telling people what
they know. They'll be pleased to think they're right, and
value your opinion. Yes, sir."

Mrs M'Kibbin could not have understood M'Coy's
argument, but for all that she abruptly challenged it.

" The wicked 'll go to hell. Now, you know that, and
does it answer you my saying it?"

" Yes, ma'am," was the instant reply. " You know the
wicked, having studied them, and I'd set value on your
experience."

" You're not to go by me. It's down in Scripture."

" If it's down in Scripture you're up in Scripture, which
I can't say I am. When you say it I take it as sure as
that there are bars in North Carolina!"

My uncle, amused, but dreading the rapid accentuation
of the controversy, intervened.

" Never mind the Sergeant, Mrs M'Kibbin. Good people
like ourselves are to get to heaven, you know."

" I don't know about the rubbish of the Street. Heaven would be a *place* if *they* got there."

The lady said this not at all offensively, but with an air of really sincere doubt about the Street, as the village of Jigglestreet was called in the district. The farmers looked with contempt on the village and its inhabitants, and a place in heaven for them must have seemed absurd to her.

" It's like you're throng to-day, doctor," she said, changing her tone, as if the claim of Jigglestreet to enter the Kingdom of Heaven made discussion absurd. " I won't keep you on the road. I hear John Joe M'Quade has a lock of oats for sale, and I just want M'Coy to bid him send me some. We sowed none the year, but just bought as we stood in need."

" The Sergeant will do anything you tell him, Mrs M'Kibbin, but I am afraid M'Quade is nearly run out. Perhaps you need more than he has on hands."

" Oh, we need only a pickle ! There's just the old mare and a pony to feed, and all the pony does is to go to meeting on the Sabbath."

" Why don't you raise oats to do you, Mrs M'Kibbin, and not leave it to chance ? "

" It's easy for you to talk, doctor. A hundred acres of land is a heavy handful for a lone woman to manage, however light we make the work ; and my heart is not set on the things of this world besides."

" Well, well, the Sergeant will give your message to M'Quade as soon as we get back to the Street. Good-bye ! Take care of yourself."

With this my uncle waved his hand to M'Coy to drive on, and we left Mrs M'Kibbin behind. But not her land, that faced us for some time—dreary, worn-out pastures, here and there patch-work of rushes and whins. Alongside of great, overgrown hedges a few gaunt bullocks turned a melancholy stare on us, looking as if, like their owner, their hearts were not set on the things of this world.

" A strange person," my uncle remarked as we drove along, " Mrs M'Kibbin may seem to you, but we have many like her here. She is religious, but her religion is partly a cause, partly a consequence of chronic mental depression. Her thoughts are the mere mechanical echo of the set phrases of meeting-house preachers. She takes

C

religion as medicine, not food, and if not rank poison little good as medicine. She salutes her friends, the Sergeant in particular, with the always novel announcement that there is a pit dug for the ungodly, that the wicked shall go to hell, and so on. Hell is the only reality for her; this earth is but a passing dream, and heaven a place that exists, indeed, but not for the sake of any that can possibly get to it. Any energy she has—it's not much—is spent in worrying over hell; if any is left it goes in wonder that anyone, the Sergeant in particular, is not of her own turn."

"Her land," I said, "clearly costs nothing to work, but how can she pay rent for it?"

"She has a mere nominal rent to pay, two and sixpence an acre."

"Even so, how can she live by it?"

"Oh, she buys young cattle and sells them again; does a poor but not unsafe business. Besides, she has some houses in the Street, and bits of land which she lets by auction for cropping. Then she lives in a poor, narrow way. Is it the case, Sergeant, that M'Quade has oats for sale?"

"Didn't he take the windmill field from her, six acres, the year, at twenty-seven the acre, and make well by selling her the grain he raised on it? But it'll not matter to John Joe, his being run out. He'll just buy in the market what she wants, and chance hell by charging as much as he can get out of her."

"Has she no family," I asked, "to help her?"

"She is a widow with a son and daughter, both grown up, but, I'm afraid, of little use."

"Use," echoed M'Coy, "leave me alone, Colonel, if she'd let them be of use in this world at least. The darter, in a sort of a way, plays the peeanee—in passing I hear it going—and grows posies in the windies and back yard. She's melancholic they do say, because their young minister didn't bestow himself on her. Alexander, the son, I've rale pity for, though the way he opens his mouth when you open yours makes you take him to be hard of hearing, which he isn't. Then he makes 'Oh, aye!' do for half the grammar and dictionary."

"I am afraid," my uncle said, qualifying as usual M'Coy's severity, "the poor lad gets no chance. His mother treats him as a mere child; if he went beyond a half silly 'Oh, aye!' she would take it as her duty to check him for presumption. Their business is cattle dealing, but she allows Alexander not a word in it. Eh, Sergeant, had you not words with her on the head of keeping Alexander in the background?"

"Yes, Colonel, when she was out with John Joe she'd have me buy for her, and I told her right away to let Alexander, and I'd help him. But John Joe fell out with her to show his value and fell in again at his convenience. He is a senator by nature, John Joe is. Yes, sir."

"Yes," my uncle said, "she employs M'Quade or a neighbour to do business for her, and does not allow Alexander even to go with them to market, to keep him from falling into bad company, she says. But the lad is really no ninny."

"That's so," said M'Coy, in a self-correcting tone. "I had it in mind, Colonel, to tell you that he asked me the other day, as if curious and no more, what money would take one to America. He was too innocent, that's a fact, and I saw that he was for getting me to infringe the Fugitive Slave Acts unknowing to myself."

"I hope, Sergeant, you did not encourage him in the notion of running away to America. What would he do there?"

"Well, Colonel, spirit would stand to him, and for a minute he minded me of old Stonewall with his pecker up. There's that spirit, when you do see you're for backing it. But I told him I never went to America yet and came back at a friend's cost, which you have a right to know is correct. But the fact is, he has an uncle, the father's brother, in Michigan, and I do believe there's writing letters, private and confidential, between the parties."

"In that case, the best thing for Alexander and his mother, too, might be that he should go to his uncle. The lad has ability, can write a clear, sensible letter, as I know. But keep out of the thing, Sergeant. There is no chance of him doing anything for himself here as long as the mother lives, and worrying over hell is apparently what she can live long on. Still it is not a case for interference; Alexander should be left to himself."

"The chance, Colonel, is that the pit is dug for him at

home. Everyone knows that no servant can put up with
the woman's ways. Only the unfortunate children have to
put up with her and be ruled by her, not being able to help
themselves. It's just America or the drink for Alexander.
That's my mind, Colonel, though I'll not interfere."

"I suppose," my uncle concluded, "we must credit Mrs
M'Kibbin with good intentions without, however, any knowledge of their destination as paving stones. It is best, on
the whole, Sergeant, to leave Alexander to work out his
own salvation. If he does that it will not be in her
way."

Understanding that my uncle had enough of Mrs
M'Kibbin, M'Coy resumed the important task of repressing
in me an assumed youthful inclination to bestow gratuitous
information on my fellow men. I was unconscious of
the disposition, and thought it a mere excuse he made to
expand his theory of human nature, which was an unusual
one in men of his class.

"Leave me alone now, Master Atty ; but however you
would put it, I'd say short that the man that mostly lives
with coyotes comes in the long run, unknown to himself,
to have the nature of the beasts. Yes, sir, without being
able to put it to himself the sort of the nature. Coloured
people, I'd say, took half the mind they have from the
wild beasts of Africa, their forefathers living among them,
and in Dixie half our mind we took from the coloured
people. The man that lives with tigers takes the nature
of tigers ; with sheep, much of the nature of sheep. Yes,
sir, not knowing it. The planter lives here more with
cattle and pigs and dogs than with men, and his nature is
according. You have the nature in them and it puts them
beyond you."

"The Sergeant," my uncle said, laughing, "carries the
doctrine of association to extremes, makes it take the place
of natural selection as the chief agency in accumulating
variations. You have read Uncle Remus and met the pro-
totype. The negro identifies himself with the lower animals,
and allows his observation of them to influence him, to form
his mind, but when one man does so all do, with difference
only in degree."

"It's deeper down than that," M'Coy said, unsatisfied by
the appreciation of his philosophy. "He don't make his

mind, Sambo ; he finds it just ready made when he's grown.
When we're tossin' about on sea he's on land, ne'er a doubt,
with his feet firm. When you and Master Atty, and maybe
Pat M'Coy, think of God Almighty, we just get lost thinking of what's not a man ; but Sambo, he's content and
happy with a cross between an alligator and an elephant.
Yes, sir."

"I hope, Atty," my uncle said, "you are taking that all
in. It is complimentary. The Sergeant never casts his
pearls before swine."

"You mind, Colonel," M'Coy went on, not heeding the
interruption, "your old nurse, Dinah Spencer ; you mind
her great, big, black man, with a stick the size of a live oak,
ready to do for little boys that dirtied their bibs. She
called, you mind, the big man God because we were whites.
Yes, sir. When it was her own she was correcting, ne'er a
man it was, but a big beast, that gobbled up a dozen little
boys at one bite and looked round for more. Being black
they understood that, and she spoke to their understanding.
Yes, sir."

"Poor old Dinah," was all my uncle said.

"But M'Coy," I asked, thinking I should interest myself
in what he was saying, "do you mean that the level of
understanding of the people here is so fixed that one must
keep to it in speaking to them ?"

"Level of understanding," he repeated after me, meditatively. "I just mean that they're baked bread and roast
meat, and 'll stand no second cooking from you, Master
Atty. I don't say but you might spoil an odd one by
putting one consate in place of another, that is, what
becomes a consate through the place it enters, and the
company it has to keep there. But the bird's stuffed, as a
rule, and done to a turn. Try Mrs M'Kibbin now, and
leave me alone if you'll get anything into her, but what
you'll get out of her under the trial 'll be amusing. Yes,
sir. And she's not the worse after all. You may go to
that school to learn, but there's no opening for a teacher
in it."

"The Sergeant," my uncle said drily, "is not at sea now ;
he finds firm ground under his feet at times. But we are
all the creatures of circumstance, and in a school that kills
those who cannot learn."

III

About a mile beyond Mrs M'Kibbin's house my uncle had
a visit to pay to a patient, a man named Sefton. The car
was stopped at a "lonin" or lane, up which we walked
until we came to a big, grim-looking house, of blue-black
stone and slate, with warped and decayed door and windows,
on which time had left only a few ugly cracked patches of
mud-coloured paint. In front of the house was the ghost
of a garden, a patch in which kale stumps stuck up through
thistles and ragweed. With the help of imagination a few
thorn bushes made a fence for it. These were cropped
down by two tethered goats, which, with a few fowls, were
all the live stock to be seen about the place.

A big melancholy-looking woman opened the door before
we came up to it.

"He is thinking long to see you, doctor," she said. "I
don't know what you'll say, but to my eye he looks to be
putting in his wee time."

My uncle shook his head.

"You know, Mrs Sefton, I could not give you hope from
the first."

It was indeed a hopeless but protracted case of malignant
disease, and all my uncle could do was to give the sufferer a
few kind words.

"What a gloomy-looking place," I said, as we came back
to the road. "But the house must have cost a large sum
to build. Is the man a dispensary patient?"

"Yes, practically, for I expect no payment for my
attendance; and yet Sefton has thirty-five acres of land in
fee-simple. But he has been ill, as you see, for three years,
and has no one but the wife and a daughter, the last working with a milliner."

" How do they live ? "

" It is hard to tell that. I suppose the only answer is that it takes very little to keep them."

" If they have the place in fee, why don't they sell it ? They would get a large sum for it."

" They might, but probably not what would pay the debts on it."

" How do they come to hold in fee-simple ? That is a rare case."

" That means a long history. Originally the farm was Church land in the hands of a thrifty and industrious man named Tilgate, who held, besides, a larger farm as a tenant-at-will. When the Irish Church was disestablished Tilgate bought out the place. On old Tilgate's death his son, who was called Gentleman Tilgate by the country people from his polished manner, built this house, and in other ways quickly got through the property left him. He had no idea of working his land, or of living the life of an ordinary farmer ; he was too fine a man for that, and, of course, ran into debt. You remember old John Kaye who lived at the Red Cross when you were here in '94 ? "

" Yes, the old moneylender the people called Minister Kaye. You remember he gave me an old Greek Testament, which I have yet, and a dozen pears which he picked himself—the very best he could get ? He was a very old man then ; he can hardly be alive."

" He was ninety, and the next winter was too much for him. He was really a good man ; it was his business fastened a bad name on him. Well, well ! he never lent me money, so I can think of him as a friend, and a worthy though rather eccentric man."

We came to the road and got on the car again.

" Gentleman Tilgate gave the Minister a mortgage on this place, and as he neither paid principal nor interest, the last soon had possession of it. Kaye never made a will, although his clergyman and myself did our best with him, but he really had no one in the world he cared for—no near relatives—and could never make up his mind what he should do with his considerable property. When he died, this man Sefton claimed to be his heir-at-law and took possession of Tilgate's farm as realty. The fact is, I know nothing about the legal aspects of the case, but no one disputed his claim except a servant man of Kaye's named Brown. It cost Sefton £200, they say, not to prove his title but to prove that Brown had no *locus standi* in challenging it. In the end, as the farm had been cropped out and utterly neglected from the elder Tilgate's time, Sefton was left in undisturbed possession."

"Who got the personalty—the bulk of Kaye's property?"

"I fancy part is still in the lawyers' hands. There were half a dozen farms through the country which practically lay derelict for two or three years, but the bulk of the estate was in mortgages, promissory notes and other paper securities which were never paid. The rascal Brown, however, must have feathered his nest well."

"It was the farmers," M'Coy put in, "who came in for the Minister's money, dead and alive. A mint of money they got from him from first to last, and repaid it by giving him the worst word in their mouths."

"Yes," my uncle said, "there is no doubt that without the form of a will they are Kaye's chief legatees, and besides, he lost large sums to them during his life. He was not hard enough for the business. His father was a Presbyterian minister—that is how he came by the title. In a cautious way, so as not to compromise his clerical position, the father accommodated his neighbours, and our minister inherited with the debts the calling, but he was a wretched financier. I often told him that he would be far safer if he put his money in Consols. He would agree and go on the same as ever, lending at five and six per cent. to farmers notorious for not paying their debts."

"But," I asked, "how could he be so wealthy if he was continually lending money only to lose it?"

It was M'Coy, always fond of knotty problems, who answered the question.

"He'd have died in the workhouse if the farmers were to be saved or bettered by lending them money. Yes, sir, he helped them to ruin themselves, and made by them under that condition. You see, he'd take a mortgage for five hundred on a farm, then the times being bad he'd get it by-and-by for the five hundred, and though it might be no bargain, by waiting, as he could, till things mended, get seven hundred or a thousand for it. Many is the stroke of the kind he made without seeing his way to it at first.

That's how he came out safe. Yes, sir, that and saving all his days."

"Yes," my uncle said, "dozens of farms dropped into his hands from the inability of their occupiers to tide over a critical period and from a hundred other causes working together, and once in his hands he held on till he got a good price. When the times are good there is plenty of money to be had on the security of land, and plenty of buyers for it, but Kaye lent in bad times to men in difficulties, almost always got their land and sold it at a profit. His intention, I have no doubt, was to tide them, if possible, over their difficulties, but that was seldom possible, and the advantage was a fair one to take."

He waved his hand towards a wide countryside on our right, dotted over with farmhouses, the majority mean in appearance.

"It would be an interesting study to work out the history of these farms for the last fifty years one by one. Most of them have changed hands again and again, and it would soon be found that the main reasons for this subsist still in full force in every house. There is, in the first place, the liability to disability from age, infirmity, sickness, and so on, telling with irresistible force on families always on the dangerous edge of things. Then there is the personal equation—vice, drunkenness, ignorance, idleness. When these factors are given their due value the legal conditions of tenure would sink into insignificance in our history."

M'Coy felt bound to dwell his own way on the text.

"Leave me alone, Master Atty, if the land, supposing it could speak for itself, wouldn't say it's poisoned keeping up Mrs M'Kibbin, Gentleman Tilgate, Minister Kaye and the like, and let the landlord down easy, not to mention the labouring man who does as little as he can help, and the working farmer who does what he can to meet rent and debt. But where is the same working farmer our model of a man? There's that countryside facing us, and the Colonel is the man to tell you how many of the farmers on it could do a day's work or get a man to do it. Yes, sir, leave me alone if you'll not find them as the rule old men and old weemen that can work none and get no one to work for them, they're that crabbit and crookit and sour. When their children are growed, away they go, as Mrs

M'Kibbin's Alexander is for doing, reckoning Michigan next door to Paradise, which by no means is the case. Then a decent servant boy 'll not stop his term to be insulted by them."

"There is much truth," my uncle added, "in what the Sergeant says, though we need not put it in so personal a way. The land, like every other kind of property, is in the hands of the aged, out of all proportion to their numbers, and the aged farmers are anything but amiable creatures. They live isolated lives, are jealous of their power, angular inclined to keep their sons and nephews in order."

M'Coy, who evidently had a bitter animus against the farmers or planters, as he occasionally called them, chimed emphasis.

"Keep them in order!—say, Colonel, keep them down ; make niggers of them. Yes, sir, you mind Archie Liddle's Johnnie, as brave a lad as a girl would care to lay eye on. You mind him now meeting us on the road driving one day, bent in two and ailing, and telling you that he was harder worked and worse treated than the servant boy in his father's house. He might have kept the secret to himself, for you knew what was wrong with him. And hasn't old Archie a grudge, sharp, against you, suspecting you know more about his running away to America than ere a one of us. Yes, sir."

"Well, I did lend the lad a few pounds, which he repaid me long ago."

"I'm not curious, Colonel ; ne'er a bit. You mind big John Master's Jessie ? Leave me alone now, if she comes Master Atty's road, I've her booked No. 2, my old woman taking a divorce. You mind remarking to her on a well-off farmer's darter going to service in Belfast, and she tossing her pretty head and telling you that she was herself at home in a gentleman's house, with good wages and light work, and nobody but a dirty drudge without a pennypiece in her father's house. Jessie wouldn't allow she was herself not being clean and rubbed down ; but it's because she's sense and grit she's booked for the vacancy mentioned."

"You would not guess," my uncle said, laughing, "that the Sergeant was raised in a slave State. He would amend the Ten Commandments by putting in the duty of parents to children, and leaving out the duty of children to parents.

"Yes, Colonel, as unnecessary, the parents doing their duty, the children may be reckoned on to do theirs; and the parents not doing their duty, the children not knowing what to do. Yes, sir. I went, Master Atty, with my State in the old days, and if I went wrong there wasn't a clergyman in Dixie knew wrong from right, not to speak of State governors, judges, legislators, newspaper men, and the rest having the telling of what was right and what wrong. Yes, sir."

M'Coy was left to continue the conversation, which he did after a pause.

"I allow that there's a differ between white and black, a mighty differ; but when I found by accident a mind of my own, it was lightning to me that the differ was no reason for making white master, and black slave. But it is against nature and reason to make slaves of one's children. Yes, sir, when my children growed, there's a big world and a chancy one before you, I said; just you out and work for yourselves; it'll have, may be, a better chance for you than ever it had for me. That's the way with the labouring men, but the farmers keep their children to work for them without wages and without liberty, without fitting them and leaving them to take the chances the world has for most. In my opinion make slaves or darned runaway cusses of them. Yes, sir."

My uncle looked thoughtful.

"Certainly," he said, "the relations between parents and children in general are more unsatisfactory in the farming than in any other class; there is more undue submission, more revolt, more friction in it. Even if the farm needed the young, and would support and pay for their labour, they run away and leave it, and in disgust and irritation at being forced to stay on it against their will and interest. In fact, our farms not being able to pay for hired labour, it is unreasonable to retain on them persons who, brought up to consider themselves superior to hired labourers, find themselves practically in a worse and inferior position. As a rule, those who go away turn out much better than those who stop, and it is no wonder that such should be the case."

Emphasis from M'Coy again.

"No wonder, Colonel, for something more than that. It's the mean cuss there's nothing in that stops on waiting till past marrying, for what's not worth waiting a year for. Yes, sir. There's Ned Boyle over yonder, a boy of fifty-six, and old Ned, at eighty-three, is as much his master as if he was coloured born. Leave me alone now, if I don't hear that the old ruffian has made a will, leaving the place to his son in Nebraska, who did the wise thing and run before he was man grown."

My uncle smiled, as if old Ned's will was a good joke.

"It is likely old Boyle has made such a will. He is quite capable of committing the monstrous injustice of depriving young Ned of the farm he has worked for years more for the old man's profit than his own."

"Working the farm, Colonel, to keep up a master is nothing to what young Ned has stood years and years, putting up with the old ruffian's capers and cahoos. Myself has heard him taunting the boy that no girl would have him, and another time daring him to bring any hussy about his place to eat him up. And ne'er a question the old cuss would be in the workhouse twenty years ago but for young Ned."

It was a disagreeable picture, but M'Coy dabbled on leaden shades to please himself.

"What kills the old man is young Ned's fiddle. If it was battering an Orange drum with the boys, he'd take it equal to quoting Scripture texts again the Papishes, but when, for peace sake, young Ned fiddles to himself in a dry ditch, he remarks that he doesn't know what possesses him to keep up an idle vagabone there's a want in."

"There is more," my uncle observed, "than the fiddle between them. Old Boyle was heavily in Minister Kaye's books, and took the Minister's death as a receipt in full for the debt. The son stupidly could not see the thing in that way, and would not be a party in denying the obligation. This irritated the old man, who looked on it not as honesty but mere craziness. But it so happened that young Ned did the very best thing he could for himself."

"I'd guess him, Colonel, not up to playing a stroke for himself. Maybe now it was you primed the piece for him."

My uncle did not heed this observation, but went on.

"For good reasons of their own the parties who took Kaye's affairs in hands did nothing to raise awkward questions as to their own position. They compromised claims knowing that they could not easily enforce them. For a nominal consideration they transferred the debt on Boyle's place to the son, the father being impracticable. If the old man has made a will, as I believe he has, leaving all to his son in America, it does not matter ; young Ned has more against the farm than it would fetch in the market."

"He did that stroke, Colonel, out of his own head! Leave me alone if I wouldn't have given him a camp-meeting certificate of innocence signed Pat M'Coy."

"Of course," my uncle continued, "the lawyers might pick holes in the transaction, but it was the best thing young Ned could do under the circumstances, and it is not likely his claim will ever be questioned."

"I'm downright ready for a glass, Colonel, on the head of that stolen march, not caring all the same for young Ned, who I say is rale mean to put up with what he did."

"I can hardly agree to that, Sergeant. Young Ned with a mortgage on the farm for more than it is worth allows the old man to play the master just as much as ever, goes to the ditch with his fiddle when he wants music, and puts up good humouredly with ill-natured remarks. I would not call that meanness."

"Now, M'Coy," I said, "is that too much for you? You made me take young Ned as a chip of the old block."

"Leave me alone, Master Atty, if I'd reflect on the old un's missus, a decent woman in her grave these thirty years. Raise her up yourself like the witch of Endor and question her as to the extraordinary means she took to improve the breed, leaving that there is nothing of the old cuss in young Ned. I'm for not intruding on her honourable retirement myself. Yes, sir. I can stand correction, but to face an old lady in the spiritual form defending herself is a thing I'll not try."

"Perhaps it is a case of atavism."

"I pass over the Colonel as a rule when he uses doctors' words, but maybe you'd give me the differ between A-tavism and B-tavism."

"A-tavism would occur if old Ned took after grand-parents or more remote ancestors, and B-tavism if young

Ned was a prophetic germ of a Boyle far away in the bosom of future time."

"Leave me alone," was the comment on this, "if the Boyles up to the Flood wouldn't vote old Ned out of their line or take his being in it as a conundrum. They'd know their own savages doin' murder and plundering straight and simple, but they followed nature as to dealin' with their children or they'd have been nowhere by this. Yes, sir, old Ned means, as all his like does, wind-up of the line not as following but as departing from nature. I'd say things come to an end with old Ned for the Boyles. You need trouble none looking into the future for more of the breed."

"I must vote with the Sergeant," my uncle said laughing. "The Boyles, father and son, vary widely from the primitive ancestral type ; they are creatures of the modern conditions of life, and yet doomed through imperfect accommodation to these very conditions. The father is sunk in the owner— the absolute owner of the common means of support—his authority becomes that of an arbitrary master, not that of a parent, and the natural dependence of the child instead of lapsing at maturity becomes protracted, exaggerated, and often perverted. This, while not confined to the farming class, obtains in that class the dimensions of a vast social evil. In it early adult life is not only deprived of the opportunity of free development but to a great extent reduced to a state servile in all but name."

A visit we had to pay in a wayside house to sickly children interrupted the conversation, but the subject was in my uncle's mind, and when we got on the car he resumed it for my benefit.

"I am afraid old Boyle is a common though it may be a rather accentuated specimen of the old men who hold so many of our farms in dependence on the labour of others. The Sergeant's doctrine, which he learned not here but in America, that all farmers are slave-drivers, open or disguised, with the mind of slave-drivers, applies here, of course with qualification. When the father, owning the farm, directs the labour of his children he tends to become a mere master, and it is well if his exertion of power does not become inordinate and tyrannical. The result, as you would find by taking a large number of concrete instances at random, is marked revolt of the young against the old, of children against parents, and the last left without help to work their farms as they best can."

"You may leave me out, Colonel, as not able to go deep into things, but didn't Minister Kaye tell you in my hearing that a farm not able to keep up a hired labouring man could keep up sons and daughters only as slaves without wages and liberty. And if ever there was a man knew the farmers it was the Minister, seeing that he lent them money with experience of loss. Yes, sir."

"Minister Kaye," my uncle assented, "was a practical observer with a pessimistic turn, who, if he reaped advantage from evils, did not on that account take them as other than evils. Yes, he often said that the farmers were always trying to live on him, on their children, their labourers, on high prices exacted from the community, on every one, and made possession of the land a means of doing so. Well, here is the temple of Esculapius, and you have had enough of the farmer for one day."

IV

BUT one could as easily escape the citizen in London as the farmer in South Tyrone. I had to hear him and hear of him all day long whether I would or would not. I had no choice but to give him thought.

The temple of Esculapius, in other words the Red Cross out-dispensary, conveyed the impression that the divinity, his priests and rites, were held in small esteem in the country. It was certainly not of the hovel style of architecture, which is peculiarly that of the dwellings of labour. Its walls were stone, its roof slate, but evidently before its consecration it had been the cowhouse or byre of a ruined farmhouse hard by, and in spite of counter, desk and shelves adorned with rows of medicine bottles, the original purpose had cost nothing to disguise. The incense which gently choked one on entering was distinctly referable to castor oil qualified by the odour of the primitive bovine inhabitants exhaled from the clay floor.

"It is well," my uncle remarked, "that I come here but once a week, for I fancy the place does not agree with me."

"Would not better accommodation be afforded if applied for?"

"I do not know that. The place is on an out-farm of old Josh Holmes, who gets £8 a year for it, and the Guardians, who are nearly all of his own tribe, no doubt think he has a prescriptive right to the rent. I found the place as you see it, and mean to leave it as I found it. I had enough of warfare in my time."

Four old women, two mothers with children to be vaccinated, and one lad, were sitting on a form in the compartment which served as a waiting-room. My uncle gave each a word as he passed into the sanctum.

He sometimes used military terms, and calling up the lad he said to me—

"Attention! Now listen."

Then speaking to the lad—

"What is your name, young man?"

"Ma name? Sure ye have ma name in yer book."

"No matter, tell me your name."

"Don't ye mind now, I was wi' ye harvest an' spring was a year wi' the ringworm."

"Well, well, tell me your name."

"Ye don't mind, ma! Sure, I live wi' wee Hughy in Corcreeghy thonder. Ma father works wi' wee Hughy. Ye mine ma father. Ye was seein' him twict. He had a crushin'."

"Will you tell me your name, or leave the place at once."

The lout gaped in distressed silence, looking deeply aggrieved.

"Why don't you tell the doctor your name at once?" said one of the young women. "Sure, doctor, he is——"

But my uncle checked her with his raised hand.

"I have to write down his name, and wish him to tell it himself. He has no ticket. Now, young man, what is your name?"

"Ada-ay."

The sound was inarticulate beyond comprehension.

"Eh, what?"

"Ada-ay."

The sound was no more definite, and my uncle looked inquiringly at the woman who had volunteered to speak.

"Sure, your honour, he is Samuel Adair, and he works with Hugh M'Laddery in Corcreeghy. You may forgive him for he is a bit backward."

The boy looked with grateful relief at the woman, as if she had given him a valuable piece of information.

"Yas. Samale Ada-ay, an' I works wi' wee Hughy in Corcreeghy. Minds his kine."

"Now," my uncle said to me, "I'll leave him to you. Probably the case is not a consultation one."

"Well, Samuel," I asked, "what is wrong with you?"

Samuel looked at me in a way that did not at all coincide with the woman's opinion of his backwardness.

" Er ye a doctor ? "

" Yes, but I have not my diploma with me."

With the air of being quite well able to ascertain the fact for himself, he drew up a dirty coat sleeve and exhibited an arm as dirty, with some circular patches of a common skin disease on it.

" Then, what d'ye call that ? "

" Ringworm."

" Right you er."

In the examinations I had lately passed no professor had expressed approval of a correct answer with more calm consciousness of right to approve. But the lad was at home with me, as I was about his own age, and his mind took its natural proportions.

" Were you ever at school ? "

The answer was given with an air of the utmost indifference.

" Oh, aye ! "

" Long ? "

" Oh, aye ! A brave wee spell."

" Can you write ? "

" I'm not good at the writin'."

" You can read, of course ? "

I could see I was beginning to trespass on his politeness in asking questions having no connection with the cure of ringworm.

" I've ten beasts ev wee Hughy's to mind, an' other work forbye, an' it's not callin' for readin' an' writin'."

" What did you go to school for then ? "

" I went to school none ; I was sent, bein' wee, to be out ev the road, an' took home when I could earn."

" I see. What is your father ? "

" He has a bit ev lan', an' works forebye wi' wee Hughy."

It was my turn now.

" Es the ringworm smittel ? "

" Well, you should not go too near the girls when you have it. You are a favourite with them, of course."

" Ye're funny. Es it in the blood ? "

" What would you say yourself ? "

" Et's for you to answer, bein' a doctor, not ma."

Then he became condescendingly explanatory.

" Ye see wee Hughy ses I gave et to his beasts, an' I ses his beasts gave et to ma. But ye see, ev they gave et to ma they gave et none to him. A smitch of et he hasn't, and he handling them constant."

" Some persons are much more apt to take it than others. The girls now and children, persons with delicate skins."

Samuel shook his head with critical dissent.

" Ma skin is none so tender, besides I sleep wi' wee Robert John, ma brother, an' he hasn't a smitch on him no more nor wee Hughy has. I ses et's smittel in a way, an' in a way et's in the blood."

" The makings of a doctor are lost in you. Do you ever argue with your minister ? "

A really intelligent smile came over the lad's face.

" Ye may talk wi' ma, ye may ; but ev ye turn the word wi' ministers, they've the hot place for ye. Na, na. I don't trouble ma minister, an' he troubles ma none."

When he left with a cure for his ringworm, my uncle took a moment to explain.

" Dispensary patients have many curious peculiarities, and among them a dislike to telling their names. They seem to have a positive difficulty about doing it in themselves. You drag first the surname, next the Christian name out of them, and you see that it is an almost painful effort in them to give it.

" That lad, Samuel Adair, was really intelligent and observant, in spite of the difficulty he had in giving you his name."

" It cannot be explained on the ground of want of intelligence. I once asked an intelligent girl how it came that she did not give her name, and the whole of it at once when asked, and yet gave the name of others readily enough. Her answer was that she knew others by their names, and had occasion to know them that way, while she did not need her name to know herself, and never used it as a means of knowing herself, so that it did not come at once to her. She meant that she had not formed the habit of identifying the Ego by name."

" That is a nice bit of psychology and reasoning both.

I suppose many traits of the kind await observation and description."

"Yes.   Attention!   You have not long to wait for another."

A curious looking old woman, mendicant all over, came forward.   She seemed for the most part head gear and raiment hermaphrodite, diffusing around an odour of bad tobacco.

"Well, Longpockets," my uncle said to her, "what is wrong with you to-day?"

"Sure it's to the doctor I come to tell that."

"You have told me Everything as often as I have told you that Everything and Nothing are more than I can cure."

My uncle only could read meaning in the twist the curious figure underwent.

"Well, well, I know you have given me up long ago as a bad job.   You look in as a friend just to see how I am getting along myself."

He gave her sixpence, which called for a protracted search among many pockets for a place of security.   When the matter was arranged at last, she said with the air of making an unimportant suggestion, and not at all as giving a piece of information.

"There's wee mon Oins' Alec ailing this wheen o' days an' your honour might look in an' see him on your way to Knocknavaddymore, the wee crature is donsy."

"What makes you think, Longpockets, that I am going to Knocknavaddymore to-day?"

"Sure, your honour sent the polis there?"

"You are sure.   Well, I hope they have something to do there."

"Deed an' one your honour didn't wish them their errand."

"How do you know?   Is Jerry M'Cue again running a still.   I would wish them their errand if they can catch him."

"That ruffin!   Sure, it's not him brings them out but his doin's."

"His doings?   Is there anything wrong more than usual at Andy M'Queen's?"

"Your honour doesn't need me to tell you that Andy

is clean away in the head an' to be took away to the 'sylum be the polis. The ruffin's doin's."

"Whose doings?"

"Jerry M'Cue's, that your honour did all in a man's power to hinder ruinin' the country with his drink—pisn, I call it. There he is now made to murder everybody an' cut his own throat, an' only for wee mon Oins and Black Mary holdin' an' tyin' him down would murder the world."

"I see. You mean, Longpockets, that Andy M'Queen not Jerry M'Cue is gone mad?"

"Sure your honour sent the polis, an' they can catch daft people right enough. Where they come short is in catching them that makes them daft."

"They caught M'Cue more than once and put him in jail."

The mass of hybrid raiment seemed to suffer a mild convulsive attack.

"I fault them, your honour, when they put him in for not keepin' him in, but lettin' him out to destroy the country with his pisn."

"Now, Longpockets, hold your tongue or give the devil his due. It was M'Queen and the other farmers in Knocknavaddy who started M'Cue at his bad work and kept him at it. The man could not have carried on for a week if they had not backed him up. There now, that will do. I have my business to mind."

"Sure, I know it's your honour that's to be thankit for reddin' the country of the ruffin. It's not the farmers' place to be huntin' him."

"If it's not their place it's not mine. There now, Longpockets, I have to get through my work."

The dismissal excited another convulsive attack caused perhaps by suppression of speech.

"The old lady," my uncle said, when she was out of hearing, "came in on purpose to tell me that Andy M'Queen had become insane, a piece of news she knew well I was quite unaware of. You heard how she told the story. She expected a long cross-examination, which she would have enjoyed immensely."

"You seem to have taken her own plan and got out of her what you wanted to know indirectly."

"Yes. If I asked her directly what brought the constables to Knocknavaddy it might be night before I would have been wiser. The shortest way was to mix up things, make a mess, and trust to get at the point incidentally or indirectly."

"It seemed strange to me that she had so bitter a feeling against M'Cue. Persons of the class generally are in sympathy with such offenders."

My uncle laughed.

"You would make a poor detective, Atty. My inference is that there is a strict alliance, offensive and defensive, between M'Cue and Longpockets, based on something more substantial than sympathy. Certainly the rascal made it a point to jibe at her, and she returned the compliment, but though she abused him, no one ever got useful information out of her, and that she often had to give. I would not suspect her if she was openly sympathetic."

"She seemed openly sympathetic with the farmers."

"That, as far as it goes, is sympathy with her porridge; she lives on them. But I fancy the expression of feeling is a mere artifice to draw me out. When she comes in to me I suspect she wants besides sixpence some piece of information. I feel excessively proud of myself when I am the pump, not she. I do best when I am in a desperate hurry and have not a minute to talk to her, and in general turn her out without apparently giving her an opportunity of obtaining or imparting information. I would never open the oyster without the trick."

"Then I suppose she is quite a depository of secrets."

"Knows everything going on in the country. I found out through her, though not with her will, all about this man M'Cue. Some years back a strange man came into the district from Connaught and passed from farmer to farmer as a servant 'boy.' Soon after his appearance the usual signs of illicit distillation showed themselves in the country, and suspicion was directed to him. He saved trouble, however, by falling one night when drunk through a trap door in the loft on which he slept, breaking his neck. But before making this end he had taught, among others, M'Cue, a small farmer, the vile business. The others, betrayed by their own stuff, were soon caught, but not so M'Cue. He had the great advantage of being a total abstainer, and had singular power of judging those he could confide in. Unscrupulous, penetrating, resourceful, he would have made a grand statesman or financier, and the application of his talents to distilling poteen was ludicrous. He was caught indeed twice and shut up, but the evidence against him was not technically valid, and though everyone knew he was guilty this helped to make a hero of him. He disappeared out of the country for a long time, and though he has returned he seems to have given the thing up. In fact, he has made what is regarded in the country as a fortune by this or some other means, and is wise enough up to the present to run no risk of losing it. But the mischief he did is incalculable."

" And did the farmers really support him ? "

" Without their connivance and support he could not have gone on. They were his customers. They have twenty-three public-houses, some of them really shebeens, in my district, and that was not enough for them."

We had some patients to attend to, but after dispatching them, my uncle resumed,—

" This very man, Andy M'Queen, who, Longpockets says, is insane, had a licensed house on his farm, for which he got a high rent. Two of the men who kept it died in succession of D.T., and for some good reasons the licence was refused renewal. M'Queen applied again and again for a renewal, and canvassed me as a magistrate to support the application. Canvassed — cajoled, bullied, insulted me. The brute was a Guardian at the time, my official superior as a medical officer, and made it plain that if he did not get the renewal he would make it hot for me. But he is a sample of the men who aim in Ireland at being magistrates, having the nomination of the magistrates, the granting of licences, the control of the police, in fact the whole government of the country in their hands. And they call betraying the people to these ruffians democracy."

" But if the people vote for the men, I do not see why the people should claim your sympathy."

" Giving the vote to Andy M'Queen's cottiers and dependants is about the same thing as giving it to his bullocks. The people have no choice. Choice depends on having men to choose between ; they have only two or three countryside bosses cast in the same mould to vote for. No outsider ever enters the local field."

"Would they not run M'Cue for their local boards or Parliament?"

"M'Cue is a Roman Catholic; he does not belong to the farmer oligarchy and has not obtained political notoriety by cursing the King or bearing arms against him. For his station he is a man of good manners, and his resistance to authority has been a nicely calculated quantity, never unnecessarily irritating."

Our conversation, which went on while my uncle was making entries in his books, was interrupted by a constable with a request to him to attend and certify in the case of Andrew M'Queen arrested as a dangerous lunatic. The procedure needed two magistrates and the medical officer.

"A real bad case, doctor," the constable said. "We found him strapped down in bed, and he is violent and can't be let loose. The magistrates are coming over immediately."

"Well, well, we are nearly done here and will follow you."

With my help the dispensary work was soon done, and we left the squalid temple of Esculapius to its witch-like custodian, who held Longpockets with skinny hand and whispered questions as we drove away with a sense of relief.

But we had our worst half hour before us. The maniac, Andy M'Queen, had in his face a note of animalism, lycanthropy, diabolism, which suggested that he was a thing to be hidden away out of human sight in a jail, asylum, or the grave. But his young wife was even more distressing to look at. Her hair, which evidently had been silky and golden, was piebald with locks bleached white. Her features were pinched and set in the fixed look of crazed misery; her large grey eyes blank in a leaden zone; her dress slatternly and dirty. The eldest child, a boy, was what the country people called an "object." He was an epileptic, and had a scar across one side of his face which everted the lower eyelid, and this went with a complexion of ghastly pallor. The scar was due to his having fallen at one time into the fire. Three other children were huddled together in a corner of the kitchen in unchildlike silence, on their wan little faces the neurotic aspect of habitual terror.

The house, which was a fine substantial one, though clearly planned by no architect better than a country mason, and rude and unfinished, was in a state of indescribable confusion. It was throughother or *durcheinander*, to use an expressive provincialism, with a vengeance. There was much more furniture in it than was at all necessary, and piles of books, but the order was that of a second-hand broker's store. In the kitchen, drawing-room chairs and deal ones were mixed together, and some of them either did not or could not stand on their legs ; from some of them indeed the appendages were missing. Two sideboards filled the side of a bedroom, in front of them a large bedstead with, not bed and bed-clothes in it, but a heap of tattered dusty books, some open, some closed, as if emptied out like stones from a cart. A valuable bookcase, with its glass doors broken and wide open, nothing in it but a few broken decanters, obstructed a small lobby so that one could scarcely pass. Tables, chairs, bureaus, clocks, china, delft, pictures, and so on, lay about in such unexpected places and positions that I longed for my camera to record the strangeness of the thing. In a stable outside I found an old white mare munching hay in one stall, the only happy living thing visible in the place, while in the other stall was a fine old Broadwood piano reared on end to make room for an old trap and a wheelbarrow, in which there was a Brussels carpet and rug tied up with a hay rope.

M'Coy, who was waiting in the yard, remarked my puzzled looks.

"You're strange to these parts, Master Atty, or you'd know Andy an' his fixins on. Remarkable they are. Yes, sir. See, now, there wasn't an auction, ne'er a one, far and near, he'd not go to an' buy slick up, drunk and sober, all one, buy slick up. You guess now how the fixins come?"

"I guess now. But the money? Cost a lot."

"Yes, sir. Considerable. But then the old man left a thousand to Andy—pounds, that is—in bank, and the place here and Kimmit's place, both in top condition and stock for every blade of grass. Then there was his uncle's place, old Martin's place in Knocknavaddybeg, he fell in for that too. Old Martin was his mother's brother and never married. Got eight hundred—pounds, that is—old Martin's savings alone. Yes, sir. Then there was the wife's fortune. Five hundred—pounds, that is. I've got, Master Atty, that I can't reckon by dollars—darned if I'm not ashamed sometimes."

"You needn't be ashamed of practical experience of pounds, M'Coy, but you don't say he lost all that by buying rubbish at auctions? Is he poor now?"

"Poor! don't the place just skeer you with the look of nothing on it. It'll never pay what's on it; and his other places, Kimmet's place and Martin's place, are clean gone, and, of course, the money went before the land. But, if what's told of him is true, he made more by buying at auctions and betting at horse races than all ever he was left. It's a fact, though again the rule, particularly the dealing being in drink. He stood to lose, Andy, buying and selling wild, but it's a fact he made, though not, I'd say, the figures reported."

"I see, he sold as well as bought—dealt in fact. It is possible that some of the things here might have been picked up far below their value, but how could the man know their value in buying and selling?"

"I'd say he didn't know it, and didn't want to know value. Andy would buy wild enough, but had nasty tricks. He'd bid wild, and the other nigger would calculate he'd not stop, certain sure of it, exactly when Andy would stop, in general with a grin that wasn't becoming on a face naturally not sweet. Somehow he got things cheap enough, Yes, sir. Then in selling he went high—twice or three times more than he gave, or smarter when he disremembered what he gave and wanted to be sure. I'd say, sir, he did come out on the safe side, dealing."

"How does it come, then, that he is ruined?"

"I'd say, sir, by giving chance the place of regular steady business and work. He made by chancy dealings and bettings, steadily losing all the time by his three big farms not being worked or minded proper. He'd buy reaping machines and have no crop worth mention to reap with them, fancy stock that he had no feeding for and no knowledge of, and keep up a lot of labour with no one to direct it, he being away most time and careless. Yes, sir. That helped, but M'Indoo was the main ruin of him."

"M'Indoo? Who is he?"

"A neighbour farmer here. If met in the States I'd say Missouri. Yes. You see Andy was for being out and out a big boss, and M'Indoo blew the wind into him to bursting point, talked of running him for President—well not exactly—Member of Parliament it was, I'd say. Then as long as he had a dime there was a farmer wanting his name to a bit of paper as a trifling form, you know, or a mortgage at any per cent. he'd fancy particular. Yes, sir. Then he'd to M'Indoo for advice, who'd say he'd sleep over it— his word that, and end by letting him in considerable. M'Indoo could do that. Yes, sir."

"Did M'Indoo make by him?"

"Ne'er a brown cent. I rather guess I'd say lost, stand-ing treats."

"Do you mean that he purposely worked to ruin M'Queen without seeking any advantage for himself?"

"Fact, that is a way of putting it. But I'd say it was just devilment neat, without a drop of water to take the edge off. Well now, supposing you in with Andy yourself, you'd have that natural anxiety to kick him that you'd be sweet and friendly with him to give you a chance of doing it. Yes, sir, I'd suspicion making real friends with a coyote."

Even M'Coy seemed relieved when the legal formalities were over and our backs turned on the unblest abode.

"Leave me alone, Colonel, if it's conny. They do say it's haunted. Yes, sir. It's a fact they do say that a baby's body was once found in a trough of pig's meat in the yard yonder; that the pigs had the sense not to eat. It's not conny. Yes, sir,"

"I have told you," my uncle said to me, "that M'Queen is a sample of our local governing element. You may note him also as a sample of the men the gulled community are about to give one hundred and twenty millions to."

V

JIGGLESTREET

It was getting dark as we entered Jigglestreet after our depressing day's work.

"God help us," my uncle said, "if lunacy goes on increasing at the rate it is, for I am afraid the help of man is vain. I am harassed with lunatics, doubly harassed with semi-lunatics; they cannot be sent to the asylum."

He was a wonderfully cheerful man considering the nature of his duties, but had sat silent and moody all the way from M'Queen's house to the village.

Passing an ugly, barn-like building, half-hidden with sombre firs and copper beeches, he spoke again, an unusual bitter note in his voice,—

"That is the Presbyterian meeting-house. There are five entrances into the Street; this guards one, the Episcopalian church another, the Roman Catholic chapel number three, the Methodist place number four, while the Baptists and Plyms make doubly sure of the last with two spiritual fortresses facing each other. Well that for 600 persons, but somehow Satan gets past them all."

We passed a metal pump, glaring in a coat of red-lead paint in the middle of crossing streets, with a single tree beside it, the state of which may be guessed from the fact that it was stripped of its bark for between four and five feet from the ground, the work, of course, of the village urchins.

M'Coy in passing levelled his whip as if it was a rifle at the pump, and remarked,—

"Leave me alone, Colonel, if anything else can be calculated on. It's the gentleman named that can't get out of the Street. Hard for him—fourteen public-houses to one public pump, and a sight worse name on the water than on the whisky."

An amusing idea brought the smile back to my uncle's face.

"Yes," he said, "we have got a new pump, but it is under suspicion, and no wonder. For a long time the water had a peculiar flavour. Got so decided that at last we sent a bottle of it up to Dublin to be analysed. Report satisfactory—a fairly wholesome, potable water. But our old pump came to a standstill, and would yield none of the duly certified element. Had to be opened up, when there was found in it a dead rat, the skeleton of a rodent of the same species nicely macerated, small bones not identifiable, box of Holloway's ointment, ounce bottle of castor oil, empty, two pewter spoons, a pen-knife, a match-box, two keys, and other sundries, all alleged to have been stuffed down the spout by certain juveniles in spite of strongly-worded testimonials of innocence from their parents. We shall very likely put the playful little dears under surveillance when the bubonic plague breaks out."

"Is the village dependent," I asked, "on one pump for water. Are there not private pumps?"

"Yes, there are five placed for convenience beside the stable, pighouse and manure heap. Ninety per cent. of the inhabitants use the street pump, and in spite of the rats it is the safest. I wrote to the Board of Guardians, *alias* Andy M'Queen & Co., that one pump was insufficient many times. Letters marked 'Read' and thrown into the waste-paper basket."

As M'Coy walked the horse up the street, I observed a street grating in front of a shop door covered with a sack, and several more carefully closed over with lids of tea-chests.

"Oh," said my uncle in answer to an inquiry, "our drainage system is that of the Stone Age, and the olfactory nerves of some of our people, like their little toes, have not quite degenerated. I report to Andy M'Queen & Co. with a secret dread that my reports may chance sometime to be attended to. So vilely is public work done in these places that it is far safer to leave things as they are. Money is worse than wasted."

A little farther on the dirty gutter by the side path

was marked by a long line of red trickling down to a grating.

"That reminds me," said M'Coy, "John Joe had two pigs to kill, and my missus gave her orders to me to get four pounds of pork chops from him. He was killing to-day, you see."

We stopped at a mean, ugly little house, proclaimed by a big painted board to all the world as the Jigglestreet Dispensary, my uncle's name, hours of attendance and "Vaccination Gratis" emblazoned on it. The spelling and lettering were doubtful, but sunshine, rain and frost had mercifully placed the artist's work beyond criticism, and the last line might have made the Anti-Vaccination League happy by passing as Assassination Gratis.

My uncle's house, separated from the dispensary by a yard gate, would have tried the conscience of an auctioneer to have called a gentlemanly residence. It was made so by the fact of a gentleman residing in it, not by any intrinsic merits of its own. But not twelve houses in the village were valued over £10, and its valuation was £12, and rent £20. That made it one of the principal houses in the village and district. Jigglestreet was indeed a typical Irish village. In a woefully-neglected park adjoining it there was a great house falling into dilapidation, which had cost more to build than did all the other houses in the parish put together. It was the seat of the nominal owner of the estate, an absentee nobleman, by repute on the look-out for an American heiress to rehabilitate his broken fortunes. The Episcopalian rectory was meant for a man with at least £800 a year, but since the disestablishment of the Irish Church its occupants had the awkward task of keeping it up on £200 a year. There was a new Presbyterian manse which had cost, perhaps, £1000 to build, and from this there was a rapid descent through a few public-houses and shops to the hovels rented at 1s. and 6d. a week, in which the mass of the people lived. It was a characteristic of the district, as I came to find, that many of the farmers lived in houses below their means and income. Men worth over £1000 could be found living in houses not fit for decent labourers, in some cases, indeed, not fit for civilised human beings.

This to some extent applied to Jigglestreet. Many of

its inhabitants who could not be called poor, lived contentedly in houses which would be condemned on sanitary grounds as not fit for human habitation. What was in particular striking was that in a place where land had no very great value the dwelling-houses were nearly all mere cribs. Some had only one room, most of them only two. Many had no rear and no back door, and where there was a yard and garden they were not larger than those seen in great cities, sometimes indeed they could be covered by a tablecloth or carpet. The place had some natural advantages; it could have been made, if not picturesque, at least, clean and pleasant-looking. It was, in fact, dirty, squalid and repulsive, simply through the savage, backward mind of the inhabitants. Without particularly seeking information, it was clear to me that the value of property in it could be greatly enhanced at small cost, but the owners of the property, mostly farmers not living in the village, did not see it. In fact, as I found, it took compulsion to make them keep the hovels at all habitable.

"You are ready for your dinner," my uncle said, bowing me in with a manner never dispensed with. "I hope our work is done for the day."

Inside, the world seemed to improve greatly. My uncle's interior was not only a pleasant home, but had a charm about it, an evidence of refined taste and culture. Doctor Atty had been married in early life in America, but his wife had died before he had come to live in Jigglestreet. His uncle and grandfather had been medical men before him in the place, and that, with a certain indifference as to where he lived, had fixed him to it. He had one daughter, and he was at peace with his surroundings, as long as she was satisfied with them and him. Jigglestreet had long ago decided that he should have married again, its way being to marry as often as it got the chance, irrespective of material and moral considerations, for which, indeed, it had no mind. But Miss O'Gara, seeing no necessity for a stepmother, and meeting no one she thought eligible for the post, the village chose a long succession of partners for its doctor, only to assert its view of things as they ought to be in vain. The impulse in the community to exert its power for the sake of exerting it, even to persecute for the sake of persecution, was strong and decided, but circumstances controlled the potent instinct. For one thing, the doctor being the only medical men available was not to be trifled with as a clergyman might, who could be exchanged for another spiritual guide, or altogether done without. For another, he was a strong individualist, or in other words had a mind of his own, which he was able with no difficulty to assert against a common mind, whose only real weapon was mindless force. The mind of country villages is wrongly accused of hypocrisy, because wrongly thought to be governed by some fixed ethical standard. The village mind understands only arbitrary power, the power of supporting by the dozen public-houses, dens of vice continually working the ruin of families before the eyes of all, and the power of persecuting the individual who ventured to think or act in any way, in the cut of his coat, say, differently from the rest. Gossip, slander, irresponsible childish criticism, in the end was only the means instinctively taken to dominate and repress the individual. In the face of it all Doctor O'Gara asserted his individuality, and the village to save its arbitrary power had to grant him and his ways a dispensation by the exercise of it.

Jigglestreet indeed had to take Miss Aylene O'Gara not only as mistress of the doctor's house but, in a way, as the queen of its social fabric. Missie, as she was called, asserted her individuality even more effectually than her father did his. Her smiles and kind words were coveted by everyone in the place. That she was an O'Gara was evident; in fact I was often made to go as near blushing as I could by being told of a likeness traceable between us. She was only seventeen, and had been ten years living with my uncle, but still, familiar with the species, I knew the American girl in her. She made my uncle's house what it was—a pleasant home—and even relieved the sombre shades of the unattractive village.

As we sat at dinner, when I looked at Missie, another face, that of the man M'Queen's unfortunate wife, arose before me through mere force of contrast. I seemed haunted by the miserable woman's aspect and that of her children, broken-spirited under a senseless terrorism. My thoughts, however, were diverted by the entrance of a clergyman. My uncle called him familiarly Father Crowe, inviting him to a place at the table. Mr Crowe, in reality a Presbyterian minister, however, did not dine so late, but would take a "half one," that is, half a glass of whisky. This he drank in grave silence, as if preliminary to the discharge of a disagreeable task.

"I came, doctor, to you," he said, laying down his glass, "about that unfortunate sister of mine, Mrs M'Queen——"

My uncle interrupted him, looking at Missie.

"Now, as our serious work is over, maybe his Reverence will let you help him to whatever you have in the way of sweets."

This was understood to mean that the painful subject was to stand over until dinner was quite done.

"This is my nephew, Atty. A full-fledged doctor now, your Reverence."

"Oh," his Reverence said to me, "I met you before, but I would not know you. Greatly improved."

"Thank you, sir," I said, at a loss for the exact meaning of the statement, and taking it therefore as a mere compliment.

"Thinking of settling in the North of Ireland?"

"No; I think I shall have to go back to America."

"You have lived there, then?"

"Yes, but I have been educated in Europe."

"Great advantage to a young man to see the world, only no one stays here when he has seen other countries."

"I don't know that. I have seen worse countries than Ireland. It agrees with me."

"Atty had malaria in America," my uncle said; "nearly died from the effects of it and bimetallism combined. Left his patriotism milk and water."

"Indeed!" his Reverence said, in a tone which suggested a man accustomed to getting rid of perplexing statements. "I suppose America has drawbacks, but then it has a sound land system. Every man there owns the land he cultivates and works for himself."

"I have heard that said here very often, but never once over there."

"But the American farmers are happy and contented.

E

They have not to be always agitating to get the Government to give them security of tenure, and to buy out predatory landlords at a cost of a hundred and twenty millions."

My uncle was amused, and smiled, perhaps, because Mr Crowe spoke as if he was repeating a passage from the Sermon on the Mount which could not possibly be open to contradiction.

"My experience," I said, "formed on the spot was quite different. I left the American farmers bitterly discontented, urging the Government to adopt a monetary system, which would have dishonoured and ruined the country, simply to enable them to pay their debts in depreciated silver. Without having any landlords to buy out, the proposal was seriously made that the Government should lend them any number of hundreds of millions of dollars at $2\frac{1}{2}$ per cent. to tide them over their difficulties."

"Now," my uncle added, "that is a wrinkle for your Reverence. When our farmers here get by agitation a hundred and twenty millions to buy out the landlords, don't let them foolishly stop. Get them to go right ahead for another hundred and twenty millions to enable them to stock and work the land. Make out the case for them, and, take my word for it, they're far too modest to turn the question with their clergy. What good is the land to them without capital and command of labour. Propose to give it back to the landlords for the hundred and twenty millions; it is worth nothing to the poor farmers without capital and labour. That is your game."

Mr Crowe had only one thing to say, and said it with a grave shake of his head.

"I am afraid, doctor, you are a landlord's man."

Then, the one thing said, abruptly changed the subject, addressing me,—

"You find the Street much improved since you were here last?"

"I was only a boy when here before, and paid no attention to anything more important than the rabbits in Ramsgate Park."

"Oh, the Street Fair," my uncle said, "did command your attention, and it is twice as big for some reason now as it was then. Perhaps it is because we have five more public-houses. These are the chief improvements we have to boast of. The Baptists and Plyms have indeed built their new chapels, but his Reverence does not reckon them as improvements."

"The doctor," Mr Crowe remarked to me, "is dead against the Street Fair, but I cannot see how our farmers are to transact their business without it."

"His Reverence," my uncle said, "ought to know the nature of my opposition to the Fair, but, as you do not, I may explain. The Local Government Board, having money to spend for the purpose, wanted labourers' cottages built in the Street, and wrote directing me to urge on the District Council the propriety of erecting them. I wrote back saying that the village was dependent on one pump for its water supply, that its drainage was defective, that a great monthly Fair was held on the streets, turning the place into a filthy cattle-yard for the time, and that there was no effective provision made for cleansing it. On these grounds, and with an experience of typhoid fever, I could not recommend the erection of houses in it either by public agency or private persons. The Local Government Board sent my letter to the District Council, as usual to be marked 'Read' and thrown into the waste-paper basket. But the letter was published in the local paper, and raised a storm in the Jigglestreet teapot, or rather tumbler."

"The general impression was that you had written to the Local Government Board in order to get the Fair done away with. That would be a serious blow to the place."

"Your Reverence saw my letter in the local paper. Did you form the impression yourself, or do you think anyone had the right to form it?"

His Reverence fenced with the question in clerical fashion.

"Oh, it is well known that you are opposed to the Fair, and your influence is dreaded."

"My letter on the face of it was simply an answer to an official communication, stating facts which otherwise would come out on the inquiry preliminary to building labourers' cottages. If I had withheld these facts I might have been called over the coals, or my integrity and motives suspected, and with reason. It was quite plain that I was simply discharging my official duty, not giving any expression of my views as a private person."

"Yes, yes," Mr Crowe observed with a pulpit air and gesture. "But what do our people know of officialism and red tape? They only know that you are hostile to the Fair."

"Is it your Reverence's business to instruct ignorance or to condone and excuse it? Suppose now our people are ignorant of the fact that this great fair held on the streets once a month makes the village a filthy, unwholesome hole, incapable of improvement, why not tell them to use their noses and eyes? Why not tell them that it depreciates property? that everyone is unwilling to build or spend money in it, but flies out of it as soon as ever he can, leaving it to the unfortunate minister and doctor, who cannot help themselves? Tell them that, and that it is all for the profit of a few publicans and the convenience of farmers."

"Exactly," Mr Crowe put in rather irrelevantly. "The poor farmers are to come in for the blame."

"Exactly," my uncle echoed. "There is one good use our Fair might serve, but which it does not serve. It might enable an intelligent and impartial man to judge how our farmers transact their business, enable him by an hour's observation to conclude that a business conducted in such a way could not be ever otherwise than in a bad way. The majority of the farmers would tell him themselves that they were neither buying nor selling, that they were looking how things went, in fact, loafing round the public-houses, treating and being treated to bad whisky. Some, no doubt, would look wise and discreetly hold their tongues, but if he intercepted them going home in the afternoon he would have no reason to complain of reserve. The men who do business with each other are a few dozen big, speculative dealers in cattle, who drop off one train, clear the market of £10,000 of stock, and are away by the next. Of course there is a lot of petty dealing, but it is ill-done in the back parlours of public-houses. The fair alone would prove that our farmers are bad workmen and worse traders."

"There may be something," Mr Crowe said grudgingly, "in what you say, but you cannot expect men brought up under the landlord system to change all at once."

My uncle shook his head and said, turning to me,—

"Perhaps you would like to know the sequel to my letter to the Local Government Board. The publicans, the only persons really anxious to keep the fair on the street, got up a memorial to someone or other against my interference with the sacred institution, and hawked it round the village for signature. Ninety-five per cent. of the inhabitants, probably about the number who drink whisky whenever they can get it, signed, and, of course, that exhibition of democratic intelligence settled me. It did not matter. If ever I had dreamed of the *rôle* of a civilising agent, the savages had long before this made me accept the inevitable."

Missie, who had vanished after dinner, reappeared with the tea equipage, but instead of taking her usual place at the tea-table, she took a seat beside Mr Crowe, a sad shade on her sweet face. The clergyman's big, brown hand lay listlessly on the table before him, and touching it sympathetically with her own little white one, she said,—

"I have just heard the sad news about your sister, Mr Crowe, and wish we could do something for her and the children in their trouble."

Mr Crowe was visibly affected, and said,—

"Dear child, I know your heart is with the afflicted. I came to consult the doctor whether her own could do anything for her, but it is a hard case; her own have been strangers to her for years, and how they can interfere now I do not know."

Missie looked at her father, who answered, directing himself to Mr Crowe,—

"When the mere shock of the thing is over, M'Queen's removal to the asylum is not a misfortune. It was bound to come, and better now than later, as things were steadily getting worse for the family. What has really to be provided against is the case of his not being kept permanently in the asylum. He may recover so far as to justify his release, and it seems to me that what is to be done now for his wife and children is, above all, to make use of the present opportunity to place them in future completely beyond his power and control. But give us tea, Missie, and then we may see our way to doing something of the kind for them."

"Yes, doctor," said Mr Crowe, "you hit the thing, but I am at a loss how to do it."

VI

DE ÆNIGMATIBUS DIABOLICIS

TWICE Missie asked our guest whether his tea was to his liking, for it seemed to choke him. He shook his head and said mournfully that it was all right. Plainly the fault lay with bitter thought.

"It is a hard case," he said ruefully. "No, Miss, no more. Don't ask me. A minister of the Gospel is bound to live up to the Gospel he preaches, but in my pulpit I stop and stammer so that my hearers—I can see it in their faces—wonder what is wrong with me. What is wrong is that I find myself preaching the Gospel of Love, of patience, forbearance and charity to them. I, I, a man who has lived from childhood in an atmosphere of hate, in enmity with father and mother, brother and sister, in a warring household. I think I am mocking them and that they must know I am."

Mr Crowe's earnestness was painfully impressive, and Missie looked pitiful and distressed. Her father, however, administered the usual kind of comfort, with an emphasis peculiarly his own.

"Your Reverence's hearers are not thinking about you in that way, you may depend; it is a line of thought they make it a point to carefully avoid. Take the families who sit under you one by one, and how many of them could you point out who have not to justify to themselves lifelong feuds with relations and neighbours. In kindness to themselves they never think of you—take it all as a matter of course."

Mr Crowe, really showing his best side, shook his head, gloomy and unsatisfied.

"They don't mind you," my uncle went on. "Can't

afford. There is that princely family of yours, the M'Killops. Why, Sandy M'Killop lived in the house with his father without exchanging a word with him for seven years. How they managed to work the farm between them I don't know. They say the mother was a kind of interpreter. Sandy is married and set up for himself, but I don't expect to see him at the old man's funeral. The same old man had five brothers and two sisters, no two of them on speaking terms. Then, as you know, old Mrs M'Killop left your meeting and went to church because, as she told everyone, she would not sit in the same house with her daughter and daughter's family. Are the M'Killops the exception or the rule in your congregation?"

Mr Crowe was unable, or did not care, to defend his congregation.

"Yes, doctor, but their minister should set them a good example the more they need it. That, however, is not the main thing. I cannot mend the past, but I want to feel myself doing what is right in God's sight now, whether people think well or ill or at all of me. My heart, indeed, bleeds for poor Lucy; she was the flower in a poor, froward flock; it would have been better for her if she had been stubborn and strong-willed, instead of being gentle and yielding, more of the nature of her kin. But it is for God's sake, to be at peace with Him, I long to make it up with my sister now after years of enmity, and my hope is that you may see an opening to do so, that you can help me."

My uncle was moved by the appeal. He reflected for some moments, and drank his tea to allow time for thought.

"Practically," he said, "you want to serve your sister, and think the present gives you the opportunity of doing so."

"Yes, yes; I want to serve her, and just as if there had never been a shade between us, as if there was no wound to heal."

"I can quite understand," my uncle said, in a questioning tone, "that you found it quite impossible to get on with Andy M'Queen, but everyone would understand that naturally arose from affection for your sister. I know nothing of the variance beyond what is common talk, and

that does not give any account of a quarrel immediately
between you and your sister."

This meant that there was something to be told before
my uncle could give advice, but Mr Crowe met the invitation to confidence with hesitation.   He took a handkerchief
from his pocket and slowly wiped some beads of perspira-
tion from his forehead.   These were the painful equivalent
of tears in a strong man.

" Our parents," he said at last, overcoming some great
difficulty, " had a good name in the congregation, and that
means in the world, which naturally is satisfied with the
opinion of the congregation one belongs to.   They had not
only the good opinion but the sympathy of the congregation
in the belief that they were afflicted with froward, rebellious
children.   But—"

Mr Crowe stopped, as if the difficulty had recurred, and
it was a moment or two before he could go on.

" But the parent has the ear of the congregation, and
while complaints from parents of children are listened to,
a child's complaint of its parent is looked on as a breach of
God's commandment.   No matter how bad the parent's
misconduct may be, everyone may complain but the child,
who is the chief sufferer.   I say this now, looking back,
because, as it seems to me, our parents ruled us harshly in
childhood, and when we grew up continued to exact
absolute submission to their will.   In this they had the
support of the congregation, so that any appearance of
resistance was an offence against both parental authority
and public opinion."

Mr Crowe was evidently trying to put the case against
his parents and the congregation they belonged to in as mild
a way as he could.

" I see," my uncle said, "in your family your parents
early gave their children the reputation of being dis-
obedient and rebellious, and prejudiced your congregation
against them."

" Yes, but not, of course, consciously or deliberately.
The fact is, our parents would not listen to a word from
us, did not allow any expression of dissent, however
reasonable, coming from us to pass unrebuked.   My father
was a man who, as he said himself, expected the man he
employed to put the horse in the cart with its tail fore-

most without a word when told to do so, and never learned
to the last that men willingly obey only intelligible and
reasonable orders.   My mother talked so much herself that
there was no getting anything into her; she could not
listen to and consider what was said to her.   I would not
say this if there was not a purpose to be served in saying
it; I am not reflecting on them."

Mr Crowe was not merely apologetic, but distressed, as
if one of my uncle's bistouries was piercing him.

"It is hard to say, but the spirit of resistance evoked in
the family seemed better than the spirit of submission;
there was both and endless trouble.   To come to Lucy's
marriage, Andy M'Queen was more than wild; he had a
bad name in the country.   But his father thought marriage
might settle him, and our parents were carried away by the
worldly advantages of the match.   Andy was an only
child, and would have the fortune of an estated gentleman.
We had no voice in the matter, least of all Lucy; a word
from us would not be listened to.   James, however, the
eldest of us, though quite a young man, had to be listened
to, and not for the first time, for he went beyond words.
He met Andy at the door, told him that he was a black-
guard, that Lucy knew that, and would not have him, and
if ever he came near the place again after her he would beat
him to within an inch of his life.   Andy knew that James
would keep his word and kept away, but though our parents
could ill work the farm without James, they made it impossible for him to live in the house with them.   I know it was
his intention to leave, that he stayed only to protect and
support Lucy, but at last the old people ordered him out of
the house, and used language to him which they would not
have dared to use to a stranger.   We, I remember, were all
on his side, but could not help him.   He went, and for
sometime we did not know what had become of him.   A
few months after he was gone Lucy, by sheer terror, was
forced to marry M'Queen ; in fact, she was given the choice
of marrying him or of going like James."

"She should have gone," said Missie, impulsively.   "I'd
have gone if it was only as a servant-maid."

"My dear," said Mr Crowe, "I said that the spirit of
submission was in the family, to work more evil than, perhaps,
the spirit of resistance.   Lucy was, if not naturally sub-

missive and yielding, yet broken-in. When James left, and she had no strong will to rely on, she became timid, and even weak in health."

"But, Mr Crowe, could you not have helped her?"

The gentleman visibly winced.

"I was at the time attending college with a view to the ministry, and that took me from home. But indeed, Miss, what I say of my sister is true of myself—I was unduly submissive to my parents; I was as I was brought up. I was brought up to believe that there was merit in obeying them, but now I know I obeyed them only in a craven spirit, for I felt all the time that they were wrong, yes, even in childhood. I felt they were wrong, but the habit of obedience was too strong, Now, when it is too late, I know I played a weak and ignoble part."

As the clergyman stopped, overcome by his emotion, my uncle, to alleviate his self-reproach rather than in a philosophical spirit, said—

"Tut, tut, your Reverence, you are telling us a common story, in which circumstance plays the principal part. Your parents and yourselves were the mere creatures of circumstances which began with Adam and Eve."

Mr Crowe did not allow this observation to tempt him from continuing his narrative under the condition of human responsibility.

"James's conduct, I remember, was disapproved in our body, and, of course, I was peculiarly bound by its judgment, as intended for the ministry. It was thought he had usurped the parents' place. They saw no wrong in Lucy marrying Andy at her parents' bidding; the wrong to them was in James rebelling against parents and inciting Lucy to rebellion. Among us, at least, it was unusual in a son to speak to and of parents as he did, and he went so far as to reflect on the opinions of the congregation."

"I see," said my uncle, smiling; "made it a personal matter with them. Put it down now, that I'd have given him absolution if he had beaten them all in company, with Andy M'Queen, to within an inch of their lives — well, the adult masculine portion of them."

Mr Crowe overlooked this and went on.

"After some time we heard of James, that through a cousin of ours who thought highly of him he had got employment in a shipping office in Liverpool, and on his own merits had been rapidly promoted to a position of responsibility. He was not only a good scholar, but a quick business man. I need not tell you the loss he was in working the farm at home, which indeed went to the bad from the day he left, but it was well for himself to become his own master, and live in peace. I believe he had intended to take Lucy away when he established himself, but, though not long about that, he was too late; she was married two months after he went away. I need not tell you, doctor, how Andy treated her from the first; you know better perhaps than anyone. What I do know is that our parents never let his ill-treatment of her near them. I was preparing for the ministry and dependent on them, just when from want of help the farm was paying ill. I couldn't reflect on them, and if I had I might have done as James did."

"Why did your sister not leave her husband," Missie asked hotly, "if he treated her badly? Her brother James would have taken her, and if he would not she would be better in service."

"Remember, Miss, I told you Lucy had been broken-in, had acquired the habit of submission, lost the power of willing for herself. But the very question did arise. After four years' absence James came over to Tyrone on a visit to the cousin who had helped him, and very soon heard how abominably Andy treated his wife. James did not go near our parents, and indeed he mightn't, for his success in life, and their own loss on the farm through want of him, only made them more bitter against him. What he did was to send a letter to Lucy, when her husband was from home, desiring her to leave him, promising her a home in Liverpool, and the custody of her children—she had two then—by legal steps if necessary."

"That was right," said Missie, "I have real love for your brother."

"I believe he is a bachelor yet, Miss, but not youthful enough for you. Three years older than I am."

This was said without a smile, and the speaker went on.

"Lucy's answer was that she would put the case to me as a brother and a minister. This brought James to me to bespeak my support for the proposal. There had been no positive alienation between us, as he understood my position—what it had been—and allowed for it, but then the position was not one in which I could hope for his respect. When he came to me I knew him at once, he had the same quick decided way he always had, but in other respects he was changed. He was indeed a fine gentleman, as well as one of those business men who take us slow country-folk aback by thinking twice as fast as we do, and not waiting till we can come up to them. I might have got on better with him, if he had allowed me an hour to do what he seemed able to do in a minute."

" I met your brother two or three times," my uncle said, " just often enough to see that he is a strong, self-reliant man, but I fancy the long, slow, painful thinking is on his side. What you take for thinking is the manufactured article—thought. He has a stock of the articles on hand marked—Made at Home."

" Yes, doctor, James always had an independent turn of mind, and put things in a new light to me often and often, and particularly on this occasion. But what can one say to a man who tells him that his morality is immorality, his religion irreligion, the God he believes in—the devil? Can we allow one man to override all the convictions and judgments which form a common mind for mankind ? "

It was my uncle's turn to put temptation to digression aside.

" I suppose, your Reverence, James holds more logically than you do, that the common depravity of human nature is represented in the common mind. But let us hear how he illustrated the position in the particular case."

Mr Crowe paused to arrange his matter. It was evidently bristling with perplexity and doubt for him.

" When he stated what he wished Lucy to do in his quick, short way, without declining to entertain the proposal, I said that the sanctity of the marriage relation and the danger of dissension and scandal in the family and congregation should be taken into account in coming to a decision. I saw, as I spoke, that he was studying me and the line he should take with me, and somehow I felt that he took me as a man brought up in submission to parents and deference to the opinions of those amongst whom I lived, and that I was rather to be overborne than per-

suaded. Anyhow he said bluntly that I was a clerical cad
and sneak, not to see in the case of our sister that the true
scandal was the prostitution of the marriage relation to
brutal ruffianism, and that the family and congregation in
not seeing what was crime not scandal, identified themselves with crime. Then he made a bitter apology, with-
drawing the terms cad and sneak, on the grounds that we
had been brought up to call mindless submission to parents,
and to the ideas of a body of narrow and ignorant louts,
submission to the law of God."

"He went at you," my uncle said in an accent of
sympathy, "with some of the most diabolic enigmas of
human life, and, after all, struck a defenceless man. Now
if he had said as much to me, I would have answered that
the louts being louts could only have the ideas of louts,
and govern lout-kind by lout-law ; that asses can only be
governed by and through the law of their nature, not by
archangels or even philosophers. But your Reverence
could not take this line ; you are committed to accommodate facts to a system of divine supernatural law."

"Yes," said Mr Crowe, unconsciously giving a good
illustration of the difficult position accorded to him, "but
I am sure I did not allow his reflections on me personally
to influence me in the least. J tried to consult conscience
and go by it. I said that the circumstances of human life
involved an incessant struggle with evil, and not only that,
but submission to evil where revolt against it but added
fuel to fire, meant meeting evil by evil. The very
proposal he made might be right from one point of view,
but it could not be carried out without creating an evil
position and an evil precedent. Lucy's position was not
an exceptional one ; it was, I had to admit, a common one,
but for that very reason I had to hesitate, as a minister, in
being a party to means which would end in making the
marriage relation a very lax one. The view in our body
was not that the relation was free from grave evils, but
that relaxation of the mutual obligation would lead to
worse evils. That view was not imposed on me ; I con-
scientiously agreed with it."

"I anticipate your brother's answer to that," my uncle
said ; "he would naturally say that every herring should
hang by its own tail. Would not accept the altruistic

position that your sister should be sacrificed to secure the institution for the benefit, open to doubt, of others."

"He would not condescend to argue the point at all. He told me that he had left the Presbyterian body the day he left his father's house, and without admitting that he had joined any other Christian denomination. He denied our Christianity in any good sense. Our body was a mere expression of force, resting on the instinct of power and love of persecution, that it would fall to pieces if it did not exert power to abolish individual thought and indulge in persecuting legitimate and wholesome freedom of thought. Our agreement, or pretended agreement, in doctrine was mere subterfuge, under cover of which we educated children to be mere puppets in a collective tyranny. His ideas were new to me, and would have taken me more time to grasp than he allowed me ; but in the particular case the end of the whole thing was that Lucy was to have perfect freedom to consult her own will and interest, the obligation to defer to her husband, her parents, the opinion of the congregation, being set aside as not only worthless, but condemned as the vile tyranny which had created her miserable position."

Mr Crowe paused to enable us to take in an argument which had taken himself time to take in.

"He went on," he continued, "to say that Lucy's history and condition proved that in requiring from her the sub-mission of a slave to her mad brute of a husband we showed ourselves that what we called Christianity was the religion of brutalised savages. When I resented the charge he jeered at me, told me he would turn the handle of the barrel-organ and grind out the corruption of the human heart. When the tune got profane I might tell him."

"Brutalised savages?" my uncle said, with a twinkle in his eye. "Now, if I had been talking to your brother I could have anticipated him. In '56 the Sergeant, myself and some more over in Missouri called ourselves Border Ruffians. Our opponents did not call themselves ruffians, which gave us the immense advantage of being candid and ingenuous. Your Reverence had to hold that your congre-gation were good people, bound to impose a divine law on your sister."

"Yes, yes," said Mr Crowe, impatient with such treatment of the subject ; " I told James at last that though it might have been wrong to have given Lucy to M'Queen, and though it might be wrong to leave her at his mercy now, still it would be much more wrong to commit her to one who had abjured the religion he and she had been brought up in, to one who had lapsed into infidelity. I became as firm as he was in tone and manner, but that seemed not to irritate but amuse him in a quiet way. He simply went back to the position he consistently held to from first to last. He was not going to do exactly what he condemned in others—impose his will on his sister. What he complained of was that her judgment and will, the solid ground of convictions in any true sense, had been over-ridden and paralysed, that by being treated as imbecile she had been made so. What he wanted was to restore her to herself, to save her from brutal tyranny. If she had religious convictions, in any sense her own, he would be only too glad to find she had any mind left, and under no circumstances would he dream of interfering with them. He was not concerned with speculative religious opinions, but with a social form which used these opinions to serve and shelter blackguards like Andy M'Queen. I was not to talk to him about religion, if in the name of religion our sister was to be bound to the devil."

" From a purely physiological point of view," I ventured to say, " I believe that constant undue repression of and interference with the will, whether it ends in paralysis or abnormal reaction in the faculty, is accountable for much mischief. I suppose your brother had some such idea in his mind."

But the purely physiological point of view was a quite unfamiliar one to Mr Crowe, who lived mentally in a region of abstract theology.

" I really think," my uncle said mercifully, " that your people did not know the worst of Andy M'Queen."

" Perhaps, and my brother did, for he never went by hearsay, but took great pains to get at facts, and with all his quickness was slow and deliberate in forming his judg-ments. I knew this so well that I did not decline positively to agree to what he wished, but stood out only for time and opportunity. I thought, indeed, that things would come to a head, so that our parents and the congregation could not but accept the separation as necessary. We separated, I leaving James under some such impression, but then I made what I know now was a false step. From habit, or as a matter of duty, I suggested to our parents that Lucy should be separated from her husband. I did this very cautiously, but it made them furious, particularly as they concluded at once that I was prompted by James. They expressed astonishment that an idea of the kind could be entertained by a minister in respect of his own sister, and said all and more than all I had anticipated. Lucy was not worse off than other women in the country, who had to put up with husbands who were not all they should be; better off, indeed, since she had not to work—which was true—but lived like a lady. God be good to the ladies who live as she has lived for years. They did not know what my ideas as a minister were, but they did know their duty to their children. Then they did their duty as they conceived it by threatening and frightening Lucy and warning Andy that it was proposed to separate them. This maddened the brute with suspicion. The end of it all was a complete breach between James, Lucy, and myself. They believed that I had not only betrayed their confidence but had acted so as to cruelly aggravate the miseries of her position. In particular, Lucy, with a bitterness unusual in her, resented my supposed heartless betrayal of her, and for five years there has been no intercourse between us. Then there was trouble in the congregation over the matter, some of the members blaming me in a very offensive manner. James blamed me for preventing the separation, Lucy for the manner in which she supposed I had prevented it, and part of the congregation for having proposed it."

Mr Crowe stopped to condole with himself under the trial, and then said, turning to me as the only one of his auditors needing the information,—

"You might think that we Presbyterian ministers, like the Catholic priests, have everything our own way, but that is a mistake. In nearly every congregation one or two members aim at power, at making the other members and the minister do their bidding."

"The same thing, for that matter," my uncle remarked, "occurs in the ward of every workhouse. One pauper with a passion for power aims at ruling the rest, and it is well for

the rest when he is not an ill-natured cur. In general the
sceptre is competed for, and the arts by which a following
is secured cultivated, so that the paupers have the good luck
to be cajoled and flattered by rivals. I suppose, your
Reverence, if the M'Queen faction went against you, the
M'Killopites went with you?"

"Yes, but it was embarrassing. Like many ministers, I
have to prevent the thing going too far, to make peace, to
prevent open war. But it is getting late and I must finish
my history. Both our parents died soon after what I have
told you, impoverished and in debt. The farm had gone
waste, my father not being able to get on with hired
labourers. What, however, was left he willed entirely to
me, James not getting anything. But although Lucy had
got her fortune—£500—when she married, M'Queen con-
tested the will, as he said himself, to bring me to terms—
that is, to get by a compromise something he was not
entitled to. I wrote on father's death to James, offering to
divide anything there was with him, but he never answered
me. He had become a partner in his firm and gone to
Australia on its business. M'Queen was, of course, beaten
at the law, and took my making no compromise with him
so ill that he left the Presbyterian body, or rather, because
for years he had gone nowhere, he would not allow Lucy
and the children to go to their place of worship, Knocknavaddy Meeting. He let them go a few times to the Plyms,
but so bad was his name in the country they were not
wanted, and of late years they have gone nowhere. The
children, I am afraid, are heathen."

"After all," Missie observed, "you might have trusted
Mrs M'Queen to her brother."

Mr Crowe shook his head sadly, but would not discuss
what could not be undone.

"When the law with M'Queen was over I had to sell our
farm, the old place we had been reared in, and which had
been in the family for generations. It was so worn out
that I got only a poor price, and when all debts and law
expenses were paid I found it would have been better if my
father had never willed it to me. But I do not mind
that."

After a pause, Mr Crowe began again in a different
tone.

"I would not trouble you, young people, in particular, with this history, only I wished my good friend here to have full knowledge of all the circumstances, and of the variance between Lucy and myself. I did not like to go to her at once, because, I am afraid, she would not trust me, but charge me with being a party to her troubles. Now, doctor, do you think you could get her to believe that I want to serve her?"

My uncle was a practical, and from his professional habits a resourceful man, and answered at once,—

"It all depends on what you propose to do to serve her and her children. It seems to me that there is only one thing you can do. You must take steps to free her from her husband's control in case he is released from the asylum. In the first place, give me your brother's address in Australia, or if you haven't it, get it through his firm in Liverpool. I shall then write and tell him how things stand, what your action has really been, and what you desire. I can, however, make but the one proposal to him : Your sister and her children must be secured against being ever again at the mercy of her husband. If our confounded laws stand in the way, we must only legislate for the particular case ourselves, and I reckon we shall be able to enforce our decisions. I may tell your brother and Mrs M'Queen herself that you mean to do everything in your power to secure her permanent separation from a hopeless ruffian and lunatic. You agree, and I shall ask your brother for his aid and influence with Mrs M'Queen."

"I agree," Mr Crowe said, "and even may go farther. From long habit and training Lucy may think that she is under some solemn obligation to her husband, the father of her children. When, however, I had time to think over what James said to me, I came to the conclusion that when general law is made to cover every case the result is evil greater than violation of the law produces. Lucy could never exert any influence over such a man as M'Queen. The connection between them ruined her without serving him ; it only gave him an opportunity of tyranny and brutality at her expense. Our people may not be able to see it in this light, but—"

"Never mind, your Reverence, what they may or may not see. My people have wit enough to respect me most when I respect them least. They suspect themselves until I relieve them of the suspicion. At bottom your people are in a muddle about our marriage laws, seeing that they make in so many cases slaves of women, and they do not respect but suspect you when you preach unqualified obedience to them. Anyhow, never mind your people. We have to find out how M'Queen's affairs stand and get legal advice, whether we act on it or not. Remember we act on it if it agrees with what we mean to do, and give it the go-bye if it does not."

This meant that having come to a decision no more words were to be wasted on the matter. Mr Crowe departed, apparently relieved by having a course mapped out for him, and promising to bring his brother's address in the morning. Next Missie, in an effort to relieve her mind from disagreeable impressions, performed a waltz round the room, a melancholy enough affair, which ended with two grave curtseys and disappearance.

"I hope," I said, as we settled down to a smoke, "your farmers are not to be judged by M'Queen or even by Mr Crowe's parents."

My uncle shook his head.

"It is enough for you to note that the cultivation of the land, farming, depends in this country to a great extent on the family relation. You can easily find out by observation that unsatisfactory family relations paralyse agricultural industry, the industry being dependent on the family working. Begin with cypher, that is where a man has no family, and you have on the other side of the equation an area of unworked land. Pass to the other extreme, to a man with a family which his farm cannot possibly support, and virtually you get the same result. Between the two a vast number of cases occur in which it is rare to find family labour really efficient. Conclusion—Agriculture in dependence on the family relation is an industrial failure."

It was characteristic of my uncle to hold me to the problem he had suggested.

"But," I said, "are many of the farmers in the position of M'Queen, able to live on the land and yet utterly neglect their business?"

"The farmer is practically never under necessity to the extent that he has to do a day's work inside of the day like a labourer, a shopman, a bank clerk, or most professional men. Many of them work very hard, but seldom systematically. On the other hand, the farmer of M'Queen's class is commonly the idlest being pretending to do business. Only in farming would you find men like M'Queen; in any other business or profession, as bankers, officials, railroad men, they would be cashiered in a month. If I did my business as most of them do theirs, and most of them, of course, are far better men than M'Queen, I would soon have no business to do."

"But how do they stand out for years if they are such bad business men?"

"Practically because they have property which it takes time to get through. The greater and best part of the land is in the hands of a farmer oligarchy, which, just like the House of Lords, is constantly dying out from vice and other causes and as constantly being renewed from a lower level. Three generations from the plough to the plough is a proverb in England, and it holds here. Andy M'Queen's father, for example, was born a labourer's son, and left two fine farms, some £5000 worth of property, to ruin Andy. It is one thing to make a fortune, another to found a family, to have children who can use, not abuse, wealth."

"I suppose, nevertheless, M'Queen is a product of heredity?"

"Heredity?—well an evolution of circumstance in inheritance. Andy's father at twenty-seven married a woman of forty-eight for her fortune, £200. She was a gloomy hypochondriac, who jealously watched him and found fault with him at every turn. But he was a cunning knave who prided himself on his ability to deceive her and every one else; it pleased him to play tricks on her, and he rather enjoyed her impotent rage and hate. The son, however, toned him down, made him wonder what he had slaved a lifetime for. What could be expected from a child bred between gloomy hate and cold indifference. Yes, they breed among themselves as they would not allow their cattle to breed."

"You raise horribly difficult questions."

"Yes, but shirk them, and you condemn the species to die out from neurasthenia and veiled lunacy. No man can hold more firmly than I do that intelligent self-control and self-restraint is the essential basis of morality, but when you have my experience as a medical man you may have reason to think that the marriage relation as it exists, in dispensing with self-control, is ruining the human species. Three-fourths of the children born in wedlock represent physical and mental incapacity in their parents ; they should not be born at all. Well, well, the world may be all the purer when there is as much left of us as there is of the plesiosaur and dinotherium, mighty monsters in their time. But you asked me whether our farmers are to be judged by M'Queen or Mr Crowe's parents. Of course not. Our patients are not all delirious ; in general, while there is grave disease, the symptoms are not obtrusively prominent, but have to be searched for and collated. That is the point of view from which you are to study our farmers. Good-night. I hope the realities of the day will not colour your dreams. For his poor wife's sake, I am glad M'Queen is in the asylum."

VII

DOCTOR CAPEL

" Eh, what do you think now of our Arcady?" asked my uncle after I had a week's experience of Jigglestreet and its district. " Of Dodona where the doves amid the oak trees murmur of their loves?"

" Your Arcady," I answered, "seems no better because free from the longing for the ways untried that, ravening and unsatisfied, draw shortened lives of men to hell. Keeps on the well-trodden paths to the destination."

Missie read poets to her father when nothing was left of the newspapers but the advertisements, and though the usual effect was soporific a stray rhyme sometimes got fixed in his memory.

" The first evening we are free from work we must go over to Lisdoheny to see Doctor Capel. I would like you to know him if—"

" Oh, I do know him. You remember he dined with us when I was here before, and made us laugh with his stories."

" I was going to say that I would like you to know him if anyone could know him. I know him, perhaps, as well as anyone does, and that means that I think the best of him is unknowable. The country people say that he is not canny, he knows so much of them and they so little of him. You must not think, however, our country people are so easily known. At work on a hot day they may make shirt and trousers do the corporal part, but they never take the heavy topcoat off their mind. That is where Capel shines ; he sees in an astonishing way what is under the topcoat."

We had been visiting patients in the neighbourhood of Jigglestreet, and were walking home through Ramsgate Park. Following a mossy avenue through brushwood or cover we came to a heavy, pretentious gateway in the earliest and ugliest stage of ruin. Standing outside was a gentleman's trap with master and servant in it, a fine but restless horse impatiently pawing the ground.

"Talk of—" my uncle said, "why, it is Capel himself."

The gentleman in the trap did not seem to heed us, but attended to the horse's movements, which became more decided as we came forward.

"One doctor he can just stand—myself. Two—gets nervous—serious consultation case. Three—has a mind to bolt—case desperate. Here, James, I'll get out and walk, it is safer. Well, permits conversation."

With this Doctor Capel handed the reins to his servant, a smart lad in regulation livery. As the official attendants of paupers, Irish dispensary doctors are, as a rule, poor men, never exciting envy by their houses and equipages. Doctor Capel, however, was as little like a dispensary doctor as his groom was like a doctor's boy or his horse a doctor's hack. He looked like a well-off English squire with the rusticity worn off by university and club life, qualified but left a marked characteristic all the same. Of professional mannerism there was not a trace; he was a squire and farmer, and yet with an air of the scholar about him. I could get so far at the first glance, but after all, what manner of man he really was I felt was beyond me to determine.

"I was driving over to see you," he said, speaking to my uncle, "or rather see your nephew here, who I heard was with you. I saw you going into Ramsgate Park, and calculated I would intercept you here. Yes, heard the young doctor was with you, and at the same time that my brother was in London, home from India with a big liver and wished me over to see him. It struck me that perhaps our young doctor here would take charge of my district for a month or so while I am away."

"Atty can answer for himself," my uncle said. "But come over and dine with us and tell Missie as usual you came to see her. Bring in business only incidentally."

"You must admit, doctors both and friends, that I have gone to business without beating about the bush, but that settled so far, I am free to admit that in addition to my usual motives for coming to the Street, I had a desire to meet our young doctor here apart from any business errand."

He stopped for a moment on the road, and turning round, looked at me for a moment with the kindly air of one seeking something to be pleased with. But the scrutiny was short.

"It may sicken you with us," he said in some connection with his survey obscure to me.

"Sicken me—what?"

"Actual medical work, Irish dispensary work in particular, contact with sick people, it is so different from theoretical medical studies."

"I was a resident in a surgical hospital and every day in contact with concrete cases of disease."

Doctor Capel smiled and then looked grave.

"Yes, and did for your cases all that could possibly be done. In dispensary work you are disheartened by finding that often you can do little, and sometimes nothing, at the expense of an enormous amount of work. I drive five miles to see a patient lying in a miserable hovel without proper food, without an intelligent nurse, without the means of applying treatment. I have to tell Murphy that I cannot see him for two or three days again, that he cannot be treated where he is and must go to the work-house hospital. Murphy takes that as sentence of death; I send the van for him; it is all I can do, and it is well if he goes. I have, say, only half a dozen patients at a time, but they are scattered over a district of 30,000 acres under these circumstances. The work is mostly travelling."

"I can cover the ground on my bicycle."

"Our roads and lanes are rather intended for Shanks's mare or mule. I travel 3000 or 4000 miles in the year, mostly driving over bad roads. It is about as much as I can do without the impossible task of curing my patients. Well, of course, cases do occur in which I am of some use, but in the main my work is travelling and keeping the dispensary books."

"Of course," my uncle said, smiling, "keeping up your professional knowledge, indulging in scientific reading and making money by farming, and even more lucrative pursuits is out of the question."

Doctor Capel went on without noticing the observation.

"They gave me, when I came to Lisdoheny, £80 a year. It was poor pay for the travelling and book-keeping, but if they had given me £8000 I could not have done the medical work."

"Lisdoheny was always a nest of poverty-stricken cottiers; the rents were too high."

My uncle made this remark, I could see, meaning something not on the surface.

"Yes, of course," Doctor Capel assented quietly, "for uncultivated land the rents were always high. The farmers who hold the greater part of the district depend on cattle - dealing, and give little employment to the labourers and cottiers—as little as they can help. They pay rent, keep up seventeen public-houses and fourteen clergymen, and collectively have a big balance in the banks. Their business is not employing and directing labour, but cattle-dealing, and, of course, the cottiers and labourers, the people of the district, are miserably poor, their means of existence precarious in the extreme."

"I suppose your farmer considers *l'Etat c'est moi*, the district himself, never thinks of anyone but himself."

Doctor Capel answered my observation with hesitation.

"The difficulty is to see where thinking comes in; the case is one rather of setting thought aside when inconveniently obtrusive. The farmer finds himself in a system which he does not in the least understand; what he does understand are the immediate personal conditions of his life. If he is an old infirm man he must subordinate his business to the fact."

"Then you would say, Capel," my uncle observed, "that the general fact is that the business is accommodated to circumstances under which it obtains its actual form?"

"Yes, the farmer's business is not carried on under the principles which should govern it as a business. There are 30,000 acres in Lisdoheny district of which 15,000 are in the hands of 100 occupiers. Now a farmer with 150 acres is tolerably secure of his means of living and able to dispense with cultivating the land otherwise than as suits him personally. Of 1200 families in the district, 700 have no land except small gardens and patches taken from farmers, and 300 occupiers have only on the average 15 acres each. Suppose now these last did cultivate on any business-like principle, they would account for only 4500 out of 30,000 acres. But 1000 families on even 10,000 acres simply means the families starved and the land starved."

Graceful gesture goes sometimes with the unconscious expression of emotion but seldom with cold expression of reasoning. I noted that Doctor Capel had the rare gift of making gesture go with and impress reasoning.

"You make," my uncle said, "your commonwealth appear an outrage on commonsense. How does it come that its members do not see it in that light?"

"Because there are not twenty men in it who have any brains, and these twenty find it suits them. A large number of the occupiers are not fit to hold or work an acre of land, and having to live by land have a problem which they call the land question. They eat, drink, and find fault with everyone except themselves. That suits the twenty with push and energy. These men elect themselves to informal control; then elect the member of Parliament, the Presbyterian clergy, local boards and officials, and aspire to appoint the magistrates and control the police; perhaps in time the nomination of the judges and the Privy Council may become the object of their ambition."

"I wish," my uncle observed, "in my district they would appoint in the meantime a midwife. I have to depend on an old woman who is frightfully deaf and despises cleanliness."

"No, sir. They pay you £25, the quarter of your salary, and though they appoint you, would not pay you sixpence if they could help themselves. They would not pay for doctor, midwife, schoolmaster; if the State pays they will appoint them, and in general wrong and unfit persons, chosen under the influence of favouritism, sectarian and party feeling. The State is to pay for everything, rent, labour, education, medical services and so on, and they are to have the whole power of the State to manage its business as they do their private business, that is, abominably ill. Now, young man, that might seem enough, but the worst personally is that we have to koo-too to this vile oligarchy."

Doctor Capel addressed me understanding that the discourse was really intended for my benefit, my uncle having practical familiarity with the system described.

"I was suggesting to Atty," my uncle said, "the study of our wonderful agrarian system, and evidently Lisdoheny presents a fine field for observation."

"Well, yes, but he can easily find more striking fields." Then turning to me,—

"You need no microscope for our social pathology; it is all an easy naked-eye affair."

"It is strange, then, that it seems so entirely to escape observation. Going by what I have read, I would say that your oligarchy was the best and worthiest of industrial systems, only labouring under landlord oppression and over-taxation."

"Yes, because our boss farmers, as you would call them in America, have political power, have members of Parliament, clergy, local officials and newspapers on their side. If, however, you take up our land question, as your uncle suggests, begin your study of it by finding out the opinions of their neighbours who have no land and who support no newspapers, opinions which have no means of expression."

"Then it is not a case of *populus vult decipi ;* there is a body of ignored and powerless opinion in the country adverse to your farmer oligarchy ?"

"I do not care for that hackneyed phrase, *populus vult decipi.* I know no wish to be deceived in the people outside the farmer oligarchy. The people in contact with it are neither deceived nor could be deceived; they are simply powerless in great part because their experience and opinion have no means of expression. The great world outside the farming class may be deceived, but it has no desire to be deceived; it is simply in the dark, and kept in the dark as to the real facts. If the opinions of the farmers' tenants, cottiers and dependents were forced on it they would be listened to."

"Yes, but would not the judgment of the farmers' dependents be of exactly the same nature as the farmers' judgment? The 700 families in your district having no land and the 300 having only 15 acres each would hold that 100 families should not have 15,000 acres between them.

Virtually, that is the case of the 100 families against the territorial landlord accommodated to a different set of circumstances."

" With a difference, yes.   Granting the position, the claim of the have-nothing with an immense numerical majority is far stronger than that of the have-something in a minority.   But I am sure you would not on consideration allow a position under which a few are bound to get the plums."

" You think that the farmers' claim, apart from being unfair to the majority of the farmers and the whole of the labourers, is radically untenable."

The discussion, however, at this point was interrupted by a little boy, a child almost, driving a dozen cows, calves and bullocks in front of us on the road.   The lad had a stick as long as himself which he brought down every now and then with frantic yells on the sides of the beasts, evidently quite unnecessarily, as they were progressing in the desired direction as fast as he could walk.   It was mere indulgence in the sense of power on his part.

" There is a lesson," Doctor Capel said, " in the way human beings exert power not only over the beasts of the field but over each other when they can.   I'd venture to say that the boy himself has experience of the same kind of thing."

Going up to the lad my uncle said to him,—

" You young rascal, why do you pound the beasts in that manner ? "

The young rascal knew Doctor O'Gara and looked at him with some awe, but more surprise at being spoken to in such a way.   He edged away as if thinking it judicious to secure a merely verbal discussion of the matter, and then answered,—

" Sure, they belong to us.   I'm Mickle John Toner's son.   They're Mickle John's kine."

" If I tell Mickle John how you beat his beasts maybe he will make you taste the stick yourself."

" He might ready enough out of obligement to you.   He was bad wi' the drink an' you cured him, an' it's like he'd think he might be wantin' you again some day.   But he doesn't mind a bit my whackin' them, whacks them worse nor me himself."

"Then, of course, he whacks you too. The man who whacks his cattle that way is sure to whack his children too."

"Yes, he whacks me sure enough an' no call, if he gets the chance. I've to leave his road many's the time, an' his tantrums is worse when he hasn't a drop. You needn't bid him whack me. I'll leave his road an' he'll not mind when he sees me again."

The boy's face was crafty and confident as his words, but one of the beasts loitering to browse on the roadside gave him a better opportunity of display than language. With uplifted stick and a terrific yell he made a run at it with the result that the herd scampered out of reach in a moment, with the lad at their heels more self-assertive than ever.

Doctor Capel smiled as he said,—

"The cattle wouldn't thank you for your interference on their behalf. When Adam took the apple, at the first bite he remarked to the lady that she might have given him something tastier than a crab—at least if he hadn't to spit, not talk. Your superior knowledge and intelligence is pure bitterness without power at its back, when any urchin may defy you."

"I suppose," my uncle remarked, "power regulates knowledge. The actual exercise of power teaches the boy that the cattle submit, and the extent to which their submission may be reckoned on. The axiom should run, Power—action—is knowledge."

"Expand the formula, and say that it is circumstance, not the schoolmaster, that really educates the youth, that really in the end determines his action and conduct."

Turning to me, Capel continued,—

"Apply that to our farmers. Their education is in a school of circumstance, and a precious bad education you will find it is."

We were entering the Street by this, and interchange of salutation with the villagers took the place of conversation. Everyone seemed to know Doctor Capel, and he showed that he knew them by using their Christian names, a familiarity which went, however, with an easy dignity. The doctor, indeed, seemed not only to know the heads of houses, but wives, children, circumstances, dealings, troubles, pleasures, everything, in a way that astonished me.

One countryman, stopping on the pathway, touching his hat, seemed to desire a few words conversation.

"Well, Robert John, what is it? He was a good lad, Samuel, and a good son. Four pounds, was it not, he sent you?"

"Thank your honour for that word. Twenty dollars American money, with the promise of more, and asking particularly for your honour. I've no right to call up my own, but it's a true word you said, better son to a father than Samuel never walked Tyrone. I just wanted to tell your honour how he asked for you, writing that he'd ever mind how you stood to him when them he wrought for were for taking away his character. You were not to be taken in by the likes of them."

"I do not think many were deceived about Samuel. Tell him I was glad to hear that he was doing well in America, and that I expected nothing else."

"Thank your honour. I'll send him your very words, and they'll please him; they'll that."

Passing on, the doctor said to me—my uncle had left us,—

"Some might take it as a pleasant history—Samuel's— because it has an amusing side. Robert John Taylor has fifteen acres of land, and seven children, the wife and himself to support by them and petty dealing. His eldest, Samuel, when barely able to work, hired with a farmer in my district, Leadlaw—the spelling of the name is its bearer's, not mine. Two or three years ago Leadlaw made an outcry about fowl, butter, eggs and sundries not obtaining due credit in the Leadlaw exchequer. He managed the department in his head, which was none of the best, kept no accounts, and never knew where he was. The plan, easy and natural to him, was to suspect the lad Samuel of theft, and suspicion was enough for him; he was too lazy and stupid to prove theft or a thief. He did indeed watch Samuel, but, as he admitted himself, without being able to find a shred of evidence against him. That, however, did not remove his suspicions, or even make him discreet in expressing them. He spoke to everyone who

would listen to him of Samuel as a thief, and so cunning a
thief that he could not be caught."

We were in front of my uncle's house, but, stopping to
hear the story out, I remarked,—

" Why did he not dismiss the boy, or why did not the
boy leave him?"

" Ah! You have no idea of our farmers, and of how
those they employ stand with them. The boy was a good
and useful lad, and Leadlaw all the time would have been
very unwilling to part with him. Most of the farmers
systematically disparage their servants and labourers, and
the law of libel does not exist for them; the lawyer does
not want such clients. There are farmers who prefer those
who have no character to lose, and others who are not
disposed to allow such a luxury. They employ rogues,
semi-idiots and poor devils liable to fits of dipsomania; ask
no questions, provided they get labour cheap, and with no
offensive assumption to respectability. I knew a farmer
and road-contractor who collected about him a number of
harmless lunatics, and grew rich by getting twice as much
labour as he would out of as many sane men, and at half
the cost."

" But what of Samuel?"

" Oh, Leadlaw carried it so far that Samuel had to throw
up his commission at last. The fact is, the fowl, butter
and eggs went on steadily disappearing, with now and then
really alarming exacerbations. Who was the thief? Now,
a nice point in casuistry comes in here. Samuel was not
the thief, but then he knew who was, and so did Katty
Sheran, a rural commission agent. For that matter the
whole countryside knew the facts, or guessed them, under
judicious reserve as to expression—farmers' affairs are
spoken of with caution. Only old Leadlaw was altogether
in the dark. He was not an observant man, and never
looked at his wife and daughters. The last were really
worth looking at, and their dress too, from the point of
view that the father was as likely to have made as paid
for it. Well, he would have had no eyes for it if real
cashmere and diamonds. The wife, too, had a failing,
indulgence in which was difficult of explanation. Leadlaw
himself indulged, as he would say by way of excuse, out-
bye—at markets and fairs, but boasted a household con-

ducted on the strictest temperance principles; except
inside of himself, a half-pint of whisky never entered it—
to his knowledge. As a casuist, to me the interesting
figure in the rather sordid drama was Samuel. He knew
the real culprits, but allowed himself to be defamed, his
character taken away, rather than betray them. He left
Leadlaw and went to America, abused and slandered by
the old man, on whom he could easily have turned the
tables with a vengeance. Never said a word."

"I fancy," I said smiling, "the key to the problem may
lie with the Leadlaw girls. Even if not in love his chivalry
was called out."

"Give me a young man to read a young man's heart.
At sixty it is the abstract casuistry of the position that
interests. No matter, Samuel was a fine lad, and I am
glad he is well out of the Leadlaw nest."

We had stayed talking outside too long for Missie. She
ran out and called Doctor Capel in.

"I was wrong indeed," he said, "to stand a moment on
one side of the door and my treasure on the other side."

"You know," he went on to me, "there are three Capels
in the world, at least to be mentioned in this connection,
my two sons in India and myself. I never hint, never
suggest; in serious matters go straight to the point. When
Francis and Antony are home on leave—three years to that
yet—I tell them in plain terms that a name has to be
changed—changed to Capel by one or other of them.
Failure—then the duty devolves on myself."

Missie, laughing, addressed me too.

"That is what they call fool talk here, but Louis can
speak sense. Always, if I don't."

The doctor bowed with ceremonious gravity.

"Yes, when I drive home to-night I shall wonder at the
sense, the fautless logic of my conversation, and, as usual,
end by ascribing it to inspiration."

The evening, a pleasant one for our Arcadian Thule,
proved, however, that Doctor Capel had graduated in
nonsense as a subtle means of sense. Without an effort,
one could not realise how, he assumed the character of a
visitor from some region of Phantasmagoria only known to
himself. He talked, indeed, of Lisdoheny and Jigglestreet,
but these prosaic districts became newly-discovered isles of

fairyland, peopled by ludicrous caricatures of humanity who behaved in an extraordinary manner, and accounted for themselves and their doings by the most fantastic theories.   But the charm of the Doll-land was its intense realism; it was a picture of humanity in which human characteristics were accentuated, exaggerated, only to make them take on not unreality, but novel reality. I was mystified, but Missie and my uncle seemed to laughingly recognise the doctor's principal anthropoids.   It was amusing, and meant to be so, but there was a recondite vein of thought in it which enhanced the skill of the caricaturist.

As usual, we smoked and talked when our visitor left.

"Missie," my uncle said, "had typhoid when she was about fourteen, and I shall never forget Capel's kindness to her and me.   He took the case quite out of my hands, and it was well, for anxiety muddles my head.   Every day he came over from Lisdoheny to see her, and has come in the middle of a wild winter night when his business there detained him all day.   He inspired her with confidence, made her call him Louis and chatter to him anything that might come into her head; I have not the knack, even with her.   He could treat her to a caricature of herself which, so far from displeasing, would delight her."

"As he was so kind to Missie I must, of course, take his duty in Lisdoheny if my doing so would be any service to him."

"You must not think of it in that way.   Capel can easily get a man to take his place.   You must go, simply because it gives you an opportunity of practice, and, if you follow my suggestion, of getting a real knowledge of the country.   I feel that Capel could not he repaid for his services to Missie and to me."

"He has really made me curious about Lisdoheny, and, as I have done Killarney and the Giants' Causeway, I may give the few months I have to spend in Ireland to matters of human interest."

"You must not expect to find Lisdoheny inhabited by curious caricatures of human beings.   Its people are as commonplace as the people of the Street.   Less variety indeed; it has no village as we have here."

"It seemed to me that what Doctor Capel was caricaturing was the commonplace, dead-level character of his surroundings, and the intolerance of the people among whom he lives for anything but a rigid conventional life. His aim was to bring out the tyranny these people exert on each other, a tyranny satisfied by servile deference to non-essential forms and formulas and stultifying individual character and conduct."

"Yes, he would give one the impression that it was puppets and their clothes he had in his mind. In point of fact each one is bound down to live, think, talk exactly as all the others do. There is, of course, an effort at revolt, but the rebels are so little able to rebel that they make themselves ridiculous by showing the fetters which the others from habit wear without display. The popery of the hot Ulster Protestant is more in evidence than the popery of the average Roman Catholic."

"He seemed to me even less polite to humanity. When the fetters are loosed a bit by some accidental circumstance his caricature comes in; the conventional clown kicks up his ugly heels and tears his clothes as his way of evincing sense of freedom. Give him liberty of thought, and he gives you in return parodies of thought. Give him liberty of action, and the mess he makes gives some other fellow an excuse for making a slave of him. The principle of conventionalism represents the fact that the individual units, as such, represent anarchy."

My uncle smiled, as if the problem had amused him before.

"I would allow revolt against conventionalism a moderately free field in full view of its childish antics. The race on the whole is worse off in slavery to convention, its members incapable of independent thought and action, incapable of true adaptation to the varying circumstances of individual life. The revolt, apart from its own details, is reaction against the worst and most far-reaching form of tyranny, everybody governing everybody, nobody free to accommodate himself to the circumstances of his own life. That in itself is as mischievous an absurdity as any that happens when the slave emancipates himself, and indulges in folly by way of showing his sense of freedom. But you will go over to Capel and settle about taking his duty?"

"Yes. I suppose the work is not very heavy?"

" Not at this season.   Chiefly travelling, as he told you.
A hundred patients in an hospital would be more easily
attended to than half a dozen scattered over so wide
an area.   But you will think little of the work, such as
it is."

Of that I was sure, and Capel was a man I felt I would
like to know and serve, so I made up my mind to the
experience of life for a month in Lisdoheny.

VIII

COUNT M‘QHAN

IT was a long, steep hill, with the slate rock cropping in places across the wild, rough road to which I was directed as a short cut to Moyclare, Doctor Capel's residence in Lisdoheny. I had written to the doctor, telling him that I was at his service, and had received an answer asking me to go over and see him.

I had just gone over a somewhat similar hill on my bicycle, and decided to walk this one. In fact for three miles I had done nothing but go up and down hills, over rain-washed gravel and outcropping rocks, speculating on short cuts in general and this one in particular. There had been occasional temptation indeed in grassy, nice-looking roadside margins to exaggerated expression of feeling. Incautiously I had ventured to try them, but the third time was enough to make me keep to the middle, bad as that was. A luxuriant spray of bramble had caught my hat, and torn my face, and in saving myself my hands and clothes had been at the mercy of the masses of *ulex europœus*, which, not content with full possession of the borderland, encroached on the road. I was in bad temper with that world of rock bramble and whin. Short cut! why, the vile path was a senseless vagary in the three dimensions of space, not twenty yards level, not twenty without a sudden turn to right or left without reason that one could see without going to the innate depravity of human nature in those that made it.

It turned, this time I allow out of deference to an old thorn tree, and suddenly consolation came to my wounded spirit in the shape of a fellow cyclist, walking, like myself, beside his machine. That there was another cycle with a fool alongside was balm to me.

Balm only as long as I saw no more of him than his back. Bad as the road made me feel, when I came up to him his face, as it turned to me, ruffled me more than ten miles of it would have done. A happy, contented, amiable face—what business had its owner on this road, or, indeed, in this world? Optimism, the natural genuine article, has always irritated me; I do not recover until it supplies a sedative in the shape of the usual foolish excuses it makes for itself. In this case, however, something else intervened, an impression of familiarity with the face which for a moment I could not account for. Then it dawned on me that Doctor Capel had fastened it in my mind by one or two of his deft touches that my fellow-traveller was one of his strange anthropoids, one, too, that had taken my fancy.

"Fine day," I said, and then, looking not at the stranger but his bicycle, "I did not expect to see another wheel on this road."

"Yes, it is a really fine day." The speaker accented the words to accent their meaning, and then, glancing at the road before us, went on, "Well, it is not exactly a road for cyclists. I sometimes thought of getting it put on the county, but was afraid it might be spoiled."

"You mean, I suppose, getting it repaired. But there seems to be no traffic on it; not a cart track."

"Oh, no; no traffic to signify, but the land just here belongs to me, and it would not be convenient to close the road."

I looked round and saw nothing but gorse, bramble and fern, with slate rock occasionally obtruding a naked face. There was no sign of cultivation, or even of cattle.

"The land seems not worth going to the expense of keeping up roads for it."

"Oh, it is the county that would pay for mending the road, and even so, half the cost would be met out of Imperial revenue. I would not dream of repairing it myself for all the use it is to me."

"That, of course, is a satisfactory arrangement; the land itself looks as if it could not be of much use to you."

The gentleman looked at me with lazy scrutiny, but seemed immediately to make up his mind to take me, as he did the road, with calm indifference.

" Oh ! the land is not so bad ; it would give good crops of potatoes and oats, if tilled, but I only graze it, and it does not stand out in grazing."

The fact did not seem in the least to displease the speaker, whose glance over the waste following mine was one of happy contentment.

" I suppose you think that it would not pay you to till your land ? "

The answer was given with an amused smile.

" Pay me ? Well, yes, it might, and so might making bicycles if I went in for the thing ; better, indeed, for I have an idea or two which might turn out worth a pile if worked out. But my vocation in particular is an easy life ; I was born a farmer, and, on the whole, I think a farmer's life about the easiest going. Of course there are men who make it, as they would any other, a hard one, but my turn is to take it as easily as possible."

The stranger's whole bearing and his plump white hand on his bicyle, corroborated his words.

" That is the landlord's principle, to live on the land without cultivating it, foregoing part of the profit in order to do so. But the farmers do not admit the principle as applicable to themselves ; they represent themselves as hard-working men carrying on an industry under very difficult conditions."

" You put things in a very unfair way," was the answer given with a quiet smile. Your statements do not correspond. You should either say that the landlords are a valuable leisured class, rendering as such important services to the community, and the farmers rendering, in their own way, similar services as an industrial class, or else you should generalise the principle the landlord goes on, so as to cover all men. Not the landlord alone, but all men, with the exception of a few idiots, aim at an easy life and are willing to pay for it. I am a farmer, for instance, and choose an easy life at the expense of half the income I might make by farming. All our farmers who are not slaves of circumstance or insane do the same thing."

"It is clear to me," I said, "that you are not a politician."

"You must allow me to say that you seem to me neither a politician nor a philosopher. If you were a politician you would make *ex parte* statements against either the landlord or the farmer, call one of them a rascal and the other a model of all the virtues. If you were a philosopher you would not limit a principle of wide generality to one set of men, the landlords."

"I am quite willing to give the principle its widest generality, but I am a polite man and do not like to give the lie direct to the farmers and their political instruments. You must admit that the farmers represent themselves as an industrial class handicapped by a heavy tribute paid to idlers. Do you give me liberty to tell you as a farmer that you want to get rid of the tribute in order to get rid of the trouble of cultivating the land and be an idler yourself ? "

My fellow-traveller laughed in his quiet way.

"Let me see," he said, "how much I have to admit as a farmer—a farmer, mind only—so as to have no further need of confession. I want, of course, ownership of my land, subject in lieu of rent to a terminable annuity open to discussion from time to time. I want the State, that is, other people, to pay poor-rate, county cess, and all other charges on land. I want poor-rate applied to support my labourers in disability and when I do not want them, and to build cottages for them, which means securing and cheapening my supply of labour. I want roads, bridges, fences and so on, this road in particular to be kept up for me. I want, above all, Protection, whereby I would get for five bullocks the price I have to take now for ten. Yes, I want a good thoroughgoing system of Protection. I want —well, well, I can be reasonable and wait on circumstances to evolve my wants. There is finality in nothing."

"You are candid. And what would you give in return for all this ? Your land here reclaimed, and in a state of cultivation."

"No, sir, something much better—a man with a life worth living, not a drudge, a slave of necessitous circumstance."

"I see. It seems to me, however, that to obtain the certainly desirable article a heavy burden has to be placed on the shoulders of a great number of men, making them more the slaves of necessitous circumstance. Then again, the farmers aim at the landlord's life without proof that that life is more particularly worth living."

"You are fond of dual statements, between which the link is not visible. What all men want is security of life, and this involves provision against disability. If men went about the task collectively, and by rational means, it might be easily effected, but as they do not do so, but leave each individual to act for himself, they have no right to complain of individual action. We farmers are left to fight our own battle for life, for life worth living, and provision against disability, and, in the absence of any collective organisation, we must leave out of consideration every interest except our own, or rather consider every interest in subservience to our own. I can understand you if you say Protection is not really in our interest, but if allowed that it was in our interest and against that of the rest of the world, I would tell you that the rest of the world may fight for itself, as we are left to fight for ourselves."

"You would go in, then, for a policy of scramble, for virtual anarchy?"

"I would not go in for a policy of scramble; what I say is, that being in a policy of scramble, being under legalised anarchy, we are quite helpless to do otherwise than make the best fight we can for ourselves."

"Do you really make the best fight you can for yourself? There are forty-one millions in the British islands, of which only a mere fraction are occupiers of land fighting for a position enabling them to live without cultivating the land. If the foreign supplies of food were cut off, a thing a few bad seasons in America might effect, the forty-one millions would suddenly become alive to their interest in the land and make it hot for the non-cultivating farmer."

"Very well, let the forty-one millions, or anyone thinking for them, formulate some plan for making the land subserve their interest, and we are open to compulsion if not to reason. But I have never seen or heard of such a plan. I have heard of plans in favour of the landlord or the farmer, in favour of the large farmer, the small farmer, the labourer; in fact, we have practical experience of such plans, but cultivation in the interest of the community has not found even theoretical expression. You have not even a shadow to oppose to us, and how then can you call us to account ? "

I was interested in my companion, and said, without any intention of flattering him,—

"You really seem to have given the subject thought, which is rare. As far as I have been able to judge, the farmer sees only his own side, and is quite unable to think in the true sense."

"Oh ! " and the answer was preceded by a bland smile, "I see my own side of the wall, and infer that it has another side, and am just as well pleased that the millions on the other side cannot see through it or look over it into our playground. But you seem to have given the thing thought too. Have you ever reduced to expression the interest of these millions in the land ? "

"Yes," I answered, "at least tentatively, and subject to criticism. I would say that the interest of the vast majority dissociated from the land is that the maximum production should be got with a minimum of organised labour, so that the largest possible contribution may be available for their wants."

"Very good, that is my idea, too. But you see, so far from the idea having any currency, it is deliberately ignored ; we have not to fight against it because no one advances it against us. What we have opposed to us is a very different idea. I admit that this out-farm of mine might make a much larger contribution towards the wants of the community, but then it might make a smaller. There are 120 acres in it, but if it was broken up into ten farms, while, no doubt, its production would be greatly increased, still it would have to support ten families, and under the condition its contribution to the wants of the majority would be much less than it is. There would be a vast excess of labour on it over and above what was necessary for its cultivation, labour which could not find employment. The experience

is a well-tried one, with the invariable result that instead
of a contribution being made to the wants of the community, the community has had to contribute towards the
support of a host of beings steeped in abject poverty.
Nevertheless, the idea of breaking up the land into small
patches is the one farmers of my class have to struggle
against, and the community, blind to its own interest,
leave us to struggle as we best can against it."

"But are there not some grounds in the experience of
parts of Europe for more favourable views of the small
occupier system?"

We were still slowly walking through wild land, though
the road had become more passable.

"I have been over most of these districts, and I prefer
this."

The speaker waved his hand over a poor pasture field,
and continued,—

"When a man has a small patch of land and no other means
of support, he must work it, of course, when and as long as
he can. Your land is cultivated, but what is your man?—a
mere drudge and slave, his life one long, painful strain,
ending, when he can work no longer, in dependence on others.
Yes, I would rather have this land as it is than parcelled
out among a crowd of Belgians, slaves of the worst master
men can have—their circumstances. I do not want the men,
therefore not the system that gives them."

"Do you not see," I said, "what your position comes to?
You would devote the land, the cultivation of which is all-
important to the majority, to the purpose of enabling a few
men to lead an easy life by relieving them of the duty of
cultivating it to its full capacity."

"I can only ask you again, as thinking for the majority,
to propound some plan in its interest. I know no plan in
the field but one which shall plant on the soil a horde of
cultivators far in excess of what the industry requires, and
therefore quite against the interest of the majority. Give
me some plan whereby the land shall be cultivated to its
full capacity in the interest of the majority, that is, making
the largest possible contribution to its wants, and you shall
find me open to consider it. In the meantime, I must hold
my position against a plan under which the interest of the

majority would suffer more than it has ever done under the *régime* of big landlords and big farmers."

This statement somehow, both in its substance and the manner in which it was given, recalled the speaker to me as the original of one of Doctor Capel's caricatures, a character which complacently disclaimed responsibility for human action on the grounds that collectively only power existed without sense of responsibility. As I was silent, my companion went on talking slowly, much as we were walking,—

" I don't blame the landlords for shirking the labour of cultivation when they were left free to do so. But I laugh at their stupidity in thinking that men would do for them, except under compulsion, what they would not do for themselves except under the same condition. In general the farmer will not work the land for himself, much less for a landlord or the public, unless under dire compulsion. What is not seen is that, given a sufficient area, he can live on it with practically little exertion, and wisely does so. His aim is always to command an area which enables him to live with the minimum of exertion, mental or bodily. There are indeed exceptional individuals who work as if work was a pleasure or duty in itself. The chief use of these few men is to serve as a cloak under cover of which the class may claim to be industrious, crazily bent on making money for other people. It is a pity our exceptions could not have a colony all to themselves to work out an awful example in the degradation and extinction of the race."

It was, as I found, the one topic of conversation in the country, the land question, and as my business after all was to listen to and elicit opinions, I maintained attentive silence.

" Nice formula that—the maximum production with the minimum of labour," the speaker went on, with the quiet air of a man who had his subject already at his finger ends. "I accept it in principle, but must throw the onus of reducing to practical form on the propounder with a *caveat*. I cannot allow the minimum of labour to be got as the maximum of labour the individual is capable of; the man would not give it, and under the actual system could not,

even as working for himself. Ten men working an area
that could be worked by two could not possibly give a
minimum of labour, particularly as the area would be subdivided as things are, so that three would have 15 and
seven only 5 acres apiece. Suppose now the 15-acre
holding gave the maximum limit of exertion in the holder,
then you would have seven men on 35 acres approximately
under a condition of minimum exertion they could not help.
Or, suppose the 5 acres gave the measure, then you would
have three men with 30 acres beyond their maximum
powers. In point of fact you have only to go to any area
of small occupiers to see that while the strain of maximum
exertion for poor results is apparent on it, the whole area
gives wasted land and wasted labour, and that invariably
and necessarily. Your plan in the interest of the community must shut out a minimum of labour, the result of
want of scope for labour."

We had emerged from Arrahantarahan Old Road, as it
was called, and got on a main road, as the speaker paused.

"I am going," I said, "over to Moyclare, Doctor Capel's
place, and as we must be near it, you may be able to
direct me."

"Not going as a patient, I hope? Well, no, I need not
ask that. I live beside the doctor, and pass his gate. You
know him?"

"Yes, I have met him at my uncle's, Doctor O'Gara's, in
Jigglestreet."

"Ah, you are young Doctor O'Gara. I heard you were
at Jigglestreet. I reckon your uncle and Miss O'Gara
among my most valued friends."

"After our chat you might make me feel that an honour,
if—"

"Oh, my name is David M'Qhan, and I live at Moyclare-
beg, just beside Doctor Capel."

"Count M'Qhan. Of course, your name is familiar to
me."

"I am a simple farmer, with no right to a title. The
country people called my father Count M'Qhan to punish
him for a stature that went with a naturally important air
and manner. I inherit the title, though not the magnitude
and manner."

" You may call yourself a simple farmer, but not meaning it as a compliment, however you came by the title, it would occur to no one to take away anything that marked you as an aristocrat."

The answer was given as if barely worth uttering,—

" Personally, I have had no intercourse with aristocrats, know nothing about them or their ways. Well, you would not call Capel an aristocrat ? "

" I would think of the doctor simply as a gentleman and not as an aristocrat. You know an aristocrat is not necessarily a gentleman. But," I added with haste, "you must not mistake me."

An amused smile, however, was all that my awkwardness of expression gave rise to.

" I agree with you that Doctor Capel is a gentleman, and as a very hardworking man, not an aristocrat. But I suppose you really mean by the term a man who is so far above the ordinary circumstances of life that he can choose his vocation freely, can be an idler if he likes. I certainly admit that I do not like to see men made slaves, or make themselves slaves voluntarily, work with furious industry for very doubtful ends, to make, say, a pile to ruin their heirs."

" You think," I said, "as an aristocrat when you aim at a life above narrow circumstance, and as a gentleman when you desire for your fellow-men what you desire for yourself. But the aristocrat seldom really desires to place all other men on his own level."

" He needn't. Our friend Capel holds that men are raised to a higher level as the result of the development of mechanical and physical science, and not by mere efforts of will and reason. Without a good timekeeper a man would make a poor effort at being punctual, and without labour-saving appliances mind makes little of legs and arms. All you doctors incline to deify mechanism and ignore mind, but I think he is right under certain limitations."

We had come by this to a gateway and lodge still gay with hydrangea, geranium and the last rose of summer. In among copper beeches, silver poplars and dark pines I could catch a glimpse of the roof and windows of a fine large house. My companion laughed and went on.

"The limitations would take us into metaphysics, so that it is as well this is Capel's house. Not many of you doctors have anything like it, and as for us farmers, we must be content if our dwellings give us the sympathy of our political friends. But Capel deserves his fine house, and is a fit master for it. You may tell him you met me and, to use your medical term, diagnosed me as an aristocrat. I may call over to see him in the evening, indeed I have an invitation from him to meet you."

We parted like old friends, and I was soon with the doctor in his study, a room testifying to the varied business and tastes of the occupant. He was a widower, and a sister, a widow, two or three years his senior, was his minister for the interior. His two sons, as he had told us, were in India, in the Civil Service. The lady, Mrs Garth, was childless, with ample means of her own, which in part accounted for the style in which the household was kept. It was a matter of wonder to everyone, but the party principally concerned, why the doctor not only retained the laborious post of a dispensary doctor, but discharged its duties with exemplary diligence.

I liked Mrs Garth at once, though it struck me that if she was safe from her brother's gift of caricature it was because she was his sister, and like him. I soon found, however, that the dispensary doctor of Lisdoheny was one of his most mercilessly treated subjects, and not at all privately. A sketch-book on the drawing-room table, open to visitors' inspection, would be open to a charge of gross rudeness if found on any other drawing-room table.

Dispensing with any ceremonious introduction when the doctor brought me into the same room, Mrs Garth came up and took my hand very quietly and graciously in both hers.

"I would know you at once," she said, "by your likeness to dear Missie. Even if we were not expecting you."

I felt my face tingling, for Missie had the grace and beauty of a poet's dream.

"A likeness in carbon-type, black and white," was all I could say, with a slight bow.

The doctor laughed.

"Not at all," he said. "All you O'Garas have a likeness not so much in feature as living expression. Just so. Missie, deeply reflective, sets her head to one side, giving the world up as a puzzle quite beyond her. There you are now with the very expression."

"I must be excused," I said, "hearing a statement I cannot understand and cannot contradict."

But Mrs Garth in a motherly way went farther.

"There now. I am sure you are a nice good boy, and that Missie would be pleased to be told you were so like her."

This was past answering, and I turned the subject by expressing my delight with Moyclare House and grounds, both of which, indeed, showed a certain rare and unexpected artistic effect.

"A Virginian swamp," I observed, "is the loveliest flower garden in the world. You seem to have stolen the plants and their natural arrangement, left the swamp behind, and made the house to match."

The doctor shook his head in dissent. "I would have preferred a reproduction from South Africa—less damp, less chance of rheumatism, but the climate of Tyrone has to be deferred to. But let us have a stroll round outside. Amelia, my sister, may show you what we have under glass."

We inspected the grounds, gardens, farmyard and stables, and though the ornamental had struck me at first sight, I soon found reason to take it as subordinate to the useful; the whole place clearly was conducted on the principle of making it pay as a farm. I had heard so much of farming not paying that I bluntly asked my host whether it paid him, particularly as his professional work took up so much of his time.

We were walking at a leisurely pace, but the doctor stopped to give emphasis to what he said.

"For the greater number of years I have spent here, I could not have held my farm unless it paid me well, and under the condition of my devoting to it only a fraction of my time. My dispensary and practice, while taking up most of my time, barely paid for the cost of working. A medical man indeed with duties such as mine has no business with anything but his profession, subject however to the condition that his profession shall support him. I soon found that it would not support me in anything but the meanest way. The pittance they gave me for a laborious dispensary about paid for the keep of a man and horse, and though I got nearly all the private practice, it was always poor and uncertain. Of course there are many districts better than mine, but the majority are worse, since there is competition in the richer areas. I had to take to farming to live, and one year with another it paid me well, much better than my profession."

"I am quite disinterested in my inquiries," I said. "I am bound to go and live with my father in St Louis, and have no intention of setting up as a doctor in Ireland."

"I know that, and that my friend O'Gara had tried to interest you in our land question. He has some good ideas on it himself, but I am afraid he would not get a hearing for them."

"Whatever may be his ideas on it, he keeps them to himself. He wants me to form an independent judgment of my own based on personal observation."

"He is right in that, but it is exactly such a judgment I fear that would get no hearing. The question is not only in the hands of blindly interested parties, but these parties command all means of expression in Parliament and the Press. Landlord and farmer have between them a monopoly, both of the land and of public opinion touching it. But I do not want to discourage you; in fact, things are coming to such a pass that it is likely the public will clear the court of both landlord and tenant, and secure a rational hearing for the question."

"I suppose, doctor, a way more natural to you of treating the question would be to reproduce an ancient but ever interesting drama, in which Punch and Judy would represent the landlord and tenant, while the audience of parliamentary nursemaids and overgrown babes, with their thumbs in their mouths, would stand for the big public."

"Thanks for the hint," the doctor said laughing. "If you don't try it I may. In reality the whole thing is so unutterably absurd, that the man who takes it seriously

H

runs the risk of being taken as the fool of the part. When is a wise man a fool? When he charges a fool with folly. Charge the public with its folly in allowing landlord and farmer to swindle it, and your charge will be resented if listened to at all."

"You seem," I said, "to think very impartially. Do you pay rent for your farm?"

"I paid rent for Moyclare at the same rate as my neighbours did for their land. Two years ago I had the opportunity of buying it out under the Land Purchase Acts, and of course availed myself of the benefit the law placed within my reach. If I had, however, been asked whether the benefit was necessary to me, or whether I had any moral right to it, I would have answered, No. What the farmers suffered at the hands of the landlords I believe has not been exaggerated; but, in spite of all that has been said, that is a personal matter between two sets of men, not materially affecting the general interest. What, however, the community suffered and suffers from the abuse and waste of the land by owner and occupier alike is a gigantic injury aggravated by the grossest fraud and deception. It was a fraud and deception to call on the really injured party to advance money to the very parties who injured it, and will certainly continue to injure it."

I was silent, and the doctor went on again after a pause.

"Moyclare paid me well, though I laboured it expensively and gave it only a portion of my time. Still I am conscious that it could have produced far more than it ever did in my hands. It covers 120 acres, and that is far too small an area to be worked to the extreme capacity with economy of labour. The labour and capital required to work my farm would not work a farm of 600 acres, but the last would not require five times as much labour and capital —nothing like it. Here it is that the injury to the community comes in. Farms of 5000 or 10,000 acres could be worked with an enormous economy of labour, because the labour could be organised in a way it cannot possibly be on small farms. The small farms exist not for the community or in its interest, but for a host of overseers and labourers whose lives and labour go to waste, and whose existence requires a price for produce not at all necessary."

" In coming over here I met a Count M'Qhan—a friend of yours—who is full of these ideas, and for a farmer an interesting man. He takes the subject out of our hands and thinks for the species first, and of economics only as determining its vital and mental state."

"Oh, indeed, accident has been beforehand with me. The Count and parson are coming over to dinner with us this evening. They are usually all the company we have here, but quality makes up for quantity. In the Count you shall find a man who can help you in a study of the agrarian question far better than I could."

" I don't know that, he seems to have settled down to a state of despair, and thinks it the right thing to make the best of it. But perhaps I am hasty in forming a judgment of him with so little to go on?"

" M'Qhan has only given you a glimpse of his philosophy. He takes human beings as he would ants or bees. There are a few—a very few philosophers of the stamp, men who get out of the human mental plane, have no mental fellowship with men. You are certainly hasty in thinking that he cares for the species. He cares for it as he does for ants and bees, only as an object of study. He might admit that the human species could be modified just as bees might only to lead you into an *impasse*. He would tell you that the collective interest is not the interest of the sum of individuals taken in time ; to obtain a modification by hypothesis desirable, more millions of individuals have to be disadvantaged and killed off in succession than ever are benefited by the modification."

" I had no idea he went so deep into things."

" He is not a very communicative man ; takes good care to know who he is making his mental confidant, and paid you a compliment if he has given you some of his more cherished ideas."

" Oh, we only touched the fringe of the land question, and it struck me that he took what he admitted to be gross abuses very placidly and contentedly."

" Yes, but that follows on his general view of the nature of human affairs. It would be to spoil that view to give it at second-hand; if you are in luck, you shall get it from himself, only you would need a preliminary course of meta-physical reading to fully appreciate it."

"But I took him as a practical man. He had a grasp of the land question although he was inconclusive."

"Inconclusive? In no way could he be more practical than in leaving you to form conclusions in your own way. But if I am not mistaken his conclusion is that you can-not change the course of the stars or of human affairs. He would tell you that our farmers are bound to a system which in the end shall sweep them off the board, and that a mere perception of the fact can alter nothing."

"He is a farmer himself, and holds this opinion appar-ently without letting it disturb his peace of mind?"

"He calls himself a farmer, not because he farms, but holds land. He has some 120 acres more land than I have, but he does not work his farm the way I do mine; his production is not half mine. He has means, partly in-herited, partly got with his wife, has a head on his shoulders, is successful as a dealer in cattle and horses, lives temperately and economically, is a good man, but a very bad farmer in the sense of a cultivator or pro-ducer. It is his knowledge of his own position, and the knowledge that it is the position aimed at and actually attained by the class of large occupiers, that makes him consider the farmer doomed. He is far too honest and capable a man to trust to falsehood, in particular to the impudent falsehood that bettering the position of farmers of his class would induce them to cultivate and better the position for the public. He knows very well that making them the owners of their holdings has made, and would only make, them act the more in their private interest, to lead an easy life. He knows, too, that there must be limits to public tolerance of the waste and abuse of the land, and of dependence on food raised abroad, that the trespass on the ignorance and stupidity of the people is going too far."

"But he holds that the small farm system is even worse."

"He gave you that side of the question? Well, if he did, I can have little to add except to say that, with our experience of the system, past and present, in this country,

it is amazing that men can be found to attempt its reproduction, that is, if one can be amazed at anything in the
politician."

" But if the position of the large farmer and the small is
alike bad and untenable, where is the alternative? We
cannot charge the public mind with ignorance and stupidity
when we are quite at a loss ourselves."

" My dear sir, I suspect your astute relative would not
have set you the problem unless he thought you were equal
to it. I would recommend you to accumulate and verify
the actual facts of our system, and trust that the procedure
will lead you to foresee, as the Count would put it, what
must happen. Your business, I take it, is not to shape or
control events, but humbly to form a mental picture of their
inevitable drift, heedless of the bye-play of politicians,
though the play is battledore and shuttlecock with hundreds
of millions of the public money."

" Your friend, the Count, asked me for a plan."

" Which shows me that he was merely skimming the
surface with one he took as a passing bird; politely accommodated himself to a conception of the unreality of
potential existence, which formally he does not allow, just
as he would say 'Good-day' to you in a snowstorm."

I saw clearly what was meant, and my uncle took
the same line, was that indications of the future form of
agricultural industry existed, that the potential form was
real, fixed and necessary, and if not actually taking the
place of the present form, was still capable of being appre-
hended. But beyond the fact that it was within the limits
of knowledge as an actual fact I did not get. It meant,
however, much to me that something more than matter
of destructive criticism lay before me as I came to be committed to the problem.

" I am safe in leaving you," the doctor said, " in the
Count's hands; you could not have a better guide. His
practical knowledge of the country and the people is something wonderful. He and I are both called landlord men
in the country, but that is simply the usual case of men not
being allowed liberty of thought. In fact, you shall soon
find that we are disowned by both landlord and farmer,
not so much because we object to their system, but because

we object to the terrorism which both equally rely on to maintain their interest, as they conceive it.   Form any independent judgment of your own, and you shall find both your enemy."

"If they are as indifferent to my judgment as I am to their enmity we shall be quits."

It was time to go in and dress for dinner, and the agrarian question did not crop up again that evening. Perhaps in my honour the company started and kept to American topics, only, however, to make me feel my own ignorance.   Mrs Garth spoke of American shrubs and alpines in a way that made me note that I had a task before me in making acquaintance with them, hitherto quite neglected.   Mrs Maude, the Episcopalian rector's wife, partly restored my confidence by talking in an astonishing way of the negro in the Southern States as not being allowed the status of a human being.   I had tender recollections of my coloured nurse and my earliest companions, her children, and some slight but sufficient observation of social exclusiveness in Europe to help me over the criticism with polite *sang-froid*.   Mrs M'Qhan, a pretty, placid-looking little lady, a fit match for her philosophic husband, was pitiful over the assassination of President M'Kinley, and astonished that such a thing could occur in a free and enlightened country.   If it was in Russia, where there was no free Press, it would be different.   Her surprise was turned on myself when I expressed no surprise at the event, and explained that while in Russia there was no free Press, in America there were hundreds of newspapers telling their readers, day after day and week after week, that the President was the most dangerous and unprincipled enemy his country ever had, depending on them to know that if they voted against him that was all that was wanted.

When the ladies left, the conversation turned on local topics, winding up with a controversy between Mr Maude, the Episcopalian clergyman, and Count M'Qhan on some metaphysical subject.   The gentlemen evidently were in the habit of fencing with each other.   The impression I retained was that, while the clergyman was too heavily handicapped by his professional preconceptions and formulas to be really free to seek truth, the Count's opinions had the value of worked-out problems of native thought, never marred by taking initial assumption for more than it was worth. The discussion seemed a logomachy to me, but the way the Count reasoned inspired me with confidence in his ability and judgment.

IX

A BIG map of Lisdoheny district, taken from the Ordnance Survey sheets, hung in Doctor Capel's study, by the help of which I soon got an idea of the area and of the holdings it was parcelled out into, like a chessboard run mad. It was no new thing for me to work a country by map, but I never had occasion to do so with such detailed care, and the exercise was not without its reward. The doctor's absence was protracted for over two months by attendance on his brother in London, but before the two months were out I knew every road, lane, farm and house in the district, as a result of methodically working by the map.

I cycled, moreover, into the adjoining districts, and on one pretence or another visited their doctors. I found the farmers, one and all, discontented with their lot, but then their discontent was intelligible, open and exaggerated in expression. It was political stock-in-trade which had paid in the past and was looked to with confidence to pay in the future. It was different with the doctors. There was an amazing number of clergymen of different denominations in the country—probably seven or eight to one doctor—but while these gentlemen, in the mere discharge of their duty, were for ever explaining their views on every subject, each to his own little circle of hearers, the few doctors were models of reserve, each according to his individual disposition practising the usual arts by which thought is concealed. I must say this was not confined to the medical men. It took some art or artfulness to get at the ideas of any individual in the country who could be suspected of thinking for himself, but whenever I succeeded I found a vein of agnosticism opposed to the conventional code of religion and morality, to which outwardly the individual yielded formal assent and deference. No matter what sect or party a man belonged to, he seldom failed, under the condition of being able to think at all, to ascribe his allegiance to his sect or party to mere matter of bringing-up or education, and by implication that that was irrational ground for his judgments. An Orangeman has told me, with a fine vein of contempt for his own side, that he would have been a Papist and Fenian if he had been born and brought up on that side, and that the extreme man of one party is only by accident not an extreme man in the other party. In the same way, I have heard many Roman Catholics give utterance to the broadest views of tolerance, which, as units in the mass, they knew well they could neither act on nor give expression to. The variance between the individual as a responsible thinking agent and as a unit in a mass, bound to give up his private thought and judgment to the formulas which hold the mass together, can be seen to lead to the striking phenomenon of widespread repression and concealment of thought, judgment and opinion. It is common to call this stupidity, mindlessness, hypocrisy, insincerity, and so on, but the bow-wow might be directed with more justice against the tyranny which engenders the evil.

If I was not one of themselves and a passing stranger moreover, I would have got little information from the doctors I visited in South Tyrone. It was easy enough to find that, like the farmers, they were in a state of chronic discontent with their position, but then the discontent was not, as in the case of the farmers, a valuable asset for political exploitation. In educated men apparent indifference and cynicism is usually a guard against the tyranny of vulgar opinion The first guard of the elderly and experienced medical men I met in South Tyrone was professional mannerism, which indeed only meant that they habitually held back instead of expressing what they thought. When I got past this I found no real indifference to the questions which divided the community, but rather cynical contempt for the collective forms of opinion. In fact, these men could not help forming unconsciously a body of opinion, only, however, to find that they had to keep it under lock and key. Even so the mass took it for granted that they did not think with it. The doctor's religion and politics, like his professional knowledge, was looked on as private property.

One of the doctors I visited was a sour and unhappy man, at least when not absorbed in speculative branches of medical study. He complained of over-work and starvation wages. His farmers certainly sweated him, but not worse, according to his own account, than they did everyone in their power, their servants and children. Another I visited, hearing he was ill, was a timid, nervous lad, who, when only just qualified, had through family interest been appointed to a large district, only to find the responsibility too much for his mental and physical abilities. This gentleman, who owed his position to a system which dispensed with the most elementary guarantees of experience and fitness, expressed bitter contempt for the knots of ignorant boss farmers who, he held, were as competent to manage the Royal Artillery as the medical service of the country. It was not the first or last time I had occasion to observe that the farmers had not the knack of making friends or gaining the respect of those who served them. This sickly young man, when I got him to speak freely, would have pleased an out-and-out anarchist by the fate he would assign the legislator, who thought by striking bedrock oligarchy he reached heaven and democracy. He was outspoken, probably on account of his youth, but under more guarded forms of expression all the medical men I met were unanimous in their condemnation of the legislation which placed local power in the hands of the countryside farmers they knew so well, and laughed at the folly of calling the mischievous blunder democracy. They all agreed that instead of giving this class power under an illusory form of election, the people, their cottiers and tenants, required protection against its greed, necessity and ignorance. They saw clearly that the pauperised element could protect itself only by driving the farmer from power and placing illiterate labourers on public boards. It was self-evident to them that the labourer and cottier tenant of the farmer could not do this, but had not only to submit to a needy master, but go through the miserable farce of voting for him. Nor, to express farther the opinions I gathered, was it desirable that the labourer and labouring farmer should assume a power which they would certainly abuse if only they used it as the oligarchical class does now. What has to be done for them cannot be done by them; the democratic interest is to be served only by the assertion of principle, and not by merely vesting power in any personal agency. Except the sick youth I have just mentioned, none of the doctors would like to see the labouring incited against the farming class, but all of them expected that the last left to its devices and under the pressure of its own narrow circumstances, would either destroy the labourer or else force him to revolt against its tyranny, to its own ruin in both cases.

One doctor, who at first I erroneously took as a humorous cynic, commanded my attention in particular. I suspected him of playing with me, amusing himself at my expense; but then apparently the only thing he took seriously was curing his patients, and even that task he qualified by objecting to the morality of prolonging the life of rascals. His disguise was effected by out-Heroding Herod. The French Revolution was a failure, because with shameful weakness it left heads on shoulders—took one head and left a hundred as bad. He was cheerful, if not merry, devoted to his profession and patients, but otherwise not taken seriously. It may be, however, that all the sermons the numerous clergymen of the district preached were barely sufficient to counteract the disturbing influence of his jests. I shall have occasion to recur to him again.

When I was about a week in charge of Lisdoheny district I was called on to attend and give evidence at a coroner's inquest, in the district of the young man I mentioned as being sick. The rule is that the coroner shall call on the medical officer of the district in which the death occurs, but in this case Doctor Smith, as I may call him, was on sick leave, and his substitute not available, so I was called in as the nearest doctor. The inquest was a mere form, and I soon saw that even the form was to be limited as much as possible. For many years the deceased was a leading farmer in the district, a member of the Local Board of Guardians and District Council, and was thought likely to be made a magistrate—the blue ribbon of bucolic ambition. He had been attending the local board of which he was a member in a town five miles from his home, and had driven himself home in the evening apparently quite well. He took ill, however, when not an hour home, and in the course of another hour was dead. The evidence was to the effect that he had been in good health, and for years had no occasion to consult a medical man. An indiscreet juror inquired whether he was in trouble over his affairs, but was curtly silenced as raising irrelevant questions.

"It is Mr Brown's death," the coroner said in a decided tone. "Gentlemen of the Jury, the cause and manner of his death, and not his affairs, you are called together to inquire into."

"But," the indiscreet juror was beginning in expostulation, when the coroner, a sharp, little, legal practitioner, cut him short by addressing me.

"Take the book, doctor. What is your name? Christian and surname in full?"

"Art Phelimy Art O'Gara."

The name was received with a pause expressive of surprise.

"What?" asked the coroner.

I repeated the name, with the remark that it should not be thought a strange one in the land of Owen Roe O'Neil, but Owen Roe might have been a pagan, and the coroner suddenly became nicely punctilious.

"What form," he asked, "of oath or affirmation do you hold binding on your conscience?"

"Any form held binding by any member of the jury I hold equally binding on me."

To prevent further discussion of the ticklish point I held up my hand as I had seen most of the jurymen do, and was duly sworn or affirmed under the form.

"I am not the coroner of this district," the official said by way of apology, "but acting for him in his absence, and, you know, the regular forms have to be observed."

My qualification as a physician and surgeon being stated,

he went on in the tone of a man who was determined to stand no nonsense.

"You have heard the evidence given at this inquest touching the death of Robert Brown, deceased?"

"Yes."

"You have made an external examination of the body of the deceased?"

"Yes."

"Have you found any marks of violence on the body, or anything to justify suspicion of violence being the cause of death?"

"I have found no marks of violence on the body and nothing to justify suspicion of death through violence. The body is healthy, well nourished and free from any signs of disease."

"But," said the indiscreet juror, to be again cut short by the coroner.

"Will you tell the jury, doctor, what, to the best of your judgment and belief, was the cause of death?"

I was in a difficulty. The evidence I had to go on was insufficient to form an approximate judgment of the cause of death. The account given by the wife, daughter, and servant maid of the sudden illness of the deceased was confused and unsatisfactory, a description of their own fright and alarm rather than anything else. The man had once slightly vomited and sank in a faint from which he had never rallied.

"In the absence of an autopsy I can form only an imperfect, a very imperfect, idea of the cause of death."

"It is for the jury to say whether in the total absence of any evidence of violence a post-mortem examination of the body is necessary."

"I do not mean to say," I observed, wishing to guard myself, "that a mere examination of the internal organs would be sufficient to establish the cause of death."

I knew perfectly well that what was in my mind was equally in the minds of both coroner and jury, but at the same time I was not sure that even chemical analysis would give a certain result.

The coroner looked at the foreman and simply said,—

" Well, gentleman ? "

" I don't see," the foreman, an elderly, rough-looking farmer said, " that there is call to go into the thing more, no one bein' charged with harming Mr Brown. No one had a word with him or again him, an' I ought to know, livin' on the march wi' him."

A murmur of assent went round the jury with one exception.

" But," began the indiscreet juror, and got no farther.

" Now, doctor," the coroner said, " the jury seeing no necessity, in the absence of suspicion attaching to anyone for an internal examination, do you say that the death cannot be accounted for by natural causes ? "

" Oh, no," I was only too glad to reply. " Confining myself to natural causes, I would say that death was due to cardiac syncope or failure of the heart's action."

" Do you consider that a sufficient cause to account for the death ? "

" Certainly. It was possibly, even probably, the cause of death."

" Gentlemen of the Jury," the coroner said with prompt decision, " you have heard the medical evidence given, I must say, with a conscientiousness which enhances its value. The object of such an inquest as we hold on the present melancholy occasion is not so much to accurately determine cause of death as to protect the living, by either negativing suspicion of foul play, or where *prima facie* evidence of guilt is present fixing it, as far as possible, in the right quarter. In the case of the deceased Robert Brown, there is no evidence that he suffered violence at all, no one is charged, as your foreman has observed, with having harmed him, and, under the circumstances, I agree with the jury and the doctor that no case arises for determining the cause of death with scientific precision. That would only be necessary if we had to fix guilt or relieve the innocent from suspicion. I suppose, therefore, Gentlemen of the Jury, your verdict is that deceased Robert Brown came by his death from natural causes, to wit, cardiac syncope."

A murmur of assent went round the jury, even the indiscreet member holding his tongue, having time to think. The verdict was probably correct, but if fair to the living it did not relieve the dead man from the suspicion of having committed sucide by taking poison. I could not, however, identify offhand any common poison as accounting for the mode of death, and saw no reason for stating an alternative doubtful in itself and extremely difficult of proof. I did not think, however, that anyone but myself believed the balance to turn in favour of the verdict.

"Queer name you have," the acting coroner said in bidding me good-bye, "but you did quite right. There was no one to blame, and no use distressing the family. They have enough of trouble before them."

"My name, sir," I said, "is so good that I am under a bond not to discredit it. Our verdict, too, is so good that we are bound not to discredit it. The chances are that it is near about right."

The coroner looked at me and shook his head in a way that meant both assent and dissent.

James, Doctor Capel's smart groom, was a striking illustration of the utility and futility of association with a philosophic reasoner. His association with his logical master made him state facts in a relation of inter-dependence, but the connection which satisfied him was often peculiarly his own, and free from pedantic adherence to the rules of induction and deduction. Doctor Capel often parodied himself, but never as well as his groom did, never with the same natural effortless effect. I had become a favourite with him, and in driving me back to Lisdoheny he gave me an account of Robert Brown and his tragical end, a philosophical account in which consequent were deduced from antecedent events so as to form a unitary picture with a background in future time. The story opened with a descriptive touch of the character of the deceased.

"Pwee, now," this to the horse. "Gee, g'long! wait till you get to your stable if it's your prayers you're thinking about. He made no will Robin Brown, they say, not but that he knew how, seein' he made all the wills miles round in the country. When not lawin' on his own account always in other people's law. A bad day it was for the attorneys the day he made away with himself."

"But the verdict was death from natural causes," I said

gravely. "The real truth is that there was not evidence to fix the precise cause of death, and in the absence of suspicious circumstances a difficult investigation was not called for."

"Pwee, now. Yes, sir. They do say, you behaved the very best considering that you and Robin were not acquainted. You see he was greatly called up, Robin, and no one was for reflecting on him. He minded everybody's business, which is saying that he didn't mind his own overly well. That takes in the country, sir. Yes, they don't see that the man who lets his own business mind itself, or helps it into a mess, is like to get other people's business into a mess concerning himself with it. Robin had a kindly turn, though mostly he got people into a mess like in a hurry. Pwee, now."

"When one minds his own business, does not concern himself with his neighbours, and is shy of helping them, he gets the reputation of being selfish."

"Pwee, now. That's so, sir. Robin was never shy of giving a helping hand to a neighbour, and was called up in consequence. But the nature of the help has to be considered. Robin's turn, I'd say, was in general to help a neighbour into a scrape, mostly into law about wonderful little. No matter how small a man is, he is ill-pleased to have his affairs looked down on as wee. Robin naturally took things big, made much of them, and if you went to him with a complaint you mightn't think worth talking over, you left him bound to fight and die over it. He'd have obliged a cock-sparrow in his wars, Robin would, only cocky mustn't take his case light, Robin being his backer. Pwee! Yes, sir, Robin made much of them, and they took it kindly."

"He must have done a lot of mischief in the country if that was his turn, and made a lot of enemies."

"Pwee, now. Yes, sir. Enemies and friends Robin had past counting. That's certain. But not long to the fore. Those Robin had dealings with for or against are not those that stand their ground in this world, but the come-and-go kind we have, passing like a show. Enemies—yes, sir, but if his enemies in their wee time had harmed him to the extent his friends of the day did, the pity for him would be

less. Pwee, now. G'long! You would, would you?
Yes, sir, I'd say, Robin served his friends as his friends
served him, and the enemies may be left out of account."

"Certainly the enemy seems to have been on the safe
side, but I heard the man had the devil's luck."

James suddenly became silent and reflective, and bestowed
more speech on the horse than was necessary.

"They say in these parts ," he said at last, as if feeling
his ground, "that there is no luck with American money."

"That is bad for me," I said; "the little I have is in
dollars."

"That's not the meaning, sir. The American is safe
enough with his own money. What's not lucky are big
lumps of American money coming over here to farmers by
the death of friends in America, legacies like. It's a real
fact that bad luck comes with them."

"I see. But the legacy might bring bad luck no matter
from what quarter it came."

"Yes, sir, it might, no question, but we have no experience to go on. It is said that a mint of Irish money goes
to England, but if our own money would do us the harm
American does we needn't be sorry, leastways when it
comes in big lumps to farmers—to what servant boys and
girls send home I never heard objection made. Yes, sir,
what harm lumps of American money did farmers in the
country is just past belief."

"Indeed! Was Robert Brown ruined by a legacy from
America?" I asked, wishing to bring James to the point.

"Pwee, now, g'long with you! You know your way,
leastways you ought. No, sir, Robin got no legacy direct
from America; the thing was not that simple. And if he
did I'd say we shouldn't be bound by a single case, but
take all cases the thing happened in, and see the luck
following them as a rule. Pwee, now! There's many a
case to be told, but Robin's in a way can stand for nigh
them all. When lumps of American money come this road
it's not one person and one generation that suffer; the luck
stands while they stand, and it's by no means the same in each
case. Pwee, now, you might know the turn without me!"

"Then it was through unlucky American money Brown
came to grief?"

I

"Unlucky. Yes, sir; to a hundred persons at least, all told, reckoning Robin in, the last of them. They do say that he was clean broke, Robin, nothing left for the family, the debts on the place being paid and the lawyers' bills settled. But they may say, the Lord be thankit, they've seen the last of the lump."

I remained silent, and let James tell the story in his own way.

"Pwee, now! It's fifty or maybe fifty-five years since one Stewart Maquade died in Philadelphia, leaving the fortune he made, no one knows how, to come by law to a brother and four sisters over here, up to that quiet, decent people as any in Lisdoheny and Ballyhannigan, with bits of farms and what kept them well. It was five thousand pounds and some hundreds that came to each of them. Well, sir, the brother, Vet Maquade he was called, being a cow doctor, went clean away in his head before ever he touched a penny of his share. They do say that he was not all there, had a want at best, and you'll allow the luck was bad luck for him, seeing he had to be put in the asylum, the Lord Chancellor keeping his money and paying for him. If it was so allowed, it would be better if the Lord Chancellor had the keeping of the whole concern and their money. I'd make it the law that he'd take charge of those money fell to, leastways till it was plain they'd not harm themselves."

"In that case you would need a dozen Lord Chancellors and hundreds of asylums."

"Pwee, now, g'long! Yes, sir, that's like enough, and kept busy, but you may come to see the necessity of it. I saw you looking curious like at the big bars on the windows of Robin's house, Knockbawn, as it is called. No wonder you looked, the same barring and cross-barring being a sight in a Christianable country. It is said to have made up Barney Magenity, the blacksmith, who forged it and put it up just as you saw it."

"It certainly did strike me. Made the house look like a jail, and one it would not be easy to get out of."

"Pwee, now! Yes, sir, it was not getting out but getting in it was again. There used to be a gate of iron bars outside the front door, and the like for the back door. Robin got them put inside and painted brown to match the name. He was jokey in turns, Robin, when he was at himself."

"Yes, I noticed the iron-barred gate behind the hall-door."

"Pwee, now! It's not much passes you, sir. Well, you see, Reed Brown, Robin's grandfather, was married on one of Stewart Maquade's sisters, and came in for her five thousand pounds, which he just brought home in gold and notes, and locked all up in an iron box, made by the same Barney Magenity we've mentioned. Pwee, now, pwee! Old Reed was mistrustful of banks and lending out, and indeed it's little he trusted anyone. He had a brave farm before ever the money came his road, and was not backward in labouring it. With the money, however, he got strange, and fell into a studying way, and as he'd neither labour his land properly nor spend a shilling of the money, his way of living was none of the best. The worst thing that could happen him or the like of him being bred to work is a studying turn. Pwee, now!"

James stopped, apparently to indulge in the vicious habit he condemned. I remained in a brown study too, but then I was smoking, and had not committed myself.

"Pwee, now, pwee! You see, sir, Reed was not what one would call a miser, but just a poor man, his money locked up and his farm gone to the bad and paying ill. He was worse, indeed, than a real poor man, for he had a fear over him day and night of being robbed. It is the happiness of the poor man with nothing that he has nothing to lose, being, so to say, robbed already, and treated as bad as bad can be by the rest of the world. Pwee, now! you know your road."

James stopped again, as if this abstruse proposition demanded reconsideration, or perhaps because it was a trick with his master to state a proposition and then go carefully back on it.

"Pwee, now!" he resumed. "Reed was never robbed his day, never treated as badly by anyone as he was by himself. Never robbed of his peace of mind by day and his rest by night except by himself. Yes, sir, they do say that old Barney the smith, who put up the iron fixings for him, did not go again his notions, but then the man maybe thought he mightn't lose a good job and no one be the better. The fact is, Reed was no miser, and allowed others more than he allowed himself. But with his studying the fear of robbers grew on him, and the robber he feared most was his own son, Archie. Reed's Archie was the only child, and when the mother died and he was man grown there was much to be said again him, though he was no robber, but just the father's son in standing in his own light. He kept company with his cousins, who were serving the devil to the best of their ability with the help of Stewart Maquade's money. They do say that, in joke or earnest, he advised the old man to sail for Liverpool with his iron box, and when fifty miles out to drop it into the sea, offering his help to do it. He had that turn, Reed's Archie, and could see deep into things."

"The advice showed sense as things stood, but I would not bet on Reed's Archie coming down on the right side of the fence."

"Pwee, now, pwee! Yes, sir, you'd not bet on Solomon doing that because he preached so fine, and Reed's Archie was Solomon wanting his crown; his wisdom an affliction and mockery. None of your gay, light-headed characters, but the contrary, that dour and melancholy that he had just to take out and play wild antics to save thought from going astray or being the death of him. Pwee, now! Yes, sir."

The words were James's, but only Doctor Capel could form a just mental picture of such a character.

"Yes, sir," he resumed, "Reed's Archie married a second cousin of his own, a Maquade, who brought him a hundred or two that was left of old Stewart's money. They do say, it was one of Archie's antics marrying, he being vast against himself as unfit for the married state. They had but the one child, this Robin we've been seeing the last of. It's allowed that Archie was the best to the wife, never touched her bit of money, and kept Reed's farm to the good for her, but otherwise now and then he took out equal to daft. It was not, however, now and then, when old Reed died, and the iron box fell to him, but just constant, and when the box was empty our man was in his coffin. One Essie Shanes told me herself that in her young days, being in service in Dungannon in a public, he came in one night carrying a flitch of bacon and ordered the whole of it to be boiled and served up to him and a crony, with a gallon of rum. When her master made objection, out he took, Archie did, a roll of sovereigns made up in paper and banged it down on the table, so that the sovereigns —there might be fifty of them—went flying about the room, and never a one of them would he gather up. Another story, I was told as a fact, was one of a neighbour who, seeing how things were going, went to Archie for the loan of a few shillings and was served with a saucerful of sovereigns out of the iron box. They say he had the face to go back, saying it was shillings he wanted, and, there being none in the box, did put up with another saucerful of sovereigns. There is nothing I'd put past some men. Pwee, now, pwee ! Will you ? You're running for the Darby, are you ? Wo-ho, easy now !"

" Reed's Archie seems to have seen into things, as you say, when he advised his father to drop the box into the sea."

"Archie was before my time," the youthful groom and philosopher observed. " Pwee, now, pwee ! Long before my time, but one can make out his turn from others. There is none of us but have something of the kind in us, thinking the one way and acting the exact contrary. They do say he'd have made a good minister, only it took liquor to loose his tongue, being silent otherwise."

"How did it come that when he made an end of the American money the luck of it followed the son ? Of course I understand how it might act through the effect on the grandfather and father, but the money itself was innocent as regards Robert Brown himself."

James pweed reflectively at the horse, as if conning over an interesting problem that had occurred to him.

"Yes, sir ; one might think that Robin went astray through the grandfather and father, that his luck was born with him, but the facts are clean again that. You see Reed died when he was a child, and Reed's Archie a year after the old man. Mrs Brown had the bringing up of the boy, and she was naturally quiet enough, and bound to be quiet, having nothing but the old farm to come and go on, which, in the hands of a woman, did not allow of capers. They do say she gave Robin overly much education and not enough of work on the farm, anyway till he was man grown he had the name of being modest, and no way given to keeping company. The only thing again him was reading books, in which for certain he did not take after the father. Pwee, now, pwee! Reed's Archie, they do say, was vast again books, and used to declare that more harm was done in the world by reading books than by any other way whatever. Let that be as it may, Robin read books, no end of them, and thought none, in which he didn't take after the father, who was always studying, studying when he was that full of liquor, he couldn't stand near steady, and was never seen to open a book. No, sir, there was nothing again Robin but his reading turn, which is allowed to be no turn for farmers. It would never be reflected on him that he thought none. You and I might pass remark on that, but country people would never notice it. It's the studying turn they notice being uncommon."

We were getting near Moyclare without getting apparently any nearer Robert Brown's luck, so I gave James a hint to hurry up with the narrative.

"Pwee! Wo-ho! Easy! Yes, sir, my belief is that Robin would be to the fore yet, and we not this errand to-day, if the American money, and its luck, didn't come in to order things. Robin was all right—a sober, steady-going young man as one could find, till one day a letter comes telling that Vet Maquade, who we've mentioned as put in an asylum, was dead, and Mrs Brown and her son were his sole heirs. The daft man's money had grown bigger than it was at first, his keep not having taken the whole of the interest, and the rest of the Maquade connection being clean wiped out there was no one for it but Robin and the mother. Pwee, now! pwee! There was no trouble or opposition about it, and no handle for the lawyers' fingers, the Maquade tribe was lost and gone, as the ten tribes we're told of, not a one of them left to dispute with Robin. Well, sir, it would not be truth to say that He went wild all at once, or indeed in a way ever. He got married, and had the three daughters you were looking at, pitiful like, I

do believe, and no more. But from the day he got the
Vet's fortune a change came over him, for all he was sober
as a judge and proper in his way of life. Yes, sir, and in
the heel of the hunt he came to be something the money and
its luck made him, something he'd never have been if it hadn't
come his road. Pwee, now! pwee!"

James stopped in his discourse, calmly confident of having established the case against American money, but willing
to allow me time to make objection if I could. I, however,
evaded the unscientific idea of luck.

"But how did Brown make ill-use of the money? I was
told that he was heavily in debt and would leave the family
penniless."

Doctor Capel was nothing if not logical, but often raised
problems only to admit they were out of reach of solution.
The groom kept close to his model.

"Wo-ho, easy! Pwee, now! Yes, sir. I say the money
made ill-use of Robin, and, as you put it, Robin made ill-
use of it. I don't say I'm right; but suppose he was given
to liquor, as his father Archie was, you'd say the main
point was the effect of the liquor on him, one of the effects
being to make him ill-use liquor in general. The effect of
the money and the manner of his getting it on Robin just
left the use he put it to a matter of course. It was the
man and his nature that was played on by circumstances
that he was not answerable for."

"The man's original nature counts for something.
Another man would have acted differently under the
influence of the possession of the money."

"Yes, sir, that's certain. We've seen Reed and Reed's
Archie and Robin took ways of their own in consequence
of the money; its effects on them differed, the one thing
sure being that they would have been better wanting
it."

"I am curious to know, from your way of looking at it,
the effects of the money on Brown."

"Pwee, now! pwee! The effect, as a fact, was to make
him the big man of the country. He was made a public
man, put on boards, made much of and had parties, mostly
with some design of putting him to use, running for ever
after him. I told you he thought none, which means that

he never had but the one notion, fixed enough, seeing nothing was put in the balance and weighed against it. Your country farmer, all the world over, is the like, but Robin's one notion was that, because he read books and had money he was no country farmer, but a statesman, like, and governor, and went in for managing and settling everything in the country. He got mixed up accordingly with what didn't in the least concern him to an extent past belief, got into lawsuits which go one way or go the other, were nothing to him. Never a day would you find him at home, running here and running there, attending meetings, making wills for neighbours or helping them to set wills aside, which is more serious, as a general rule. Settling everything settled Robin, that and not knowing when to give way and knock under to what couldn't be helped, seeing things out. Pwee, now ! pwee ! It sees you out, persevering too far, that turn."

"I suppose, then, that all that proved expensive for Robin ? "

"Expensive ! Wo-ho, easy now ! You know your road. Here we are now, a good, steady forty minutes' run it is from Knockbawn, though the doctor has done it under many a time. Expensive—why, for years the people have been on the look-out for Robin's wind-up. I'd say they had more idea of where the man was, what he had and what he owed than ever he had himself. He had a way, sir, Robin had, of not seeing himself or his own affairs, not wanting to look particular. Pwee, now ! I'm not equal to him, I allow, but you get the doctor to touch him off, and fill up with a word or two from the Count."

"I think you have given a pretty good sketch yourself. Brown seems to have been cut out for Parliament, Congress or comic opera."

"Yes, sir. I never heard him spoken of for opera whatever that is, but they that wanted to blow him up did talk of him for Parliament. Once there was serious word of it, and the objection made was that he was one that would do no man's bidding. He had his notion, Robin, and there he was, you could make nothing of him ; your job would be to hinder him jumping down your throat. Yes, sir, he'd allow no man his liberty. He might in the end be as reasonable as the farmer men that would put him in, but he'd take the bit in his mouth and not acknowledge them. I don't say I'd fall out with him for that if he had sound judgment of his own, but there's where the failure comes in.   Pwee, now !   Here we are."

We were at Moyclare, but before parting with James I put in a word for American money.

"The fault is not with the money, James, but with the people who get it.   It is just as likely that any other great advantage falling their way would have the same effect, only a few deriving benefit from it."

"Yes, sir, I've heard the doctor go over that, but right or wrong there's a bad name on American money come over here, and that of itself is a fact.   Yes, sir."

X

DOCTOR JOHN

In a routine of dispensary work my time passed quickly in South Tyrone, and just because medical work brought me in contact with a large number of the members of the community, I became quickly and unconsciously, rather than through deliberate study, familiar with the agrarian system. But mere familiarity with the system brought with it the danger of taking it with all its glaring evils as necessary and inevitable. The hundreds I met who were familiar with it, bred up in it, took the subordination of agriculture to the personal conditions of individual life, the holding and management of land by persons under disability, as a matter of course, a matter that never called for thought or discussion. That, in reality the factor raising the land question, never assumed in their minds the form of a problem. Fortunately for my study of agrarianism there were exceptions, singularly few indeed, and without weight or influence, but yet singularly competent. The varied forms under which disability, physical and mental, occurs were ever under the eye of the physician, made up his natural and necessary province of thought and work. Doctor Capel and my uncle knew as a matter of course that the majority of mankind is under disability, and that no discrimination against disability obtaining in the class occupying the land, the class was utterly unable to discharge the task of cultivating it; all it could do was to make a desperate struggle to live by it under the condition of disability. In their mind, too, the agrarian system was all of a piece; the landowner and occupier were alike under the necessity of meeting the condition, their conflict a mere expression of individual necessity. Both wanted to live on the land without cultivating it, but one stood in the way of the other doing so as far as it could possibly be done by the other.

But the medical men, both in an official and private position, had to hold their tongues, room or place for expression of their knowledge and judgment there was none. The nominees and creatures, once of the land-owning, now of the farmer oligarchy, their livelihood and their interest is and always was dependent on discreet silence, often on ignominious subservience. The critics who have eyes and caustic censure for this position, a common one for educated men, are usually singularly blind to the brutal terrorism which creates it.

To one medical man in South Tyrone I owe the step from destructive criticism of the existing agrarian system to constructive ideas, the conception of the transforma-tion which the system must in the end undergo. I men-tioned visiting the doctor of a district adjoining Lisdoheny, a humorous cynic, I called and took him to be at first. His name was John Devine, but in the country he was simply Doctor John. He was a farmer or occupier of land as well as a medical man, but there was mentally nothing of the farmer in him. When he allowed me to know him, to get beyond his cloak of mannerism, I found him a thoughtful man with the modesty which comes to men baffled at every turn by disease and death.

He was much more popular with the farmers than either Doctor Capel or my uncle, and had a large practice. Apart from skill and experience in his profession, as a farmer and the son of a farmer he was at home with farmers. Yet while they could form some idea of Doctor Capel they stopped short with Doctor John, stopped where he meant them to stop, which meant that they could seldom take him seriously. For some time indeed I was unable to take him as in earnest, not until, as I thought, he had formed a judgment of my object, that I was worth being taken seriously.

Soon after coming to Lisdoheny I had visited Doctor John, but professional work brought me in more immediate contact with him. I had taken over a patient from

Doctor Capel, and, distrusted on account perhaps of my youth, was required to call in a consultant.

"As papa seems no better, doctor, maybe you would like to have another opinion. Two heads, you know, are better than one."

Miss M'Whillan wanted another doctor to see her father, not because two heads were better than one, but because one was on the shoulders of a strange young man she knew nothing about, who had come in Doctor Capel's place, and the strange young man thought it a very good reason.

"I do not look," I said, "on your father's case, Miss M'Whillan, as a very serious one, but if you wish to have another doctor I am willing, of course, to share the responsibility such as it is. Is there any medical man in particular he would prefer to see?"

"Oh, we always call on Doctor Capel when anything is wrong, and leave everything to him. We depend on him as an old friend as well as our doctor. Perhaps you might like to call in your uncle to assist you?"

I knew at once that this was said out of politeness, and did not express what was wanted.

"Doctor O'Gara, I have no doubt, would come if asked, but if your father has consulted any other doctor with Capel, or, in his absence, he would be the man to call in."

"Papa had Doctor John from Frayne when Doctor Capel was away before, two years ago. Do you know Doctor John?"

"Doctor Devine of Frayne. Yes, I called on him only a week ago and liked him. I believe you could not have a better man. Would your father like to have him?"

"Oh, papa knows Doctor John, and would be sure to get on well with him."

"Then get him. I will write a note asking him to come over as soon as he can. It is not far to Moyclare, and if you send me the answer I shall come over and meet him."

The lady was evidently pleased to have no more diplomacy over what her mind was made up to do.

"That will do well. I can send a messenger to Frayne at once, and when I get the answer send it over to you."

I told Doctor Devine that the case did not need a second doctor, but that I wrote to him at the desire of the patient, who had confidence in him, and his coming would be of service. The answer was to the effect that he could meet me at Mr M'Whillan's at 5 P.M., and restore the depression of spirits which he anticipated would be contagious in M'Whillan's case by going over to Moyclare and spending the evening with Mrs Garth and myself.

The consultation, a mere form on the medical side, was no form with Mr M'Whillan, who expanded with Doctor John in a way he had not done with me. I knew, of course, that his ailment was aggravated by mental anxieties, but had had no opportunity, not knowing what they were, of meeting the case. Not so with Doctor John, whose skill in drawing out our patient and applying remedies, from kindly sympathy to airy ridicule, I could not but admire.

" You know, doctor," Mr M'Whillan said, "it ill fits me to be laid up. Here is this big farm on my hands and not a soul to look after it but myself, though, dear knows, I've contracted the business of it these years past within the smallest bounds possible. I haven't a man about the place I can trust buying and selling to, and though Lena does what she can she has the house to look after, and they just play on her."

" Yes, I know," Doctor John answered, and it struck me he knew much more than the patient told us. " I know all that, Mr M'Whillan, but you are just to let things slide—go to the devil—which there is not the least fear of them doing. More fear of yourself if you don't keep your room and your spirits up. That's your business at present, and just stick to it. If I was in your shoes, why, I'd not open my letters —well, unless I was sure they were pleasant reading, Let things slide, Mr M'Whillan."

Somehow this address had not the effect of a sedative. The gentleman, after a pause of nervous thought, asked with a note of surprise and curiosity,—

" What put it into your head, doctor, to talk about letters ? "

" Just one I got this morning, Mr M'Whillan, that I guessed should not be taken at breakfast."

" And what did you do with it ?   Didn't you open it ? "

" Certainly not.   I laid it by until I was fasting and in so bad a humour that I could give it a proper reply."

Mr M'Whillan was not exactly agitated, but some vexation and trouble going with his illness made him painfully nervous.

" Do you know, doctor," he said with hesitation, " I got a letter, too, this morning, and—"

" I see," Doctor John interrupted, " you opened it and it made you think you should have two doctors when one was barely necessary."

Mr M'Whillan was a little composed by the doctor's interruption, which was, of course, meant to reassure him as to his ailment, but his letter was on his mind.

" You know, doctor," he said, " I have two sons."

" Yes, Mr M'Whillan, and that you may be proud of both of them—one the manager of a bank, the other a member of the Colonial Parliament in Coral Britain.   In the Government, is he ? "

The public might be satisfied with the two gentlemen, but clearly their father was not.

" The letter was from Andrew in Australia.   But maybe you have heard something about him, doctor ? "

Mr M'Whillan was hesitating and half-inclined not to go into particulars.

" Not a word, Mr M'Whillan, beyond the fact that he is a leading man in the Legislature, which means, of course, that he is feared rather than liked by his fellow Senators."

Our patient smiled at this.

" That's the fact anyhow.   They liked him so little that they put him in jail.   It seems he told them that their Parliament was a gang of ruffians, and they clapped him in jail because he'd not withdraw the expression and apologise. I could have told them that he wouldn't.   Andrew was no man to call names in a passion without reason or design. He was moderate with the workers here, and slower to fault them than I was ; he never said a thing but there was some design in it.   I expect he knew what he was about when he called them ruffians, and they didn't know what they were about when they suspended him and put him into jail.   Anyhow they had to let him out and take his seat again, when his first word was to tell them that he was ashamed to sit with them, and wouldn't if public duty did not require him to do what was highly disagreeable to him. I don't understand these things, doctor, but I am sure Andrew had some design in it."

"We doctors, Mr M'Whillan, never tell a lunatic that he is mad, but we have to pass our word to the world that he is only fit for an asylum. Your son's certificate was intended for the world, of course."

"I am sure that Andrew would never have called them undeserved names, but that has to do with me only, as, thinking he was not getting on overly well with them, I wrote to him to come home and mind the farm, as at my age it was getting past me. My heart was set on this, and I told him I'd give him the whole management and not interfere with him. I quite expected that there would be no difficulty about it, seeing that it was a fine property and be made over entirely to him. But the answer is, that though he would come to see me, he would have nothing to do with Irish farming, that his property in Australia promised him far better results than any he could hope for in Ireland ; as it was, it was really worth far more than my farm."

"I am sure," Doctor John observed, "with your son's welfare at heart, that ought to have pleased you, Mr M'Whillan. As you said, however, he had a design in giving his Parliament a bit of his mind, and it seems to me that he is not the man to throw up the sponge and leave them to their devices. He means to be their master."

"I did not think of that, doctor, but it is like you are right enough, though he does not mention the subject. What is plain to me is that when my place comes to him— I always intended it for him—he'll not come and live on it, but just sell it, a thing I can't bear the thought of. Andrew was always quite against things as they are in Ireland, and was for altering them. Our minister, the Reverend Buchanan, told me that he was a Socialist and as much against farmers as landlords, but I never heeded his opinions. You know things take their own way, no matter what we may think. I left Andrew free to think as he liked."

"And he thinks in consequence," the doctor said, with a smile too innocent to be free from suspicion of being artificial, "that he can have things as he likes. No matter, I am sure the Reverend Buchanan applied correctives."

"Oh, Buchanan did talk to him, but it was useless: Andrew was so ill-pleased with Buchanan that he told him that all he ever did was to impose ideas on other men and never reason with them, that his profession did not leave him open to reason himself. I do think there was something in it; Buchanan was overly given to lay down the law."

"I see, Mr M'Whillan, it was your son that applied correctives."

"Oh," said the gentleman, returning to what was uppermost in his mind, "Andrew was ill-pleased with more than Buchanan; not with me, for I gave him his liberty, but with our people and their ways, and would go to Australia, though I was against it; but, as I said, I gave him his liberty. He always said that Ireland was bound to go from bad to worse, and was no country for a man to stop in. But when I wrote to him I thought, seeing the scrape he had got into, he had learned that other countries had their faults too."

"You are wrong, I believe, in thinking that he had got into a scrape. You said that he had some design, and I agree with you. You ought to be satisfied that he has wealth and a career before him in the colony. You have, to be sure, a good farm and position, but still it would evidently be dragging him down to a lower position to make him take your place. Besides, Ireland, as we are all agreed, is going to the bad, and he might go to the bad here with us."

Mr M'Whillan looked intently at the speaker, and asked, with peculiar emphasis,—

"Do you really believe, doctor, that the country is going to the bad, and that Andrew mightn't hold his own as well as I have done?"

I was curious to see what the effect of this direct demand for a sincere opinion would be, but Doctor John met it with silence, as if lost in thought.

"The reason I ask," our patient went on by way of explanation, "is just because Andrew uses nearly your very words. He says that the conditions of labour are so changing in Ireland, and everywhere else, that he could never work the farm as I did, never make it pay as it has done in times past, not even if he got it free of rent, and that is impossible, though our rent is only half what it was. He says that the farmer's profit is going the road of the landlord's rent, and both will come to be easy of reckoning. He says just that he'd be beaten in the long run, and knew better than to go into a business in liquidation."

Mr M'Whillan spoke in the tone of a man both sick and anxious, but the doctor, unwilling, I suppose, to express his sincere opinion to no purpose, made an adroit move.

"Would you mind, Mr M'Whillan, allowing me to read the letter? I would like to advise you for the best, but to do so would need to have all information available."

The sick man willingly complied, drawing the letter from under his pillow, with the remark that it was a long one, but short for all it meant. The doctor, taking it, read it very carefully, and when he came to the end went back on some passages, running his finger along the lines with an intently thoughtful eye. The painstaking perusal evidently gratified our patient and inspired his confidence. His satisfaction, however, was damped when the doctor, having finished, leant back in his chair and laughed very gently, as if he was indulging in thought all alone.

"What is it, doctor; what is there to laugh at in it?"

"Oh, nothing, Mr M'Whillan; nothing in the letter itself. The fact is, there is nothing in it that can't and shouldn't wait till you're quite well. Not a letter, clearly, to answer until you can think over it with a sound mind in a sound body. You put it aside just now, and when you are well you shall have no difficulty in answering it to your satisfaction."

But the doctor leant back in his chair and laughed again.

"It is at your son's parliamentary colleagues I am laughing. I have only your son's word for it that they are ruffians, but their acts for it that they are idiots. Now, if he had used the expression to me, I would have told him that he was only reflecting on our common human

K

nature, giving in vulgar language the theological truism that all men are desperately wicked, and be quits with him. If, however, instead of giving him word for word I gave blow for word, I would have proved his case, and be an idiot to prove myself a ruffian. They made a mistake when they put your son into jail, Mr M'Whillan. They should have passed a solemn resolution that, in an assembly of ruffians, the conduct of business peculiarly required the ruffians to be mannerly to each other, which would mean that your son was an unmannerly ruffian. That would have been quite enough."

But Mr M'Whillan's interest in his son's parliamentary escapade was slight.

"If they were not a bad lot, doctor, Andrew would not have called them names, and without knowing that most people would believe he was only telling the truth. But that is small concern to me. You see, I have to settle my affairs, make my will. I don't doubt what you and the young doctor tell me as to my getting into my usual state, but all the same one can never be sure at my time of life. Maybe Andrew is right enough in not coming home and taking my place, though I expected he might. What troubles me is that he'll not come back, and will sell the place when it falls to him. You see, he says I should sell it myself if I can get a good price. The best price wouldn't tempt me to part with what has been in the name so long, and I want to leave it to him so fixed that he cannot sell it."

"I see, Mr M'Whillan, what is your trouble. But your son in the bank, is he not the eldest? What would he say to leaving the place to Andrew? And your daughter?"

Mr M'Whillan's answer was not given at once, and was hesitating.

"Oh, there is money to the good for their share; what may satisfy them. I always put by when times were good and I could look after things. Then William put the money into things that made well. I always told him that it was for him and Lena, and he was quite satisfied."

I saw that Doctor John was mildly surprised. Apparently he was not aware that Mr M'Whillan was wealthy enough to leave his farm to one son and yet make a fair

division of his property. All the same he remarked, with
an air of careless indifference,—

"I really thought you had bought land with your money,
added to your farm, you know."

"I bought Creeve forbye," our patient went on, reassured
by the cool way Doctor John took his confidences; "and
if I had it to do again I'd let it stand. To be sure it lay
in to me, but I paid too dear for it. My father left me
this place bare enough, and I only got a hundred pounds
by my poor wife, but I made by farming when times were
good."

"Good times, good times," ejaculated the doctor, "I
never knew you. When will you come back again? You
are a smart man, that's the fact, Mr M'Whillan. But what
do you say to consulting your son in the bank? He is a
business man, I am told."

The suggestion did not seem to be acceptable.

"Yes, doctor, William is a business man. He just looks
at you, and listens to all you say when he has time, but
gives no opinion except he knows, and mostly says he
knows nothing out of his own line. He was put into the
bank when he was quite young, and has no heart for this
place. Then the wife is that grand, she'd not look near it.
The fact is, they're rich, and quite above us. They go to
church, and are high in their ways."

"The case is beginning to look serious," the doctor said,
glancing at me.

"I do believe," our patient went on, with a melancholy
fidgeting, "William, if he said anything, would go with
Andrew, and be for selling the place, there being no one to
labour it and make it pay. He'd say he could invest the
price to bring in more than it makes."

"Now, Mr M'Whillan, can't you have sense, and not be
asking our pity? The place is a rubbishy old place which
has served its turn, thanks to your wit and prudence;
raised men far too big to live in it or bother about it. I'm
mistaken if Andrew does not mean to kick that Parliament
of his into its senses and be Prime Minister of Coral
Britain. Then William, if he would only overcome that
bad habit of saying nothing about what he knows nothing
about, and defer to the wife, may get into the Mother of

Parliaments, and culminate in fireworks by expressing profound contempt for it. But what about Miss M'Whillan ?"

" Oh, Lena is very good—the best; but the price of a store beast might be five pounds, or ten, for all she knows, and it's by a pound in the price of a beast, one way or another, that money is made in farming. She would give up farming and live private, as she'll be able to do, only she thinks more of me than she does of herself. The very best is Lena."

" Make a good wife," the doctor said, with a glance in my direction.

" She could have married, Lena," our patient said, noticing the glance as little as I did, " but she would not leave me; said it was enough to have a farmer for her father."

" Hum ! open, perhaps, to reconsider the matter if the proposal came, say, from a doctor ?"

This being quite unnoticed Doctor John went on, addressing me with reasoning intended for the sick man.

" That's the way, O'Gara, with our farmers. As a rule, when they make by industry, prudence and thrift, it is only to ruin their children. In the case of our friend here we have a rare exception. His children cannot be spoiled and ruined by what he has done for them. They have made the most of the start given them, raised themselves in life and got a cut over a farmer or a poor devil of a dispensary doctor."

Turning to the patient the doctor addressed him with an air of finality.

" Now, Mr M'Whillan, your business is to get well, and you have shown us that there is no reason why your farm and money should stand in the way of that. It would be wrong of you to bring Andrew home, even if he would come. As to your desire to keep the place in your name and family, it is natural enough, and, perhaps, may easily be accomplished. Your sons evidently are under no compulsion to sell, and if you express an earnest wish in your will that they shall keep it, very likely they may be willing, as they are able to keep it. If this is not enough you can consult a lawyer as to any more binding form.

Speaking, however, for myself, I would feel more bound by a friend's wishes, under the circumstances, than by any legal forms, which often may easily be evaded."

Mr M'Whillan seemed relieved and gratified by this view of the matter.

" I do believe, doctor, that William and Andrew would feel the same and regard any wish of mine in reason more than they would law ; Andrew, in particular, would not regard law if he did not think it right."

Another thought, however, occurred to depress the patient.

" But then, doctor, neither of them living in it, the place would go to desolation, like many another in the country ; a labouring man in the old house that did me my day, and the land let every year by auction. What is a farm without a farmer on it ? "

Doctor John leaned back in his chair and laughed as softly as a girl.

" What," he repeated, with the intonation of amusement, " is a farm without a farmer on it ? Why, most of our farms would be as well wanting the farmers we've on them. My own, now, would make me blush, if it was a thing I could do. Well, Mr M'Whillan, I don't suspect you, as I do your son, Andrew, to have an eye to the public interest in the cultivation of the land ; I take it that you are just sentimental, have a nice sentimental attachment for the old place that did so well for you and your children. You have a soft side I like, Mr M'Whillan."

" Well, doctor," the gentleman said in a distinctly apologetic tone, " I allow I'm a bit soft about the place. It goes sore against me to think of it going to wreck and ruin like Allan Rowan's place in Ballyhannigan beside you."

" Like scores of places all over the country. I am told Allan is making a pile in America and keeps his farm of whins and rushes—damn the rent—just to be able to brag to the Yankees of his old ancestral domain in Ireland. Allan was that turn anyhow. I wish, Mr M'Whillan, I was as sure of a quarter of what I want as you can be sure of all you have any right to wish for. Fine view you have here "
—the speaker gazed out of the window on an expanse of

pasture land—" but an artist would consider it improved by being a bit wilder—a bit less artificial; object to these thorn hedges. Now, if only the Prime Minister of Coral Britain, or William M'Whillan, Esq., M.P., would keep the place as a shooting lodge, the very desirable improvement would certainly be effected."

For the first time since we came in Mr M'Whillan smiled. The doctor evidently had succeeded in getting him to take a less gloomy view of the future of Cairnbane, as his place was called.

" I was in doubt, doctor, about speaking to you about what was on my mind, but I am glad I did now. I can face a thing and make the best of it when it is straight before me. My trouble was that I could not see anything before me."

" It is really likely, Mr M'Whillan, that your sons will respect your wish to keep the place. They'll see that it would make a shooting-lodge, and proud you ought to be at the idea of their being able to make it one. They may buy a dozen of these small holdings about and make the place really worth sentimental attachment. You are safe with me, but most people would think you had no right to the luxury on the strength of a farm—nothing out of the common. They might laugh at you."

The sick man smiled again.

" It's little, doctor, I minded people laughing at me my day. It was always turn about—they one day, I the next —and when the laugh was mine it was none of theirs."

" Just so, Mr M'Whillan. You have some years of life before you if you only let things slide. If they laugh at you because you have no son to take your place, you can laugh at them—your sons by-and-by able to keep Cairnbane without it keeping them. That's the sort of place to have a sentimental attachment to, and not the bit of land one has to knock a poor living out of with hard work. But it is at yourself you are likely to be laughing before there is occasion for that will of yours."

Doctor John had treated our patient with consummate skill. The talk alone over what occupied the man's mind acted to compose him, making him take a calmer and more reasonable view of his troubles. He wanted, as he said,

to see his way to what he should do, and though the doctor's
advice was practically to do nothing for the present, still
that was a plain and easily-followed course once it appeared
that the future of the old place might not be as black as it
seemed. We left him greatly cheered, and, as we had anticipated, he was soon in his usual state of health.

Having sent on the doctor's trap we walked over to
Moyclare, a matter of only a mile. My companion was
reflective and our pace leisurely.

"I really laughed," he explained, "at old M'Whillan
bringing the son home to vegetate on that farm. Couldn't
help it. It is well for us that there are other breeds of men
than that raised on farms. In every species there are
varieties expressing process of extinction; in *homo* the
variety is *agrestis*. *Qualia nunc hominum producit corpora
tellus.*"

"Indeed," I said, "that is quite contrary to the popular
idea."

"To the popular idea, yes; to the mind of the dispensary
doctor of Frayne, resting on observation and experience,
no."

"Do you mean to say that the agricultural population
represents the element of extinction in the human
race?"

"That is put in a nice scientific way quite unnecessarily.
The fact needs no scientific determination or expression;
homo var rusticus is becoming extinct all the world over,
and here in particular."

"But you stated the fact in a scientific form as a mere
fact of natural history."

"The dispensary doctor of Frayne is nothing if not
scientific. He is no crank, running counter to popular ideas
out of pure cussedness."

"His ideas must be valuable, then?"

"Valuable, yes, but not appreciated. I expect to have a
big funeral and all the people at it, kindly forgiving me my
queer notions, with the remark that I wasn't so bad a man
after all."

"Naturally, if you are a scientific man your ideas must
be almost unintelligible to country people."

"Not allowed. If you hear me coming out with an idea

which you think a child could not understand, please tell
me.   As it is, the dispensary doctor of Frayne is never unintelligible, as far as he can judge, to those he speaks to.
The fault is the other way; he finds the ideas of those who
speak to him unintelligible."

The doctor stopped short, and then waved the subject
aside—

"Their mental is like their physical pabulum, generally
very improper.   Mind and body half-starved or ill-
nourished, but they can't help it, and get to dislike
wholesome food.   It's a big world, Cairnbane, to old
M'Whillan, and I suspect we have not got him to understand how small a one to his son Andrew.   Of course
he would be right if Andrew was a simple-minded rustic,
content with the paternal acres and the paternal life;
but then he isn't.   That's the way, the able men cut
farming and farming cuts the weak men—wipes them
out."

"Indeed!   M'Whillan seems to have made well by
farming."

"So well that the farm is doomed.   Our patient's
father was an idle, thriftless, drinking creature, and his
sons might have been as their grandfather, in which case
our patient's life-work would go to make the wreck the
bigger.   M'Whillan himself is an exception.   The rule is
given by his father, and his sons in abusing or using
opportunity."

"It is a very obvious fact that the agricultural industry
is altogether at the mercy of the circumstances of individual life, but somehow it never struck me forcibly until
I came to this country."

Doctor John looked at me rather suddenly and inquiringly.

"Agricultural industry," he repeated slowly after me, as
if conning over the phrase.   At the mercy of the circumstances of individual life.   Oh, indeed, when you have got
so far, you must be thinking over the subject.   You take
an interest in it?"

"Well," I said, "I have eyes in my head, and cannot help seeing the farms and their farmers.   I have
ears too, and since I came to Jigglestreet I have heard

little talked about except compulsory sale and the land question."

"And correcting your ears by your eyes you have concluded that no one sees the farms and their farmers, or like myself that the ideas presented to you are unintelligible."

"They are intelligible to me only in this way: The farmer wants the land, the landlord wants to keep it, and both use arguments which, whether true or false, would not affect the issue; have the value of speeches in Parliament in affecting votes."

"But they inform the public?"

"They may determine the public mind, but it is by misleading not informing it. Both parties avoid touching or deliberately conceal the essential facts on which our judgment should rest."

The doctor smiled.

"You are horribly intelligible, young man; have the knack of an expert carpenter with a hammer and nail. But are the ideas presented to you under condition of concealment of the essential facts not unintelligible to you? I keep to my position."

"I find," I answered, "not one in a hundred of the farms with any decent pretence to cultivation. I find the farmers, the majority of them, from age, infirmity, and other forms of disability, unable to cultivate or to direct and organise labour. The idea that change in the form of tenure, if put as any remedy for disabilities incidental to individual life, is quite intelligible to me as a monstrous falsehood, and if concealed as a monstrous deception."

"The ethical system, not less the logic of the dispensary doctor of Frayne, requires falsehoods and deceptions to be taken as unintelligible ideas. He takes them as expressing the fact that man is predominantly a non-intelligent animal, in proof, accounting for his acts by *ex post facto* ideas, that is, consequent is put as causative of antecedent, a highly unintelligible procedure."

I laughed at this.

"The air of South Tyrone must be conducive to metaphysical speculation. Doctor Capel, Count M'Qhan, and my uncle even, always in the end lapse into metaphysics, and the dispensary doctor of Frayne clearly is in the fashion."

"The last-named insignificant person believes that all questions rest on a metaphysical basis, and cannot be said to lapse into an atmosphere habitual to him. But he has ninety-six acres of land for which he pays £80 a year rent, which he has to earn as best he can."

"And the possession under the condition is a necessary antecedent to his reasoning, gives occasion to *ex post facto* ideas unintelligible as such."

"Well, yes, a certain set of unintelligible ideas occur in his mental field, which somehow, perhaps because he is of the same profession as Doctor O'Gara—a thinker *longe intervallo*—he cannot accept in the crude state, but submits to rational examination."

"I need hardly ask whether with any definite practical results ? "

"From having the farm I find in my mind the idea that in order to be under the proper inducement to cultivate it I should own it, that the State should make me its owner in consideration of the advantage its due cultivation would be to it. Now that idea, if I held it, would dishonour my intelligence. On examination I find that last year I planted two acres of potatoes, and ploughed four or five acres of lea for oats, which is about all I ever do. I did not do it with any intention of cultivating, under any impression of duty. The fact is, there is a còttier family on the land, with a sort of prescriptive right to employment, otherwise I would prefer to sublet or graze the farm ; if it paid the rent that is all I would ask. I have therefore no right to any benefit on the ground of being a cultivator, nor would any possible benefit, such as making me its owner, induce me to cultivate it. But you would say, nevertheless, that it is abuse of language to call the first-mentioned idea unintelligible ? "

I could only answer this by an attitude of attention, implying that the position allowed of development.

"Well," said the speaker understanding me, "we may take another idea which, as a matter of fact, you would find our people look on as utterly unintelligible. It may be, it is indeed said, that as I am unable or unwilling to cultivate my land it should be taken from me, and its cultivation otherwise provided for. To take the land from those, whether landlords or farmers, who do not, and cannot under any circumstances, cultivate it, is to those concerned an unintelligible and anarchical idea."

"Oh, indeed," I said, "you make intelligibility depend on the exercise of intelligence."

"I make cooking depend on ability to cook in an agent cooking, not on any potentiality in the article cooked. The bullock eats turnips raw, the natural man swallows ideas unreasoned and unintelligible, and has a decided predilection for them in a form which saves him the trouble of the long process of reasoning necessary to make them intelligible, and it may be not at all to his taste. In general men like their ideas as bullocks do their turnips —raw."

"The dispensary doctor of Frayne, an exception, goes in for French cookery."

"Now there is that idea of taking my land from me," the doctor said smiling, "it is a raw turnip, nothing better. In every hundred human beings the efficient working element is represented by nine or ten men of mean adult life; the ability of the remainder for work is, if not *nil*, small or negligible. To make, therefore, ability to labour the title to property would mean absolute dependence for ninety per cent. of us. The title of the worker again would hold good only while he was efficient; on occasion, and in every case, he would ultimately pass into the ranks of the dependent. But in the particular case of the land a large part of the efficient element, passing from it to other pursuits, would forfeit title to possession, leaving it to a minority varying according to accidental circumstances, including cases in which virtually the whole element might be drained away, or reduced numerically to inefficiency. Thus ability to cultivate, including the case of willingness, as title to possession would not secure the end proposed, but rather accentuate the dependence of the incapable majority on the capable minority."

"Your argument," I remarked, "is one in defence of the institution of property in the interest of women, children, the aged, infirm, and disabled. From this point of view however, you must admit that the institution has been grossly perverted and abused in the conceived interest of the capable element, not merely to relieve it from the necessity for labour, but to gratify inordinate desires in it."

"Really, young man, you are tempting me to expand in a way I seldom venture to do. My rule is to chaff at the bullocks and their raw turnips. Of course, my land is wasted and abused, the institution of property grossly perverted, but I am not going to take all that as a raw turnip; I hope for some reasoned-out intelligible ideas on the subject, but I have not to go far to find that the murderer and robber is the man physically able—the strong man who likes raw turnips, and can digest them. I would prefer to be robbed of my land by a mediæval baron who just said he was the stronger man, than swindled out of it under false pretences by labourers and Parliamentary humbugs. The old-type rascal would make no attempt on my common sense and judgment."

"But allowing that your land is wasted and abused you would allow that a state of things exists calling for correction."

"My admission is a far larger one, I admit, assert if you like, that all the land of the United Kingdom is wasted and abused. What I do not admit is that handing over the possession of it to those physically able to cultivate it would be a corrective, simply because the plan has been tried exhaustively, with the result that the physically able devote their abilities to getting rid of the necessity for labour by robbing the weak and incapable of their only means of subsistence. Of course, the modern crusade in favour of the strong man glosses over universal dependence on him by talk of old-age pensions and humane poor laws, but we are not to be caught by that salt on our tails. The majority of mankind is in disability, and, to a great extent, in dependence, and that dependence, so far from being increased, should be diminished; everything possible should be done to secure to it independence of the means of existence. The land is wasted and abused simply because it is in hands unable or unwilling to cultivate it, but I would let it remain wasted and abused before I would make its occupiers, such as they are, dependent on the able-bodied rascal."

"But," I objected, "the actual crusade is of the very opposite nature. It is to enable the aged, blind, lame and halt, the widow and infant, the idiot, imbecile and lunatic, the doctor, clergyman, shopkeeper, jockey, cattle jobber, absentee, and so on, to hold land under the easiest possible conditions. In fact, the conditions of the individual occupier's life, far more than the conditions of tenure, are behind the land agitation, and, as the agitation never meets the essential conditions, it is endless and futile. When the State compels reduction of your rent, and compels sale to you, the crusade is altogether in your favour, and, to use your own term, is a very unintelligible proceeding."

"So unintelligible, wild and random, that its action, a favour one day, may be a blow the next. It has not been a blow up to the present, because the tenant had no definite form of property to be robbed of, and his incompetence really served him. The outcry against the landlord arose in great part exactly because he made feeble and stupid attempts at meeting the case of disability by evictions which reflected on his humanity. Now, and more so by-and-by, the occupier, as owner, shall have something tangible to be aimed at, cannot escape responsibility for the condition of the land, and shall visibly be open to the charge of having obtained favours from the State under false pretences."

"I really do not understand," I said, "your position. You anticipate that the occupiers of the land shall be exposed to serious attack on the ground of their obvious disability for the task of cultivation, and yet hold that their disability does not invalidate title to ownership."

The doctor laughed with the air of a man who had completely mastered his subject.

"My present position means that I have, to my surprise, met a man who does not run the risk of choking himself by bolting the raw turnips called *prima facie* ideas. Our position, as you will allow me to call it, as medical men demands the protection of the interest of human life, therefore the securing as far as possible mastery over their means of subsistence to women, infants, the aged sick, infirm, and so on, not leaving them at the mercy of the strong man. Now, having arrived both at this elementary position and at Moyclare, the discussion must stand adjourned, but not *sine die*."

XI

THE REVEREND CINAMON

WHEN we came into Moyclare House Mrs Garth, after exchanging greetings with Doctor John, told me that there was a clergyman waiting to see me on some dispensary business. She then said to Doctor John,—

"You know him—the Reverend Cinamon, the Covenanting minister of Tyrkane."

Missie, who was staying a few days at Moyclare, and Doctor John were trying which could smile sweetest, but the doctor fell out of the running at once, and made a grimace at the announcement.

"What can he want with me?" I asked. "This is no time for dispensary business."

"Oh," Mrs Garth said, "my brother would see him at any time—likes to talk to him, and I asked him to stop for dinner. His business is something about a hole in the roof of a house of his. He has been talking to me this half-hour, but really I do not know what he wants."

"I do," Doctor John said in a decided tone. "His Reverence wants someone to do something he does not want to do himself."

Then, turning to me, he continued,—

"You are not quite up, I suppose, in dispensary work, which sometimes touches legal matters, and it may be as well that I should see Mr Cinamon with you. Of course, I shall not say a word unless I see occasion."

"I would be glad of your assistance. I have no experience in part of the dispensary work."

We went into Doctor Capel's study, where our visitor was awaiting us. He was a big, elderly man, a country farmer, I thought, under a clerical veneer. I, however, only took him in by degrees; his aspects, indeed, were histrionic, and formed in the pulpit, not the commonplace outer world.

Doctor John, after shaking hands and telling him he was looking too well for the company, introduced me to him as a gentleman and green gosling, a disingenuous hint that I might be played on. I was duly and clumsily shaken hands with. The accompanying remark, to the effect that Capel was not the man to leave anything else in his place, was not nearly as ambiguous as the smile that went with it.

"I came about a small matter of business," the gentleman went on after this preliminary, "just to get an order from you as medical officer to have a house closed as unfit for human habitation."

I looked at Doctor John in the hope that he might put the clergyman right, but he had settled down at a table, and was apparently deep in a medical journal. I knew this was assumed, and meant that I was to act on my own judgment.

"I have to ascertain, Mr Cinamon," I said, "in the first place whether I have power to give such an order. I believe a certain procedure must be followed."

"Oh, yes, there is a lot of forms, of course, to be gone through—a lot of forms—but the thing is often done, you know."

"Red tape," Doctor John remarked, showing that he was not inattentive to what was said; "a lot of red tape, Mr Cinamon."

"Red tape," the gentleman echoed. "A lot of red tape."

"What is done, Mr Cinamon," I asked, thinking trespass was attempted on my inexperience, "the medical officer giving orders or houses being closed?"

"Oh, houses closed as being unfit for habitation. There is, of course, a lot of forms to be gone through."

"That seems to me to mean putting out their occupiers, and I am sure the medical officer cannot order eviction. The legal forms have to be followed, no matter what opinion we may entertain of them."

"Then let us," Mr Cinamon said, with a pulpit gesture, "bow the knee to red tape, begin with the forms. What is to be done first?"

I looked at Doctor John, but he was of set purpose absorbed in his journal, and I am sure wished to know how I would act left to my own resources. I was not wholly without experience, as the sanitary officer had given me instructions in the case of some notices served on me in Doctor Capel's dispensary.

"In these cases, Mr Cinamon, the sanitary officer reports to the medical officer, and the last, after inspection, to the sanitary authority, the District Council. In general, an offence is committed by the owner of the house in keeping it in a dangerous or insanitary state. If the house you are concerned about is inspected by the sanitary officer he notifies me as medical officer, when after seeing it I report to the District Council."

"Is that all the medical officer can do? Cannot he issue an order, or at least warn the occupier to leave the house?"

"That would be exceeding his duty. He merely reports the matter to the council and recommends what in his judgment should be done."

"Then the council issues the order on the recommendation of the medical officer?"

"I am not aware that the council issues any order whatever. It has a notice served on the responsible party to abate the nuisance complained of."

"Then who issues the order, doctor?"

"No one that I am aware of."

"Then what is done in case the notice is not attended to?"

"I believe in such case it is the duty of the council to summon the responsible party before the magistrates at Petty Sessions to answer for an offence actually committed. The magistrates convict if the offence is proved, and possibly in some cases may order a house to be closed, but they might be chary of making the law an instrument for eviction."

This explanation was evidently unsatisfactory to the reverend gentleman, and falling into the vein of the thing, under the suspicion that he wished to make use of me

L

for his private ends, I did not attempt to make it otherwise.

"A nice roundabout all that," he said in an aggrieved
tone. "Is that an end of the red tape?"

"Oh, no," said Doctor John, suddenly. "Not at all,
Mr Cinamon. The nuisance may be questioned, the
responsibility of the parties questioned. Everything
questioned. Case may be appealed. No end of trouble,
cost and red tape."

"Now," said Mr Cinamon, in a tone the persuasiveness
of which verged on the wheedling, "in this case couldn't
you, doctor, tell the man in the house that it was not fit to
live in, and that the law would not allow him to live in it?
He might believe you, and it would save a lot of trouble all
round."

By this time I was sure that the gentleman knew the
law better than I did, and that his real object was to make
use of me to escape the legal procedure which would
tell against himself. But out of politeness I pretended
insincere reflection for a moment.

"Doctor Capel might, perhaps, do that, but acting for
him I am bound to be particular in using his official
position. I think in nearly every case the law would not
put the tenant out and close the house, but compel the
landlord to put it into a habitable state, punish him even
for having it otherwise. I am afraid I would make a very
lame attempt at getting the man to leave the house."

Doctor John suddenly looked at me. His face was a
singularly expressive one and I inferred at once that he
did not wish our visitor to be disposed of so quickly.

"Really," he said, "you two gentlemen have a way
I don't understand. You are settling a case between you
without having it in concrete form before you. Give
particulars, Mr Cinamon, give particulars, and the thing
may take another aspect. O'Gara, of course, must treat
the case from the official point of view, but tell us con-
fidentially and as private persons what it is all about and
we'll treat it in the same way, and may be our unofficial
advice will be enough."

There was a sly twinkle in Mr Cinamon's eye which
conveyed the impression that he had something "rich" to

tell. He probably relished preaching sermons, and had the enjoyment of a *raconteur* in telling stories in which the *raconteur* is the central figure. Then he had the perfect self-confidence of the man who believes that everything he does is right and can easily be proved to be right. It was the nature of the man, but a nature fortified by long pulpit training. It was amusingly consistent with this that he began in the modest self-depreciatory manner of the man who allows no one to contradict or blame him but himself.

" Oh, the case is quite simple, and altogether due to my own careless, easy-going way, taking men as they ought to be, not as they are. Chiefly out of kindness I engaged a man, Culkin—a man they say there's a want in, not all there, you know—to work for me when I wanted a worker. I gave him a house and he was to come and do my work when called on. Well, one day when I called on him he said he was working for a neighbour, and being engaged for the day couldn't drop the spade out of his hand and run to me, that he had to earn his living, and that I should give him notice beforehand when I wanted him. I told him to begone out of my house, that I wanted him no longer. I was short with him because he answered me, a bit hasty, you know, but the fact is, there is no standing these workers nowadays. I allow I might have managed the thing more quietly."

"Did you make," I asked, "any formal or written agreement with him ? If you did, of course, that should rule the case."

" Oh, no, that is not usual here. I just told him that he might have the house if he came to work with me when I called on him. That is often done here."

"Then there was no rent fixed between you for the house ? "

" Oh, the rent was paid in the man's work. He left that to me and I might stop a shilling or sixpence a week for rent out of his pay. I was not hard on him, you may be sure, and there wouldn't have been a word if he hadn't answered me."

I thought Mr Cinamon was a man who would expect a full quota of work from a labourer, and servile deference into the bargain, and had taken means to secure both, but merely said,—

"I suppose the man would not leave your house."

"Oh, no. He said he was willing to stand to his bargain and work for me when called on if I would give him notice beforehand. He just defied me, and told me he'd go out when he was put out."

"But does not the law provide means for putting him out ?"

"Oh, yes, with a lot of trouble and expense. Red tape, you know. I have had plenty of experience of it with workers and want no more. That's why I thought if the house was condemned as unfit for human habitation the man might go, or would have to go."

"But," I said, "instead of the house being condemned, it is likely the sanitary authority would compel you, as the landlord, to repair it, having nothing to say to the occupier's title as a tenant. But is the house really in so bad a state ?"

There was a sly twinkle in the reverend gentleman's eye again.

"Why, there is a big hole in the roof which lets in the weather, and I would not say but the whole roof might fall in. There should be an order to have the house pulled down entirely ; it's not safe for cow cattle, let alone human beings, and it's not fair to ask me to build it up and roof it against my pleasure for anyone, let alone a man who pays me nothing for it in work or money."

"Was the house in that state when you let it to the man under the condition of being paid rent for it in work ?"

"If it came to law I'd leave it to the lawyer to say what the conditions were ; it's no business of mine, the law of it. It was no great things of a house, but good enough for no great things of a character like Culkin when he came to it. He wouldn't be so keen to stop on if anyone would take him and give him better."

"But if the roof has fallen in part, and is ready to fall in altogether, and the man's character not good, you may have some charge against him of damaging your property or, at least, not taking reasonable care of it."

The twinkle in Mr Cinamon's eye became something near a roguish leer.

"That's not exactly the way of it. The roof was sound enough when Culkin came to the house a year ago, and I have no charge to make against him of damaging it. The house belongs to me, and I did the thing myself. Seeing that Culkin wouldn't leave, I just watched when he was away with the Orange drums one dark night and put a live coal in the thatch. I thought there would be a brave blaze and the whole roof away, but the thatch was too rotten and damp to make a bonfire. Anyhow, when my boy came back, there was a fine big hole over his head, the night would be on the short side for reckoning all the stars he could see through it."

The speaker laughed, perfectly satisfied that he had done a very smart thing, and one that he was able to defend as proper and justifiable under the circumstances. He knew very well, I had no doubt, that he had committed an offence in point of law, but he placed his judgment far above the law, particularly law that was not likely to reach him.

Doctor John looked up from the journal which he held in his hand, although all the time an attentive listener, and observed in a tone of gravity,—

"Did you take any steps towards making a claim on the county for malicious burning, or talk of making such a claim? You might be suspected of doing it yourself if you didn't."

"Oh," the gentleman answered with a chuckle, "I wouldn't do that; it wasn't necessary. I let it be thought that I set no value on the house, and that I was not in any great way about Culkin staying in it. I wouldn't let him think he was spiteing me. I know who to trust, and never said a word about the thing to anyone but you two gentlemen. Took it quite unconcernedly."

"Your Reverence is quite safe with us; but what do you think, O'Gara, should be done?"

Doctor John looked curiously at me as if he would like to know the opinion I would form.

"Is the house," I asked Mr Cinamon, "in a really dangerous state—in any danger of falling on the man and injuring or killing him? That might make the case an awkward one."

" There's a want in Culkin, but he is not as bad as all that; he'll take care of his skin. I hear he put props under the roof, and patched up the hole with old boards and sacks. He is not a fool all out."

I did not think we should do anything to help our visitor, even if able to do so, but looked at the doctor, who responded this time.

"I really think, Mr Cinamon," he said, "your best plan would be to give Culkin a pound or two to go out quietly. You see it is said that we farmers treat our tenants and labourers far worse than the landlords treat us, and it would be as well to give no colour to the statement, particularly just now. Besides, our young friend here, although, of course, he will respect your confidence, has no sympathy for us. He would be sure to recommend the District Council to compel you to repair the house, and if you went to Petty Sessions you would be fined for having kept an occupied house in a dangerous state. Then if you took legal steps to put the man out—"

"Oh, I'll not do that," hastily interrupted Mr Cinamon. "I had enough of that to make me give up keeping houses for thankless people. I have three houses on my land shut up, and when Culkin is out there'll be four, which may drop before I'll let anyone into. No matter what happens, make or not make, I'll have no houses on my land. I've made up my mind to that. I don't like giving a rascal like Culkin money for my own house; but I agree with you, doctor, it is as well not to raise any stir just now. In this world, you know, one cannot have everything his own way; one must submit to be imposed on. I am always giving in to people, but the more I give in the more I find I have to give in to downright imposition. Well, well, as a clergyman I have to set an example, and, as you recommend it, I'll try and settle with the rascal quietly and without any law."

As he reached his concluding sentences Mr Cinamon's tone and manner rose equal to the occasion—a tone and manner of calm resignation challenging admiration. The undoubtedly sincere acting had a certain rare though rough perfection which those who had the privilege of listening to him in his meeting-house must have been

impressed with as embodying the ideal man—the man as
he ought to be—and have been happy in the thought that
they had as their minister one qualified to make the
embodiment.

It was time to get ready for dinner, but in spite of
this recognition of Mr Cinamon's ability, when I
brought Doctor John up to my room I remarked to
him,—

"I do not quite see why you should have given that
man good advice."

"Indeed. Why, because he badly needed it, and we
invited his confidence under the condition of giving advice.
Besides, I am to some extent in sympathy with him."

"I would not have thought that possible."

"Yes, but think what you may, it is a fact. He
belongs to a Church which sets itself above the State,
recognises no law but virtually what it makes or sanctions
itself. Of course it has to submit to *force majeure*, but
that does not affect the principle."

"And do you approve of or sympathise with such a
principle?"

"Of course I do. Why, if some person or body of
persons were not for ever setting themselves above the
State, and the rules it makes, the human race would have
gone to the devil long ago. You and I, in principle, set
ourselves above the law, call it in question, condemn it,
and the pity is that we can do so only very ineffec-
tively. Cinamon may err in detail, in principle he is all
right."

"As usually put, it is said that while we have a right
to question a law, and take means to alter it, we are
bound to obey it while it has the force of law."

"Do people obey law under that impression?"

"Well, I suppose their obedience is partly from unintelligent habit, partly from compulsion."

"Therefore the law is conditioned to unintelligent habit
and compulsion, therefore in antagonism to intelligent
apprehension—let me see, apprehension? Yes, sir, the
term may stand—to the elementary step in reasoning."

"You are an Anarchist."

"You are another. Only difference between us is that

you hold to one anarchy, I to another.   Well, perhaps we may find some base of agreement."

After dinner Count M'Qhan dropped in to have a chat with me.   It had become common with him.   He had a rooted objection to late dinners, and would drink nothing but a single cup of coffee.   He said his digestive apparatus was, like the rest of him, otiose, given to idleness and ease. How an idle man could have come to know so much, and have a mental grasp which no reading, no matter how wide, could give was a mystery to me.   He was never laboured, never confused or obscure; if he did pause to think, the interruption only emphasised his fluency and ease of expression.   He had helped me greatly in forming a general view of what he called agrarianism, or the agrarian system, had indeed created in my mind a solid, coherent idea of the thing in its unitary sense.   Of the system in that sense he had wonderful knowledge, the result of actual observation in Ireland and other parts of Europe.   But beyond giving me a true mental picture he did not go.   To himself indeed criticism seemed never to suggest change, at least without at the same time suggesting objections to change not easily got over.   There was indeed a grim vein of fatalism in him; the child because it wanted thought was happy; the man who thought and tried to order life by thought invited unhappiness if only through failure; to amend in thought the conditions of human life was to misunderstand these conditions; on the average a hundred savages were as well off, as happy, as a hundred so-called civilised men.   Thus I usually found myself ending in an *impasse*, a blind alley, with him, and his calm acceptance of the circumstance was rather irritating to me, and would be to anyone, who held that casting our bread on the waters we should be guided by abstract ideas of right and wrong.   It may have been a matter of mere temperament, but I could never find peace and content by his way of thinking.   I would never have interested myself in the agrarian system as he described it, if its monstrous follies and crimes did not excite feelings of revolt and anger, demanding, as a matter of course, expression as a duty.

"Do you know anything, doctor," Mr Cinamon asked

after the ladies had left the room, "of the sale of the Shaneglish estate to the tenants?"

"Oh," answered Doctor John drily, "I know something of the sale of the majority of the Shaneglish tenants to a lady patient of mine with a turn for speculation, rather kept in check by rheumatic gout and an uncertain temper. Mrs Jones consulted me before she bought—"

"I wish her luck of her purchase," said Mr Cinamon, with the meaning that the purchaser badly needed the wish. "You didn't advise her to buy the hole of a place, doctor?"

"I waited, of course, your Reverence, to see whether she had made up her mind. When I found she was quite resolved to buy I advised her strongly—well, to go as far as £800."

"Eight hundred pounds!" ejaculated Mr Cinamon, in a tone which might be one either of sincere surprise, or the primary note of a cattle dealer in a country fair.

"Yes, your Reverence, eight hundred pounds, but she got it dog-cheap at six hundred and seventy. You see there are fifty-two holdings on the estate, of which thirty-eight are in the village and not under the Land Acts, open to anyone to buy. Let me tell you, Mrs Jones knows a good thing, or wouldn't have remained a widow these twenty years."

"But, doctor, do you mean to say that that lot of poor tumbledown houses can ever pay her?"

"I mean to say that at £800, allowing an ample margin for repairs and even improvements, it would pay 7 per cent. But as she said herself, the rents under the old landlord were ridiculously low—houses at 6d. and 1s. a week that could easily fetch 1s. 6d. and 3s. a week. She says she'll soon make it pay her 10 or 12 per cent., and it is likely in a little time, and with a little outlay, she'll do better. Oh, no, Lucinda is no goose. Wouldn't have remained her own mistress if she was."

"But what about the land, doctor? I heard that the price was eighteen years' purchase, and the hanging gale of rent forgiven."

"You are about right, the price works out at about seventeen years' purchase, and barely pays the first mortgagees who forced the sale to make themselves safe. You know there are two townlands, Shaneglish and Gortnamuckley, in the estate and fourteen tenants. One of them, Sandy M'Laine, gets £2000 from the Commissioners to buy out his holdings, and the same gentleman could command £4000 at a day's notice."

"Then," I said, interested by the last statement, "the State lends a rich man £2000—or, say, fourteen men £14,000—to buy out their holdings, and leaves thirty-eight holders to be bought up by a speculator for want of an advance of £670. Is it because the security for the repayment of the last sum is bad?"

"No, sir. If the householders were directed to pay their shilling or two shillings a week for their cribs in the village of Shaneglish, with the intimation that at the end of seventeen years said cribs would be their own property, that £670 would be as good as Consols. Payment to be made weekly into the post-office."

"Then why are they not given the same privilege as the farmers?"

"They are not given the same privilege because they always paid their rent without demur, were peaceable, law-abiding, never agitated, never shot anyone, never put themselves above the law, were not worth anything to the politician. Were just a poor-spirited, mean lot."

Oh, now, doctor," Mr Cinamon observed in his severest clerical manner, "a man in your position should not speak in that way. There is a vast difference, as you know, between a farmer and a man renting a house or a room in a house—a vast difference."

" And what am I saying, your Reverence, but that there is a vast difference. The man who pays 1s. a week for a house in Shaneglish knows very well that another man's labour and money built the house, and decently recognises the other man's right. He has wit enough, besides, to see that if there is no rent for houses no one will build houses for him and his class. But no one has any title to the land, on the ground of having made it. The landlord and tenant are on a level in that respect; the title is simply a legal fiction, which has no real binding force on the judgment or conscience. No man has a valid title to the land, therefore every man has a right to scramble for it. Now, Mr Cinamon, you have no *locus standi* in asking me to go down on my knees to the law and law-made titles."

This last was in answer to more than one gesture of dissent coming from the reverend gentleman.

" I would not ask you, doctor, to put human laws over conscience and judgment, but to go by facts." Mr Cinamon, with these words, laying two fingers of one hand on the open palm of the other, assumed an attitude of exposition, which the doctor met with one of his peculiarly benign smiles.

" It is a fact, doctor, that human law no more made me a farmer than it made me an unworthy minister—a minister, though an unworthy one, of the Church of the Covenant. That Church exists, not as a fact of law, but as a fact of resistance to law. I need not tell you what it has gone through in order to be barely tolerated. In the same way the farming class exists as a fact of resistance to law; if the law was left to its own sweet will we would have been destroyed long ago. The landlord trampled on us indeed, but we exist because he dared not use the power the law gave to the uttermost, that is, because, one way or another, we resisted him. Death was the gift of the law; we gave ourselves life."

" Bravo, your Reverence. Now, O'Gara, there is another Anarchist for you. But, Mr Cinamon, as a present fact, the law protects you in the enjoyment of considerable property against men who have nothing."

" The law," was the answer, with a variation of the expository gesture, " took away, and takes away, from us our natural inherent right of self-protection, under the false pretence of protecting us; as far as it could it left us at the mercy of rapacious landlords, who would, and did, deprive us of our means of existence. As far as we could we saved ourselves by asserting the original right of self-protection. That the law may leave me to save my life again by saving my means of subsistence is a quite possible case, to be met by my protecting myself. I am a clergyman, but I have a rifle in my house, and could reckon on my neighbour farmers making common cause with me. Now, that is our title to our land; the title to our means of living is the

same as our title to our life, and it is a mere fact of
experience that human law robbed us of our living, our
lives and our liberty of thought, as far as we were unable
to resist it."

The reverend gentleman waved a big, strong hand, as if
farther discussion of the position would be absurd.   Doctor
John, smiling with inscrutable calmness, looked at Count
M'Qhan and then at me, as a call to us to take part in the
discussion.   The Count, with a look, passed on the invitation to me, and, daring much, I entered the lists with the
doughty champion.

"While, Mr Cinamon," I said, " I was admiring how you
talk and think, a saying of an English writer came into my
mind, to the effect that, while hundreds can talk for one
who can think, thousands can think for one who can see.
The fact is, your position holds good only under the condition that forty millions of persons can't see.   What they
can't or don't see is that, relatively, only a minute fraction
of them occupies land, and, again, that only a fraction of
that fraction has an appreciable interest as occupiers.   But
the last fraction can be, but is not, seen to cultivate the
land as suits itself, or as it is able; in point of fact, only so
as barely to support itself.   The consequence, quite unseen,
of course, is, that practically the forty millions, including
the larger section of the agrarian population, are in enforced
dependence on foreign countries for their means of existence—their food.   They have been told over and over again
to open their eyes to this dangerous and precarious state of
things, and to the land of their own country lying waste
and uncultivated.   I suppose they have to learn to resist
law.   But, as it seems to me, you do not see, too.   A mere
accident might at a week's notice throw them for their
means of existence on their own land, in which case their
necessity would override yours, and, like yours, know no
law.   Their title to life and means of life would have irresistible force to rest on."

The clergyman answered in a tone of non-committal.

"Oh ! we see and know all that.   The struggle against
landlordism has been based all along on the principle that
the land, in order to be cultivated, must be in the hands of
the actual cultivator.   Why, one of the farmer's means of

protecting himself was by not cultivating, not improving his holding. If he raised it in value he would be put out or his rent raised on him."

I looked at Count M'Qhan, under the impression that his truthfulness would impel him to answer this statement. He responded in a lazy and unexciting way.

" I suppose, Mr Cinamon, you are right in thinking that necessity determined the action of the farmers, and that their title rests on necessity as opposed to law. But the necessity, while greatly intensified by absolute power in the landlord was primarily and unavoidably due to the circumstances of the individual occupier's life. His struggle was to maintain himself not when able, but when unable to cultivate his holding, to live by it when he couldn't work it, when he became dependent on others to work it for him. That condition has to be met now as much as ever, and practically is met by minimising the labour of cultivation. You should not denounce landlordism, Mr Cinamon, the principle of it is that the land should support you and me, as well as the landlord, when unable or unwilling to work ourselves."

Whether this position accorded with the clergyman's ideas or the Count was too unexciting, he went off in a tangent indicative of curiosity, in my direction.

" You seem, doctor," he said to me, with an air of kindly interest, which I scarcely appreciated, " to take an interest in our land question over here, and for a stranger and a young man to have considerable knowledge of it. I am myself an extremely moderate man in my views, and do not at all favour the use made of the tenant for political agitation. But, I suppose you have some object in devoting so much attention to it ? "

" I certainly have not as an object making use of political agitation to advance the tenants' interest as they conceive it. But my poor help is not wanted."

Doctor John, with his hands clasped together, leant back in his chair, and said laughingly—

" Really, your Reverence, you and I are on the one tack. Ever since I came to Moyclare this evening, I have been wondering what O'Gara is up to. What is your object, O'Gara ? Out with it. You are among friends."

I thought this a piece of acting on the part of Doctor John, with the intention of taking "a rise" out of the clergyman.

"An unimportant object; just gathering information for my private gratification."

"Do tell! A young American gathering information with no practical object. Has been all round Ireland, your Reverence, valuing it as if he was studying the price he'd go to for the bit of an island. I'd say he has down in his note-book the valuation of your farm, how many acres in it, how many you till, how many beasts it carries and might carry, and so on. Knows maybe more about it than you do yourself. No object in all that, eh?"

Mr Cinamon was evidently mystified by the doctor's exaggeration, and even the Count looked as if his curiosity was excited.

"Now, O'Gara," the doctor went on, in a tone that took everything as settled, "just confess at once that you were sent over to examine and report on the island by a syndicate of big American capitalists who are thinking of taking it over and running it as one farm instead of half a million. They feed the Britisher from their own continent at considerable disadvantage—distance, dear labour, drought, blizzards, and so on. Naturally enough, they think that if they come next door to the critter and take up land, every acre of which is worth all round four in America, they can improve on the job. Oh! you may just admit at once; there are things we can't see and things we can."

"I am obliged to you, doctor," I said, "the idea is worth consideration, but—"

"Well, I know," he interrupted artfully, "we must not ask you to commit a breach of the confidence your employers repose in you. The thing, of course, must be taken for the present in a hypothetical way."

I laughed but it was at Mr Cinamon, who assumed an aspect of calculated reserve, evidently taking Doctor John as having some grounds to go on as to my personal object. Like many clergymen, with a fine substratum of invincible ignorance, he was a gullible man, and I was not inclined to spoil sport.

"Oh, doctor," I said, "if the project is really in the air

and comes to anything you will be entitled to a founder's share."

"I quite disapprove on principle," Mr Cinamon said in his most solemn manner, "of these great combines as calculated to destroy free competition."

"I have made up my mind, your Reverence," the doctor said with a good imitation of the gentleman's gravity, "to hand over my ninety-six acres of land to the syndicate if I am offered anything like reasonable terms, and let free competition be destroyed."

"Well, of course," the clergyman said with the assumed indifference of a dealer, "if a combine offered me a fair price for my land, I would give the matter consideration. I was only thinking of the principle of the thing."

"You are thinking, your Reverence, just like myself," Doctor John said bluntly, "how the thing would affect you personally. Now, O'Gara, if you can, without a breach of confidence, will you tell us how the project would really affect us ?"

The doctor leant his head on his hand in an attitude of profound attention, which impressed one, at least, of us as serious.

"Oh," I said, accepting the situation, "I can only give you my own ideas or suppositions. A combine is a combine, and would not buy your land, but offer you—the landlord, mortgagee, tenant—a share in its capital equivalent to your interest, a matter which, no doubt, would not be settled easily. It would then take up your land, relieve you of its management, and instead of rent and farmer's profits you would get dividends depending on the success with which the association worked the land. It might prove a better thing for you than an investment in the best of the South African mines."

I added the last sentence with a serious intention. As I was speaking, the advantages of the transformation of agricultural industry in the direction indicated suddenly dawned on me. I saw that the change would meet the case of disability, the radical fault of the present system, without depriving the disabled of ownership, of an independent hold over their means of existence. With this also came the conviction that Doctor John was only leading me to express or entertain ideas formed in his own mind, that he was playing both on Mr Cinamon and me at one and the same time. But, as is often the case, ideas on their first occurrence do not readily find or even seek expression. The necessity for thought silenced me. But Count M'Qhan relieved me.

" The idea," he said, in his calmest manner, " of working the land on the joint-stock principle has often occurred to me, as it has to many others ; some attempts, indeed, in the direction have been made, and failed. In fact, industry at the present time has two forms—the ancient, represented by agriculture in its existing state, and the modern, represented, say, by a railroad. Imagine a railroad worked by its owners as actual overseers or employés, and you have an idea of our system of agriculture. But to apply to agriculture the modern form of industry—the form which as far as possible eliminates disability from actual management, selects and trains the agent for his allotted task—I consider altogether impracticable. A land association which would take up a large tract and cultivate it so as to be able to undersell the foreign producer would, of course, undersell us farmers too. Any stick does to beat a dog with. It would be accused of destroying freedom of competition, of monopoly, extermination, murder, and robbery ; it would be defamed and legislated out of existence. That is one of the difficulties it would meet—only one, but enough."

" I was averse," Doctor John said, imitating the Count's manner as nicely as he did Mr Cinamon's, " to old M'Whillan bringing his son Andrew home to vegetate on a farm, but I would not object—I would indeed advise you—O'Gara, to recommend your syndicate to employ him to defend its interests in Parliament ; the man is cut out for the job, and your big capitalists would have no trouble in getting a seat for him—it would be a mere matter of money —even if Andrew couldn't talk himself into one ; call a spade a spade. As for the rest, we farmers would soon see that the option for us was to join or go into the Court of Bankruptcy.

The last sentence made Mr Cinamon assume a controversial attitude, which, however, came to nothing, as Count M'Qhan rising to go was a hint to him to go too, their way home being the same. The Count, a model of punctuality, never allowed discussion to detain him beyond his accustomed hour.

But although Doctor John had five miles of a drive before him, he remained a short time longer with me. If he thought I had no practical object in taking an interest in the land question, he assumed I had.

"If you can do nothing else," he said, "write about it. I saw when you referred the condition of the farmer to his own disability, you had a grasp of the question. Don't kill the patient, don't let him kill himself. Find a cure for him."

M

XII

BOTH my teachers, as I may call them—Doctor John and
Count M'Qhan—were bold and independent thinkers,
trained in the actual field of experience, and never allowing class prejudices or narrow views of self-interest to affect
their judgment. But there was a great difference between
the two men. The Count simply photographed the agrarian
system in its native ugliness, and leaving the feature of
human responsibility in the background, called no one to
account for it, and imposed on no one the duty of amending
it. If the system injured or destroyed those under it, or
even the human race, that was a feature in the transcript,
and it was enough that it should find due reproduction
in it.

The doctor, on the other hand, was an artist whose means
were found in language, whose picture was a cinemato-
graph, and therefore gave a sequence which put the
dependence of events one on another in the foreground;
presented it immediately to thought, a difficult problem, but
one that could not be evaded. If, as he put it, agrarianism
was one long chapter of cupidity in the exercise of power,
of stupidity in passive submission to the evil exercise—in
sum, of ruffianism—the very note of wilful criminality in
the term implied responsibility for human action, and that
left hope for mankind, which the conception, open or disguised, of irresponsibility, did not. Thus while the Count
seldom blamed anyone, the doctor freely blamed everyone
and believed in the utility of doing so. If the Count had
been a doctor and got any patients he would be unintelligible to them, but Doctor John was never more

intelligible to his many patients and never more implicitly trusted by them than when he dwelt on the effects of their own conduct as contributing to their ailments.

The teaching of the Count, however, just because it was so much actual fieldwork, was a first and necessary step for me. Doctor John led me to compare the agricultural with other forms of industry, but before I could do so I had to form a systematic conception of the first, free from any theoretical assumptions.

Within a mile and a half of Moyclare there was an eminence called Tyrkane Fort, one of those raths so common in Irish landscape. As it was the highest point in the country and famed for the prospect from it, I arranged with the Count to ascend it some day I was not occupied with dispensary work. The path to the fort led us past Mr Cinamon's farmhouse, and on our way to it we met that gentleman. It was on his land and he kindly acted the host and came with us. It was evident that the Count meant more than mere enjoyment of the view, for he carried a map and field-glass. He was a lazy man, but somehow, where the average man was careless and superficial, he found a task to do and did it easily, because methodically.

It was a fine clear day, and when we had got to the crest of the hill, or rather little plateau, the Count asked Mr Cinamon an apparently commonplace question.

" You have been up here oftener than any of us, as the fort is on your land. How many farms would you say we can see looking all round ? "

Mr Cinamon looked half surprised, half amused.

" Why, I never thought how many ; why should I ? Well, I suppose, hundreds, or, with the help of the glass, over a thousand."

" Oh, we can be more accurate than that. There are two ways of reckoning them—one by actual enumeration over the definable area, the other by roughly fixing an area and calculating the number from the average area of each farm for the district. Let me see."

The Count unfolded the map, and looking from it to the wide expanse of country before us, went on in the most placid, matter-of-fact way possible.

"Now, there is Ballyconnell Fort five miles from us to the north, the Seven Mile Hill the same distance to the south; between Annaghbeg and Lissan, east and west, is another ten miles. Within these limits we see 64,000 acres, and the average area of our farms being thirty-five acres, there are some 1820 holdings in view. Too large a number for us. Suppose we reckon 100 near us."

Mr Cinamon laughed and asked,—

"What is it all for? You'll get tired before you reach twenty."

"Ah, well, we'll stop, of course, when we get tired. Now, O'Gara, out with your note-book and dot down particulars. We begin here—No. 1, Townland, Tyrkane; occupier, Rev. David Cinamon; seventy-eight acres. No remarks. That may do as a model."

To the north, at no great distance, we saw under us what was evidently a gentleman's seat, though not at all of the first class—not at all, indeed, indicating wealth or great estate. We could see an old stone house with a garden and out-houses, the neglect and dilapidation of which neither distance and enormous overgrowths of ivy, nor under-growths of wind-torn bushes, effectually concealed.

"No. 2, Townland, Keggan," the Count went on in his calm, business-like way. "The Misses Legard, owners-in-fee; 180 acres, Mr Cinamon, is there not in Keggan demesne?"

"Yes, but forty acres are under wood, such as it is—not a stick worth five shillings in the whole of it—whinny braes the most of it. Then there are forty acres of flooded bottoms which used to be good land enough in old Colonel Legard's time. He kept the drains open. I might bring an action against the ladies, for there are ten acres of my land flooded from the way the Keggan drains are left stopped up, but I would not like to be hard on them."

"The Misses Legard," the Count went on, "are two ladies who live in Switzerland, I am afraid in genteel poverty. They are the nominal owners of the two town-lands of Kegganmore and Kegganbeg, which brought in about £1000 a year in their father's time. When he died their brother neglected and dipped the property, and when it came to them the rent reductions left it worth little.

Poor ladies! they must be on the wrong side of sixty now, and from the way they were brought up their trial must be a sore one."

"But," I said, "the demesne and house might be worth a great deal more if kept in order."

"It would matter nothing to them if they were kept up," Mr Cinamon remarked. "I hear they have an allowance of £150 a year out of the place. Somehow the mortgagees could not help it, though the whole rent wouldn't quite cover their claim. The title is such, they can't sell and can't let the ladies sell."

"Anyhow, O'Gara," the Count said, "you may put down 180 acres; owners, two elderly ladies living in Switzerland; agent, John Perkins, solicitor, Dublin. Land let by auction every year; worn out and uncultivated. House untenanted and dilapidated."

Somewhat nearer us on the right was a small farmhouse or labourer's cottage, to which the Count pointed.

"Curious enough, we have another absentee to deal with here—on a small scale, though. No. 3, Townland, Kegganmore; occupier, James Brown; area, twenty-eight acres; reduced rent, £17, 10s.—correct me, Mr Cinamon, if I make any mistake. Occupier in California for the last five years. House and garden let to a labourer at a rent of 2s. a week, or £5, 4s. a year; land let by auction every year. In poor condition—worn out."

"Are there many farms in the country the so-called occupiers of which are absentees?"

It was Mr Cinamon who answered my question. He was beginning to see the drift of the Count's proceeding.

"Oh, there are a good many gentlemen's places, covering a big area, with no one on them, but not more than four or five farmers like James Brown."

"No. 4, Townland, Kegganmore; occupier, Alexander M'Laine," the Count went on, imperturbably; "area, fifty-five acres; reduced rent, £40.

"The new rent," Mr Cinamon corrected, "is £36, 15s.; it is a poor farm."

"An out-farm of Mr M'Laine of Shaneglish. M'Laine got it through a loan to the former occupier, and means to sell if he can get a purchaser. Only grazes it for the present."

" Are there many out-farms of this kind in the country ? "
I asked. " They seem to be equivalent to holdings in the
hands of absentees."

"The first time I met you," the Count said smiling,
"you were admiring an out-farm of mine on Arrahantarrahan Old Road. The area they cover is more important
than their number. There are, however, several kinds of
them. I know some farmers with half-a-dozen separate
patches from half-a-mile to a mile apart, a state of things
which increases the cost and trouble of working. Again, a
large part of the land about villages, like Jigglestreet, is
held by persons living in the town or village, and as they
have other business to attend to they are bad farmers.
But men like M'Laine and M'Qhan hold a considerable
area as out-farms, and—well, perhaps, Mr Cinamon may
tell you how we treat them or they treat us."

But the reverend gentleman was suspicious, and merely
shaking his head would not commit himself.

" No matter," the Count proceeded. " No. 5, another of
the Legard tenants, Townland, Kegganbeg; occupier,
Andrew M'Spaddan ; area, 41 acres ; rent, £33. By the
way, Mr Cinamon, how old is M'Spaddan ? "

" Oh, M'Spaddan is at a standstill as long as I mind.
He voted against O'Connell and Catholic Emancipation,
and is always uneasy that he'll be late in getting into
Dungannon to do it again. They have been saying that he
is a hundred these ten years."

"That is a point we have neglected, O'Gara, the age of
the occupier." The Count spoke gravely, conscious of a
lapse. " But, in point of fact, by running over the names
of the occupiers after we have taken a hundred, we shall
find sixty of them over sixty years of age. Now, Mr
Cinamon, how is M'Spaddan's farm managed ? "

Mr Cinamon laughed.

" Oh, easier than the man himself. There is no getting
anyone to live with him and mind him. The place was
assigned over to a cousin of his, Gawn Geddes, who lives at
Gortnacopple, the other side of Dungannon, ten miles
away, on condition of making the old man an allowance.
Gawn manages the farm, but it's not often he shows near
it ; the old man threatens to shoot him."

"Well, O'Gara, you can put down : Farm waste and uncultivated."

The Count was taking the circle of farms immediately surrounding Tyrkane Fort and farm. The next he came to, lying to the east, was evidently in point of culture a vast improvement on those we had passed over. The house looked clean and neat, and the land in great part bore the marks of tillage. But the Count's accent was unchanged.

"This farm is on Lord de Villeroi's estate, as is Tyrkane. No. 6, Townland, Shanvegan ; occupier, Hugh M'Ilgorm, a man about forty-six years of age ; area, 62 acres ; rent, £49. Now, O'Gara, you know M'Ilgorm ; I saw you speaking to him yesterday. Would you say that I was his senior ? "

The Count looked a man of thirty-six, and although close scrutiny might induce one to add a few years on, it would be with some doubt. M'Ilgorm, though a strong, muscular man, was quite grey, and life's burdens deeply marked on his face. I had taken him to be near sixty. I answered, however, with the discretion of a medical man.

"I never guess age until I have examined the heart and felt the arteries."

"Well," the Count said smiling, "I happen to know M'Ilgorm's age and my own ; he is forty-six and I am forty-seven. I am just as certain that if I lived the life he did, and worked as he did for even ten of the forty-seven years, I would not be here to make the statement."

"Hugh," Mr Cinamon corroborated, "has been a perfect slave ; I would never have gone through what he has, but he be to work and save. His father, old John, had five daughters and the one son, and when he died it was found that he had left the place to Hugh, charged with fortunes of £50 to each of the girls. It was a poor joke for him, seeing that the farm if put to sale would not have fetched £250 at the time. But he just set himself to do the thing, and has done it. When, however, the place was freed two years ago, his son left him and went away to Australia, and there he is, left to struggle on with two younger children—a boy and girl—bound to fly his life of hard work as soon as they get the chance. He is a brave man, I allow, Hugh M'Ilgorm."

"A brave man," the Count echoed, "whose life, industry, thrift, and ability have been wasted. Well, well, O'Gara, you can put to his credit that the farm is cultivated and in good condition."

"That's what you can't say for the next," the clergyman said with a chuckle. "Hugh M'Ilgorm proposed to all the farmers round to go in a body and cut down the thistles on it, just to save their own land being sown over, but they wouldn't. Farmers never can be got to agree."

"No. 7," the Count went on, "Townland, Shanvegan; occupier, Lawrence M'Parlin; area, 39 acres; rent, £27; under lease. Well, Mr Cinamon, do you think M'Parlin should be made the owner of his holding on the grounds that he grows thistles enough to sow the country side?"

"Oh, Lawrence, every one knows is a lunatic. There should be a law to meet such a case."

"So there is, only with no means of being put in force. You have down, O'Gara: Farm waste."

Our eyes next fell on some twenty houses not far apart from each other, and an area of land, which was nearly all used for tillage purposes, interrupted here and there by bosses of rock, partly overgrown with whins. The Count, after considering the uninviting prospect for a moment or two, remarked with some hesitation,—

"These holdings are well worth being taken separately, but to save time we may take them *en bloc*, noting some of the more striking particulars. I know them pretty well, having gone over them before. Nos. 8 to 29—there are twenty-one of them—townland, Shanvegan; occupiers hold from 3 to 15 acres each; total area, 180 acres; rent, £185; therefore much higher than that got from the larger farms. What is your opinion, Mr Cinamon, of the value of these holdings?"

The gentleman addressed looked as if he had never formed an opinion on the subject, and then gave one which he had got second-hand.

"Oh, I suppose, their chief use is keeping up a supply of labour in the country."

"It would be interesting," the Count said, with a calmness which would be cynical if, by any chance, he could be cynical, "to know how much these twenty-one holders of land here make by working as labourers at home in our own neighbourhood. They tell me next to nothing; that it is only when they go abroad, or to England and Scotland, the members of their families make anything. How much employment, Mr Cinamon, do they get on your farm or mine, or on any of the farms we have gone over?"

"It takes us," Mr Cinamon allowed, "all our time to keep ourselves up. They can't expect us to keep them. Besides they are bad workers, and make a compliment of working for us."

"They are certainly poor, unsystematic workers. There is ten times more labour on this 180 acres than is necessary for its cultivation, and, of course, the occupiers are idle and untrained. How can we pass their land as in good condition and well farmed, O'Gara?" Look at those little fields with their enormous fences. There is probably not a horse on the whole area, and not more than two or three cows."

"I am afraid the tenure of life on it is more precarious," I said, "than the legal tenure of the land. The houses look very unfit for human beings to live in."

The Count inclined his head gravely, and, turning to the south in his circuit, went on,—

"Now, here is a group of six holdings all about the same size, 20 acres, under the same landlord, Lord De Villeroi. Nos. 30 to 36; area, 124 acres; rent, I suppose, £95. The occupiers happen to be four old men and two old women. Now, Mr Cinamon, has Isaac Slavin over there any one living with him?"

"The sister, Martha. She has been out of her mind since she was a child, and she must be over sixty-five now. It is curious, he gets on well with her, and that's more than he does with anyone else. The neighbours put in his crop for him. You did it last year."

"And you, Mr Cinamon, the year before. Well, the next is the widow Hoolahan; her grandson manages for her, and pretty well too, though she has the name of being hard to put up with—her neighbour, Bella Lynass, says so, at least, which is injudicious, as the widow retaliates by casting doubts on the existence of Bella's husband in America. There can be no doubt, however, as to the existence of Bella's three daughters, who have good situations as cooks, and keep the farm for her."

"Oh," Mr Cinamon said, laughing, "there can be no doubt about the husband. I knew him well, and he really owns the farm if he is in the land of the living. The mystery comes in with the daughters."

"No matter, Mr Cinamon, we are dealing with a purely economical question. The daughters keep the farm, and the farm keeps no one, which, as you know, is not an uncommon case in the country. But you must put the farm down as ill kept, not in good condition, O'Gara."

"It seems to me," I said, "quite wild."

"Oh, not worse than my farm in Arrahantarrahan. The next two places are held by two brothers, Cormac and Barney M'Cusker. Cormac is a widower over sixty, with a houseful of young children. He keeps house, cooks, washes, minds the children, and works his land, and not badly, as you see."

"As well as the brother Barney lets him," the clergyman remarked, with his usual tendency towards personal criticism. "You had to bind Barney over to keep the peace twice, and it's six months in jail each time he should have got."

"And would have got if Cormac had pressed the case. No matter. The farm to the right is Barney M'Cusker's, and it is a fair index to its owner. You may put it down, O'Gara, waste and uncultivated."

"I think," Mr Cinamon observed jocosely, "the doctor does not care to be going through a mere form—is tired of the thing."

"Ah, well," said the Count with his usual calmness. "Take the glass, Mr Cinamon, and pick out for us out of the 1800 farms in sight those you consider in good condition and well cultivated. It shall certainly save time and not tire us, particularly if you do not care to reckon in farms which have, as in M'Ilgorm's case, worn out and prematurely aged their occupiers."

Mr Cinamon's big hands were in his coat pockets, and went deeper down in them at the Count's proposal. He would not touch the glass.

"Oh, now, Count," he said, "you know very well that I allow the state of the country. I don't want to make out that it is any better than it is by picking out odd cases where men above the common have overcome the difficulties bad laws have put in the way of all of us. The country is under the curse of landlordism, and you needn't ask me to weaken the case against it."

The Count looked at me as if the statement made was more for me than him.

"I understand the Count," I said with an attempt to imitate the gentleman's calm philosophic manner, "to mean that a hundred or a thousand occupiers of land should be taken at random in the actual field, with a view to determine precisely the conditions under which they live as affecting their ability to cultivate their holdings."

A grim, or even hard, and sardonic smile came into the clergyman's face as he took me up.

"I know very well, gentlemen, what you are at. If you go deep into the thing maybe I can go to the bottom of the well with you and maybe I can't; it doesn't matter in the least. There's a place, I allow, for the discussion of true fact and principle, but the place is not a battlefield. There is a time for the discussion, that is, when you have reason to think it may lead to a decision; otherwise, it is idle disputation, which should be refrained from. The issue between landlords and tenants is simply a battle in which principle and the interpretation you set, on facts has no weight, and the fault is not the tenants. The landlords, with their territorialism, entail, primogeniture, settlements, and titles which were no titles, raised a dust in which no principle could be seen; all we could see was that they had made themselves masters of our lives by making themselves masters of our means of living. They call us robbers, but we are just men fighting for our lives, and if they had any sense they would be thankful if they get off with their heads on their shoulders. Land purchase, indeed! If I had my way they wouldn't get three ha'pence, and I say that more as a clergyman, bound to resist evildoers, than as a farmer."

But Mr Cinamon, in speaking, had quite dropped the clergyman, and was the natural man, sincere because intensely bitter. What he said, however, added nothing to my stock of information. My own observation, and the opinions of those I had come in contact with, had taught me that as a mere fact the landowners were not simply unpopular, but, irrespective of any question of interest, had estranged the popular mind by persistence in their barbaric and antiquated system. Men who were entirely opposed to land agitation in its actual form, nevertheless I found tolerated it through disgust at the unteachableness of the landlords and the perception that all along the line they had yielded only to brute force. As Unionists and Protestants they had a following; as landowners they stood alone, and were even suspected of making use of the Unionist and Protestant interest to protract the life of their own system.

"The exercise of force, Mr Cinamon," the Count observed with, if possible, increased calmness in his tone, "calls for an exercise of thought and discretion even more difficult and rare than that necessary in what is absurdly styled academic definition of principle, simply because immediate responsibility for action goes with it. Grant that the tenants are fighting a battle, the smoke the landlords fight in is no reason for adjourning the performance to midnight; we are bound to make the best use we can of what light is available. As a rule when one side wins a battle, it is only to find itself face to face with new enemies and new difficulties. We cannot take the landlords' position and undertake their responsibilities without being exposed to criticism on the ground of principle. You say the landlords defied and outraged principle; would you have us, simply taking their place, do the same thing?"

Mr Cinamon was really of a somewhat mobile temperament, and while the Count never changed either his position or tone the clergyman became a clergyman and put on charity.

"Now, Count," he said, "though I am down on landlords all round, you know I am not a hard man when I come to my fellow-man, no matter what he is. In fact, I allow that it is out of place for one man to be down on another without first putting himself in that other man's shoes. There are those Misses Legard—I pity them more than I can tell you, remembering them in my young days, kind and good to the poor of the country. I have said that there is a battle between the landlords and tenants, and I don't draw back from that. What I do say, however, is that the battle would have gone against them long ago only for what kindliness, charity and forbearance there is in the world, and which many of them deserved full share of. You, with your cold, dry reason, would have been far harder on them than ever I would have been; you would have reached them quickly and sharply where we go roundabouts, willing to let them down easy. I allow that the farmers have their failings too, but it's a case for charity and forbearance."

The Count was amused and smiled.

"Shall we go on, O'Gara," he asked, "with our review of these holdings under us or be satisfied with establishing the method of examination? In reality the method is not new to me; I have taken several areas in different parts of the country, and always obtained a practically invariable result. Taking a hundred persons at random—to be certain would need a much larger number, but no matter—only ten of the hundred would be able-bodied men, capable of, say, military service, and seventy of them would be under one form of disability or another and a burden on the capable section. If, then, ownership of land is vested in persons under no condition of ability to work it, seventy per cent. would be wholly incapable, twenty per cent. partially incapable, and only ten per cent. fully capable. I find the actual result in the field is even more unfavourable. There is a contant drain of the capable section from the land, the drain is from the areas on which there is a great surplus of labour; this surplus is of bad quality, intractable and untrained, and is not at all, to the extent imagined by loose theorists, available for the areas on which there is a deficiency of labour. Mr Cinamon and every other practical farmer of the same class says the same thing of the small farming class, that labour is in excess in it, but at the same time not available for the purposes of the large farmer—unreliable and not at command when wanted."

" I agree with that," Mr Cinamon said, evidently as expressing painful experience, " and allow that, when we get rid of the landlords, our difficulties with labour shall remain, and may be too much for us."

" Yes, Mr Cinamon, but you are to note that we are simply describing an actual state of things under our eyes without attributing blame for any evils we may observe in it to anyone, and, therefore, not giving them a dispensation under the form of charity and forbearance. Anyone wanting to form an honest and, therefore, a sound and useful judgment, can, and must, do as we have just done, only working on a larger scale, must take the farmers one by one, and, from a large number, estimate their ability to cultivate the land. If seventy-five, or even sixty-five, per cent. are under disability and inefficient, the case is one, not for charity and forbearance, or even dry cold reason, but for the inevitable operation of economic law helped or marred by wild outbursts of political agitation."

" But, Count, you must allow that, if the farming interest is relieved of the incubus of landlordism, it shall be in a better position to cultivate the land."

" I allow nothing of the kind, Mr Cinamon. It will be in a better condition to meet the case of disability under which it labours, that is all. Old men and old women, sick and infirm persons, can hold on better when they have little or no rent to pay, but their ability to work or direct and organise labour must remain unaffected."

" Well," the clergyman said, driven back to a defensible position, " they have a right to do that. The landlords do nothing ; the farmers do what is done, and if it is not up to the mark, you gentlemen would fix, still they have the best right, having done something to be safe against disability. If disability is no charge against the landlords on better grounds, it is no charge against the farmers."

The Count, with a calm dignity which was enough to earn him his title, answered, with a gesture in my direction,—

" Well, yes ; but there are men in the world like O'Gara here who hold that, when a clear case of disability is made out against clergymen and doctors, they should be relieved of duty, and the cure of souls and bodies provided for otherwise. The interest he considers is not that of the clergyman and doctor, but that of those they serve. He draws no distinction between landlord and farmer, but, having determined as an actual fact that the land in their hands is waste and uncultivated, and that that fact depends on the other equally clear fact, their disability, he holds that the community is grievously injured, and in a possible case may act on the principle that necessity knows no law."

In speaking hitherto, Mr Cinamon had occasionally hesitated as if needing time to think, but now he looked at me with a shade of contempt, and spoke with marked confidence.

"I suppose," he said, directing himself to me, "you are one of those who go in for what is called Land Nationalisation, that is, that the Government should own the land and manage it in some wonderful way in the interest of the people. I have been in no countries but Ireland and Scotland, and you have been, as I have heard, in America and other parts, and if you say you have found a people anywhere ready to trust their Government with complete mastery over their means of living, well, I am open to reason, and shall consider what you say. But unless you can give me one instance, at least, of a people ready to hand over their land and lives to Government, I cannot give up the beliefs of my Church and people, founded on painful experience of Government in past and present time."

It was easy for me to answer this. The constitutions of every American State I knew, framed by thoughtful men with experience of so-called democratic government, showed in every line profound distrust of the mechanism called into existence, and of the legislative bodies, even more than of the personal officials. The framers of these instruments evidently only expressed the popular mind in making the most elaborate precautions against what was taken for granted, the almost incurable proclivity of legislatures and executives to grossly misuse and abuse power. This was equivalent to an express denial of the position that, because the people under universal suffrage elected their agents, these last therefore acted either under compulsion or of their free will in the interest of the people. It was again equivalent to a definition of principle, meant to meet the invariable tendency of the agency, however constituted, to escape and evade limitation and indulge in arbitrary power. I had not only no instance to give of a people trusting its Government, but no instance of a Government that was not provoking distrust by violation of principles rooted in the mind and conscience of mankind.

But I was not bound to explain this, since the clergyman's question was mere evasion of the issue raised by the Count, and to that issue I stood firmly.

"To change," I said, "the body of landlords for the Government, whether the Government was trusted or not, would change nothing in the agrarian system, and meet none of the objections made to it. If these occupiers paid rent to the Government instead of their present landlords, the case of disability proved against them would remain in full force. Changing the landlord, or doing away with him entirely, would still leave from seventy to ninety per cent. of the occupiers under the disabilities incidental to human life, disabilities in by far the greater extent calling not for charity and forbearance, but for recognition, as necessary and unavoidable. Again, the land would be left just as it is, broken up in deference to personal rights into fragments, disregarding all relation to its efficient and economical cultivation, barring due organisation of labour for the end."

To think with Mr Cinamon was to lose the confidence which the habit of glib repetition of formulas fosters. But his thinking took an airy turn.

"When you doctors," he said, "cure old age, infirmity and sickness, make a bargain beforehand with Government not to undo your work, or you shall have your pains for nothing; or, rather, you should do nothing of the kind, for you could hold it to nothing, and the very nature of the thing is to abuse every advantage a people may gain. Suppose we farmers, by any plan, were to cultivate the land so as to make the United Kingdom independent of the supplies of food from abroad—a thing I admit could be done—our Government would lose any sense it has, and never rest till our last estate would be worse than our first. I trust no Government; none of us really do. Get us a sane Government that we can trust, and then we may talk about what would immensely increase its power and its irresponsibility in the exercise of power."

The Count's peculiar smile told me that, though the words were Mr Cinamon's, the reasoning was his, or inspired by him. It was quite in his line to paint the agrarian prospect in the most sombre tints, and not only leave it so, but ignore what others might take as a bright-ening ray on the horizon. But Mr Cinamon's mind was not a truly responsive one, since, in imputing blame to Government, he admitted responsibility in human affairs.

"Very well," I said, adopting the Count's calm manner as the other had done his reasoning, in part at least. "You should aim at getting a sane Government by squarely charging the Government you have with criminal insanity, in proposing to bolster up 50,000 to 100,000 persons—seventy-five per cent. of whom are under one form of disability or another—in occupation of the land, by giving them the use of £120,000,000 of the public money. I say 50,000 to 100,000 persons, because an insignificant fraction of the money would go to numbers in excess of this. This crime and folly is a direct act of Government, justifying to the full the profound distrust with which, as you say, the institution is regarded. With you the feeling rests on traditional or historical, with me on actual present ex-perience. Nothing Government ever did in the past in bolstering up a few thousand landlords by giving them absolute power over the means of subsistence of, not the people, not even the actual labourers on the land, but a few hundred thousand tenants, is more characteristic of Governmental action than this proposal in principle actually accepted. Bad as it is that the millions of the people should be in dangerous and precarious dependence on foreign countries for their food, their own land waste and uncultivated in the hands of incompetent occupiers, the sting of the thing lies in the mind your Government has for its mindless people. Yes, Mr Cinamon, it is your

N

precious Government that has to be begun with ; but do it, bring knowledge, reason, judgment, to bear against it, and because you object to deception and fraud you are called a Red, an Anarchist, an ally of assassins ; any stick will do."

The Count smiled blandly, as if I was merely filling in a shade or two in his picture with Indian ink. The clergyman—what clergyman would ?—did not allow me the last word, but what he said did not influence my judgment.   I had had opportunities of cultivating Doctor Devine's society, and, perhaps because we were medical men, and looked on social evils as we did on the ailments of our patients, as things we were bound at least to attempt to cure or mitigate, his influence prevented me from lapsing into cynical indifference or despair.

XIII

MEGILLO'S CORNER

I GOT into the habit of going over to Doctor John on Sunday afternoons, and if I had to miss the Sunday visit I knew that Saturday was his dispensary day, and was glad to accompany him on his professional errands. His ways of thinking were instructive to me, although, like my uncle, he was often merely suggestive, indicating a problem and leaving me to work it out myself. If we saw a patient together he left the diagnosis of the case, if an interesting one, to me, and did not hesitate to correct me when his opinion was different from mine; always, however, with perfect impartiality, giving the reasons for both his own view and mine.

On one of my Saturday visits I drove with him to a place in his district called Megillo's Corner. Megillo, he explained to me, was a mis-spelling for M'Gillow, which, again, was a corrupt form of the name M'Guffin. A number of roads and lanes converged at the place, and a family named Megillo had, time out of mind, kept a public-house at it. The house, which was no better than a shebeen, had been closed up for thirty years or more, and for twenty years no one of the name of Megillo had been known to reside in the neighbourhood. Ten years ago, however, a man stated vaguely to be from America, and who called himself Leveson Megillo, had bought the public, as it was still called, and the bit of land attached to it, and resided in it for three or four months at a time, then would suddenly disappear; back to America, his neighbours said, without any grounds for the statement. They knew nothing about the man except what he told them, and that was confined to one particular. The old Megillos, who kept the shebeen in past times, bore in the traditions of the country the very worst reputation. It was said that pedlars, the only travellers who frequented the house, had on many occasions been murdered and robbed, the legend adding with nice precision that their corpses were built up into the walls of the house, which were, in places, of great thickness. But the one point which Leveson Megillo made known about himself, and that as if proud of it, was that he was the direct and lineal descendant and representative of the Leveson Megillo whose name, on a stone in the hall, attested the fact that he built the house in 1717, and of his lineal descendants, who had occupied it for 150 years afterwards. This claim of the newcomer was strongly corroborated by certain old crones in the country, who declared their willingness to take any form of oath prescribed to them that the stranger was the very picture of the Megillos they saw in their youth. This, with the man's own statement, was enough to attach to him the reputation of the tribe, of course made blacker by revival. The Corner was made up of a group of houses occupied by farm labourers, all, with the exception of the public, of the poorest description. But the dozen houses were rich in dogs, fowl and children, who swarmed on the road in free and unrestrained social intercourse. If, however, Leveson Megillo chanced on the scene only the least intelligent of the animals—the fowl—remained unconcerned; the children, some with a run, some with a crafty pretence of having seen no one, slunk behind the ruined walls, which were the characteristic feature of the place. The dogs, after a moment's reflection, decided that though the movement was incomprehensible, still it might be better to follow the example set by superior intelligence, and disappeared one and all. How Megillo took it all was what Doctor John did not know, and he was a man who never admitted total ignorance, only to supply its place by hypothesis.

"The man never sent for me before," he said, "though I believe he suffers from occasional turns of bad health. His housekeeper, old Jane Macklemunn, has, however, been a patient of mine, and she told me that she knew nothing against the man except that he read books and kept to himself. I needn't put *sic* to the statement for you."

"No; but how does it come that he manages to get a woman to live with him if his reputation is so bad?"

"How did Nero and Caligula manage to get Prime Ministers, mistresses and valets? If Megillo is as rich as they say, I expect he would easily get a nice, tidy, young wife, glad, in fact, of an opportunity of showing us all that she did not regard our opinions when they stood in the way of doing as she pleased. Jane Macklemunn is neither young nor nice, but age has not diminished her irrepressible wilfulness. Then," was the thoughtful addition, "she may be right, there may be nothing against the man."

"It is strange that he should have excited prejudice against himself by avowing immediate connection with a race of murderers and robbers."

"I did not say, O'Gara, that the Megillos were a race of murderers and robbers; the stories told about them would be simply vulgar trash if so explicitly and rudely outspoken. All I know is that certain interesting and mysterious legends surround their old house at the Corner, which would be quite spoiled if, instead of being dim and awful, they assumed the form of proved fact. Suppose, now, it was on record and beyond question that the great-grandfather of a certain young Doctor O'Gara was hung for sheep stealing and manslaughter, the fact would be rather in his favour than otherwise, and even with sensitive girls between seventeen and twenty. No, sir, the children would not run away from O'Gara and Devine because they are descendants of a long line of sheep stealers, who never hesitated to kill their man in pursuit of their calling, provided always the thing was no mystery, made no demand on imagination."

This was a favourite position with Doctor John, one he made extensive use of. Men, he held, were comparatively easily managed, were rational when rationally treated, rational to the extent of patiently enduring suffering and evil, the nature and cause of which was plain to them. They become irrational, their action incalculable, when they are mystified, kept in the dark, and their emotions played on. This led to the farther position with him that all authority exerted over them, the authority of parents, of the clergy, of rulers, was deeply vitiated by the idea that it was not only right but necessary to make use of their mental frailty and ignorance to guide them through, not their intelligence, but their want of intelligence. From his experiential point of view, that on which he rested to the exclusion of *prima facie* reasoning, emotionalism and sentimentalism were, as he called them, sub-acute insanity, and those who cultivated emotionalism as a means of controlling men were simply developing lunacy and action under diseased and weakened self-control.

" I am curious," he said, " to know what effect the children of the Corner, running away at the sight of Megillo, has on the man. How he takes it may show us the strength or weakness of his mind. The imps, if he murdered one of them, their parents and instructors would be more to blame than the man himself."

" I was called to see a child," I said, " the other day, who went into spasms of terror at the sight of me. The parents, to get it to swallow a dose of oil and make it good under the difficulties of colic, had threatened to bring a doctor, who would think nothing of cutting it open. Minus the dose the child had taken, the pint of castor oil, with a dirty mug, was on the table, and, as the child would not allow me to examine it, I went through a farce of insisting that the father and mother should finish the oil between them. I was, however, only gently persuasive with them, which the youngster, interested and amused, did not fail to observe, and before I left the house it would have done for me what it would not have done for the silly parents."

" Oh, I have had many similar experiences, but, as you see, familiarity breeds contempt. The imps of the Corner are not afraid of us."

We were at the Corner, and surrounded by over a dozen young people who, as they were not expecting us, were not in Sunday clothes. The doctor was driving himself, and three or four of the older lads hustled each other for the honour, with the prospect of sixpence thrown in, of holding the horse. A lad, by no means the biggest or stoutest of the lot, speedily settled the matter to his own satisfaction, and even Doctor John yielded the reins to him as a matter of course.

" Walk him up and down, Roddy—he is hot—but don't go out of sight."

" It's all right, doctor, you know. We'll be here whenever you want us."

The doctor had confidence in Roddy, for he walked into the public without casting a look behind him. The public was a heavy-looking, squat, stone building, with a long row of small, diamond-paned, iron-framed windows. Its porch was of blue, big stones which, rough above and below, were greasily smooth where exposed to contact with those that had frequented it in times past. Inside the porch were two similarly polished stones which had served as seats, a half-door and behind it a whole door, both plain boarding, but of oak nearly black with age. The doors were open, and Jane Macklemunn, the housekeeper, stood ready to receive us. Doctor John on entering stopped and looked round him as if testing his memory.

" I have been in the house before, Jane, but it must be thirty years ago. Well, all the change I see is that it is much cleaner than it was then."

" I suppose, doctor," the woman answered, "it was in the Foursides's time you were in it. They were noways particular. I have not overly much to do, but what there is to do is done."

A screen after the fashion of Irish houses of the class was in front of the door, and behind it was a large room which served as hall, kitchen and reception-room. There was no grate or stove in the room, but a great hearth on which a fire was burning brightly. The furniture was of the common kind—clean deal—but the ceiling was of dark oak, and a curious, old-fashioned window, broad but low, and with bull's-eye glass panes, looked out into an orchard.

The doctor, standing in the middle of the room, remarked,—

"Some changes have been made, but I can't tell what."

" Oh, the Foursides made changes from what it was in old times, but beyond cleaning, nothing has been done in my time."

" Where is Mr Megillo, Jane ?"

" In his room, doctor ; he said he wouldn't rise till after he saw you."

There was a stair, half a ladder, of old and much-worn oak at one end of the room we were in. This we ascended to an attic or loft, at one end of which a door led into our patient's bedroom. Mrs Macklemunn simply directed us to the room and left us to introduce ourselves. With a tap on the door, which met an immediate response, we entered a large and airy room, which, like the rest of the house, was scrupulously clean without losing the air of homely antiquity. Mr Megillo was sitting up in his bed wrapped in a great-coat, with a dark felt hat on his head. He was a man about sixty-five years of age, with a beard half red half white, clipped rather close, but the hair which showed under his hat was dark red, with only some few threads of white in it. He was a man, I said to myself at once, who had struggled against ill-health and perhaps other untoward circumstances by cultivating self-control and temperate habits. There was nothing sinister or repellent in his appearance, but at the same time nothing to command attention or, indeed, excite notice. To the trained eye of a medical man, however, a point for interest would occur : he was evidently suffering from the effects of malaria of old standing. Another point that struck us was that he had lost one hand.

He was expecting Doctor John, but not me, and he looked at me at first with a little surprise which suddenly became self-inquiring, as if he was trying to remember someone he had met before. The same thing happened to myself ; it struck me that I had seen the man before, but without being able to recall where or under what circumstances, which meant that he had made no lasting impression on my mind.

Doctor John had quietly taken a chair by the bedside, and feeling the patient's pulse, remarked,—

" You have two doctors come to see you instead of one. This is young Doctor O'Gara, a nephew of my friend in

Jigglestreet, who you must often have heard of, if, indeed, you do not know him personally."

"Mr Megillo's look passed from me at once just as if he had all the information he required as to me. He looked instead at Doctor John, and I could note in him a certain confidence in his own ability to read the character and mind of those he came in contact with. The scrutiny, which was short, seemed to inspire what he said.

"I often thought, doctor, of calling on you and consulting you, but I have been with many doctors and they have all told me much like what I know myself—that I can never be cured, just relieved at the time, that is all."

Doctor John said nothing to this, but following a rule with him, silently made a careful examination of the sick man from the objective point of view, and then proceeded diplomatically to subjective details.

"How did you manage to lose your hand, Mr Megillo— an accident?"

"Not exactly. I served in the Civil War in America, under Sherman, and lost the hand at Chattanooga, or rather it had to be cut off in hospital."

"I hope the United States Government give you a pension?"

"Yes, I get a good pension, but the loss of my hand at twenty-two has been a serious drawback on me. I would have done much better in life with my hand and no pension."

"You must have got intermittent fever or malaria when comparatively young, after your soldiering came to an end?"

"Yes. After the war I became what you call over here a pedlar, travelling over the middle States. It was at this time, when under thirty, I got the fever which has injured my constitution, left me liable every now and then, indeed, mostly, every fall, to attacks of hæmorrhage which bring me to death's door."

"And, I suppose, threw you altogether on your pension?"

"Well, no. I had really become a commission agent for a bank that lent money on real estate, mostly on mortgage to farmers, and having got a good connection,

I could manage my business as suited me. Then I got to deal in real estate, in which line I made and lost large sums. The usual way, you know."

"Were you ever married, Mr Megillo?"

Megillo had spoken of the loss of his hand, his health and his money with a tone of cool indifference, but there was a tremor in his voice in answering this.

"Yes, but my poor wife died two years after our marriage, and her death affected my health—somewhat."

The "somewhat" meant an effort in the speaker to maintain a stoical attitude.

"No children?"

"Yes, we had one—a son. He is grown up, an official in the Pennsylvania Railroad Company, is married and has three children. His name is Leveson Megillo, and you can easily find him in the Company's head office in Philadelphia."

Mr Megillo directed himself to me in saying this, as if he knew I might be in the city named. His expression conveyed the impression that he had some knowledge of me.

But Doctor John, returning to business, asked a number of questions to complete his information of the patient's past and present state of health, and not until these medical points were fully ascertained did he touch on his personal history again.

"What is not clear to me, Mr Megillo," he said, "is why you live here; I suppose, as you were so early in life in the Federal army, you are a native of America?"

"No, doctor, I was born in this very room, and lived as a child in this house. I am Snuffy Leveson's second son."

"Oh, indeed," Doctor John said very gravely. "I attended your poor father then in his last illness—and his daughter, Ally."

The doctor spoke with reluctance as if fearing to call up painful memories. But Mr Megillo spoke with the calm of a man who had trained himself to take the ills of life stoically.

"I am well aware of that, doctor, and although I sent for you on my own account, it was also because I always meant to make you some acknowledgment for your great kindness to them in the last sad days of their sad lives. I should have done so when I came over here first, but really it was not till lately, when I was last in America, that I came to know our family history. Of course I knew it in part, but the fact is I am not in the habit of uselessly raking up unpleasant matters, rather for the sake of my peace of mind avoid seeking or dwelling on them. But they cannot always be avoided, and much has been forced on me which, with the exception of your kindness, has been very painful to me. But, perhaps, doctor, you are aware of some of these circumstances—not all, I know well."

Doctor John visibly hesitated, as if what he knew might be even more painful than Mr Megillo anticipated.

"Your father, Mr Megillo, I suppose you know, died in great poverty, and had been weak in mind for some years before. Your sister—"

"Was also weak in mind from childhood, and naturally, doctor, you think I knew the facts and should have done something for them?"

Doctor John was far too honest and prudent a man to make professions which would lead Mr Megillo to think him insincere, and awaited explanation in silence.

"My father had a brother, Alexander, in America, who came over to Ireland when I was a little lad of thirteen, and brought me back to America with him. I had an elder brother then, Leveson Brown Megillo—we were all Levesons, my uncle was Leveson Alexander and my name is the same, called after him. My uncle was a carpenter in Alleghany City, but belonged to a peculiar sect of Methodists of which he ultimately became the leading minister. He held what I look on now as strange and narrow religious views, but, of course, as a child and youth I formed no opinion about them, though they affected me unconsciously. He called me a brand he had plucked from the burning, and created the impression on my mind that my people at home were lost sinners and, perhaps without meaning it, estranged me from them. A widower with one daughter who was three years my senior, he acted under impulses which he ascribed to revelation, and as his daughter firmly believed in him, I naturally followed her example."

"I understand now, Mr Megillo," Doctor John said, wishing to give him an opportunity of avoiding farther explanation, but the sick man went on with the air of one who had made up his mind to discharge a painful duty.

"In fact, Belinda and myself often were unable to distinguish whether he spoke under inspiration or was conveying information he had got in the usual way. Thus, two years after leaving Ireland he told me that my brother, Leveson Brown, was dead, adding once more that I was a brand plucked from the burning. This I took him to know by some supernatural means and literally believed that some dreadful fate had befallen my brother which I had barely escaped by a miracle. He was greatly excited when the Civil War broke out, and solemnly commanded me to join the Federal army—a mere form, as I was set on doing so myself. Of course, when I got out in the world I began at once to understand the atmosphere in which I was brought up, and my faith in my uncle came to rest only on his kindness to me and on a belief that his intentions were good. That was enough to prevent me from ever discussing matters of opinion with him, and we kept on good terms to the last. One feeling, however, I was unable to shake myself free from—"

Mr Megillo stopped, and taking a box of cigars off the table beside his bed, opened and held it towards us. When we had each taken one, he said in the level tone with which he had been speaking,—

"I am in your hands now, doctor. Will you allow me one?"

The doctor nodded assent, and Megillo trimming, fingering, and fixing the cigar in a holder, resumed where he had left off.

"I could not get over the feeling, a superstitious feeling, that association with my people in Ireland was to be avoided as evil and defiling, although every trace of the old queer sanctimonious spirit had been rubbed out of me or replaced by prejudice against the Britisher."

Mr Megillo lit his cigar and we puffed away for a while in silence.

"I hope, doctor," he said at last, "I am not taking up too much of your time. You may have other calls to make?"

"You may make your mind quite easy on that head. Business is very slack just now."

"It's the one thing I do, doctor, with some success— making my mind easy. A tough hide, I find, stands to me. I don't mind in the least what would fret most men."

Mr Megillo whiffed at his cigar just long enough to keep it alive, and then went on,—

"I would probably never have come to Ireland, never have thought of my people over here if left to myself. My uncle, however, who lived to a great age, and was the same to the last, sent for me some ten years ago and in his usual way commanded me to go over to Ireland, the house of bondage he called it, and take possession of the place of our forefathers. When I sought more definite information he told me to take the ransom of the place, which would be 1500 dollars, with me ; he would give it to me if I was not willing to use my own money for the purpose. I knew that he was acting under an impulse which, however, I was past taking as a revelation. When he told me that all my people in Ireland were dead and gone, and their place in the hands of strangers, it dawned on me that he had information obtained in the ordinary way. My curiosity was excited, and I wished at least to see the place in which I had been born, and which I dimly remembered. I was in a position to go anywhere I liked, as I had retired from active business, and farther, several doctors had recommended me at one time or another to go to Europe. As for buying the place, of course, I let that stand over till I saw what I had to buy and whether it was really in the market. To get more out of my uncle than he chose to tell me I knew would be vain, so I obeyed him, as somehow or other I always did. When I came over here I could not but suspect that the transaction had been arranged beforehand. Forsyth, who owned the place, seemed to expect me, and his price was just the 1500 dollars."

"I heard that John Forsyth got £300 for the place, and thought the transaction a strange one. The £300 just paid John's debts, and it was said that if put up to auction he would have got £450."

To this remark of Doctor John's Megillo replied by

puffing at his cigar meditatively as if recalling a problem to
mind.

"The transaction surprised me at the time, doctor, but
not as much as did the man, Forsyth. When I asked him the
price, he said at once £300 to me. I asked whether he
was sure he could not get more, that I did not want to take
any advantage. He said that the price to me was £300,
and that he would take no more from me or from anyone
else, and no less, for the money was none of his to give away.
But, perhaps, you understand that; you knew the man."

Doctor John nodded doubtful assent.

"When the bargain was completed I found that Forsyth
had for himself only the price of the furniture and chattels.
When I asked him what he meant to do with himself, his
wife and two small children, with only £20 to the good,
he shook his head and said that the Forsyths came to the
place full, and not till they left it empty could they
hope for the hand of God to guide them. He'd just wait
till the morrow when he'd give me up possession, before
he'd think over what was to be done."

Megillo was husbanding his cigar, taking as much
enjoyment as possible out of it, like a man who has to
exercise moderation in smoking. He made what he was
saying help him to do this. So after a few moments'
leisurely puffing he went on again,—

"The very morning he gave me up possession I received
a letter from my uncle commanding me in the usual terms
to send over to him the man Forsyth and his family, paying
their passage, and making every provision for their comfort.
When Forsyth gave me up possession I read the letter
to him, adding that both my uncle and myself were
able and willing to find employment for him in America.
The poor man fell on his knees in the kitchen below,
thanked the Almighty that the light of His countenance
should be turned towards him at last, and declared to
me that he was heart-glad to be free of both Megillo's
Corner and a country in which he never had but troubles
and sorrows, not of his own making, that came from God's
hand. At the time I did not understand the man, but just
took him to act like my uncle—under religious feelings and
impulses which were beyond my comprehension."

Mr Megillo finished his smoking silently and then said,—

"You attended my father and sister, doctor, and know the history of the country. Perhaps if you told me what you know of my family it would leave me less to say."

"History, Mr Megillo," Doctor John answered smiling, "when of our own time dare not, when, therefore, of our fathers' times cannot, be told. What I know I am quite sure shall never enter the page of history; what I cannot tell now can never be told."

"Yes, doctor, I was through the Civil War, and it just amuses me when I read histories of it. But you might tell me how it came that my father was reduced to poverty, and then I can tell you whether my uncle and myself knew of the fact at the time."

"This *quid pro quo* had no immediate effect on Doctor John, who was inclined to be didactic.

"You have heard, Mr Megillo, the nice line which tells us that Governments do little or nothing to cause or cure the ills men suffer from. I always admired the way the rhymester jingled cause and cure together, but after all it is the common trick whereby a half truth is made the bigger lie."

Megillo looked longingly at the box of cigars as if he needed another to help him to maintain his composure, but his self-restraint triumphed.

"Oh," said the doctor reading the man's mind, "what I say is strictly to the point, decided your father's fate. In the middle of the last century the British Parliament passed an Encumbered Estates' Act, and established a court under it for the sale of encumbered estates. The Act was by way of curing the evils which the same governing body had directly caused, by treating insolvent and nominal owners of land quite differently from other insolvents and bankrupts, and, of course, caused a fine crop of new evils. You are aware that the Megillo's Corner estate, as it is still called, was originally the property of a family named Trafford?"

"Yes, my ancestor, Leveson Megillo, who built this house, held under lease from a Sir Milo Trafford. I know that."

" A lease of forty-one acres of land for lives renewable for ever at a nominal fine, the rent £15, 15s., or 7s. 6d. an acre."

This practical particular made Megillo at once look a keen business man.

" I am aware that a lease had existed, but it was lost, and I did not know the exact terms, doctor."

"Lost? We have to come to that, Mr Megillo. Somewhere about 1859 the Trafford estate was sold in the Encumbered Estates Court. The Act, framed altogether in the interests of a class, gave the purchaser what was called a Parliamentary title, one which could not be called in question, but of course the titles of the occupiers, of which in general there was no record, were not ascertained or secured, were left a happy hunting-ground for the lawyers. Nor was any provision made that the purchaser should be solvent, not himself an encumbered landowner. It so happened that the small Megillo's Corner estate adjoined, lay into, as they say, the big Frayne estate, which then brought in £14,000 a year, and the managers of the last thought it a fine stroke of policy to buy the small estate. The Frayne estate, to be sure, was heavily dipped—the Earl of Bosworth got, it was said, only £4000 a year out of it, but that did not matter. Who were the managers of the estate? Certainly not the Earl ; he was a young officer in the Guards who was much too busy spending all he could lay hands on to have any time for business, and the charge of such an estate would mean a great and engrossing business. It was said that his grandmother, the sister of an English Duke, a lady who never put her foot in Ireland, inspired everything, acting through the family lawyer, whose first and last visit to Ireland was on the occasion of the purchase of Megillo's Corner estate. You are following me, Mr Megillo?—these details are essential for the understanding of your father's case."

" I am attending to every word you say, doctor."

" Well, the Bosworth people bought the estate, bought it dear, and borrowed every penny of the price. The rental, in fact, fell considerably short of the interest on the borrowed purchase-money, but that at the time could be and was remedied. The two estates had been managed on very different lines. On the Trafford estate there were a dozen leaseholds like your father's, and about a dozen tenancies-at-will; the holders, however, having been allowed freedom to buy and sell, had paid £20 to £35 per acre for their interest. This, of course, was left quite unprotected under the Act. The Frayne estate, on the other hand, had gradually been brought under a rigid set of office rules, the rents were higher, the power of arbitrarily changing them kept alive, and the tenant-right, a fixed sum of £5 an acre, paid into the office by the buyer and by the office to the seller, a new contract being entered into, usually involving a rise in the rent equivalent to the reduction in the tenant-right. There were many other office rules, all calculated to keep the tenant in a subservient and dependent position. I tell you this, Mr Megillo, because you are an American, and may not be aware of the state of things here some thirty years ago."

"Oh, doctor, if I don't know, it was not the fault of Irishmen over the other side. In general they used language more calculated to impress the memory than you do."

"Well, Mr Megillo, not being in the clerical line, I would let them down easy. Anyway, when the Bosworth people got Megillo's Corner, they proceeded immediately, and in a mighty high-handed way, to apply the Frayne rules to it. They cut down the tenant-right price at first to £10 and then to £5, and took every opportunity of raising the rents to the Frayne level. As in your father's case, all the buildings had been erected, all the improvements made, by the tenants. At one blow not only was this property taken from them, but a pigsty they would not be allowed to make on their farms without permission from the office. So far, however, the new landlord was acting within the law, but there is more to be told before we get to your father, but I fancy you know what happened?"

"Go on, doctor," Mr Megillo said quietly, "whatever I know I would like to have confirmed by you. I do not suppose you would be prejudiced, but think like a judge on the bench, and that is the kind of opinion—the opinion of a judge—I want."

"The Bosworth estate," the doctor went on, "had very rigid rules bearing against the tenant, but was for all that loosely and carelessly managed. The Earl left everything to the agent, the agent, a fine gentleman, who was seldom at home, left everything to the head clerk in the office, and the clerk in turn trusted to the reports of the bailiffs on the estate. If a tenant had a grievance, the difficulty he had to face was to find any one who would listen to him ; he was driven from pillar to post, baffled, forced to cringe to the bailiff. On this estate in particular money was always being wanted, and from the agent down every one employed on it held their position as they found money— increased the rental. The bailiff who secured a few more pounds of rent to the office had a passport to favours and effective protection from complaints. The bailiff on the Megillo's Corner estate, you know, was Davy Forsyth, the grandfather of the Forsyth you bought this place from."

"Yes, doctor, I know that."

"Davy, Mr Megillo, was the tenant-at-will of a small farm on the estate, and apparently a great friend of your father's, indeed I think in some way related to him."

"Davy's sister was my uncle's wife—that's all the relationship there was between the families. I never saw her ; my uncle was a widower when he took me to America. I know, doctor, you have to dissect Davy, and you needn't spare the knife on account of the relationship."

"Davy, Mr Megillo, didn't spare your father on account of it. There were, I told you, a dozen holdings like your father's on the Corner estate—for-ever holdings, they were called. Now there are only two, and we would need to call up Davy from the dead to learn how the title to nine of them lapsed to the advantage of the office. About one, your father's, there can be no doubt. Your poor father was fuddled and weak-minded from drink, and did not know how he stood at the time the Bosworth people bought the estate and for a few years after. Before he died, however, being unable to get drink, he became comparatively clear and collected in mind, and adhered consistently to the one statement—a statement he repeated to me when dying, and knowing that he was dying. He said that he distinctly recollected giving Davy for two years his rent to pay into the office, and that Davy did not mind

giving him a receipt, but said it was all right. At the end
of the two years Davy, however, insisted that he was
several years in arrear, and that if he was not he would be
called on to produce the receipts. These he had never got
for two years, and could not find those for previous years,
though he knew they used to be in his desk, tied up in a
bundle. He suspected Davy of having stolen them. Some
time after Davy began saying that there was something
wrong about the old Trafford leases, that the office had
been examining them, and did not allow that they held
good. In point of fact the same threat had been made
against the other leaseholders, whether by the office or its
underlings does not matter, with the effect that some of them
—poor persons, ignorant and powerless—apparently voluntarily surrendered their leases and became tenants under the
office terms. Finally, Davy got him to give up his lease to
the office, under the plea that he, Davy, had become
responsible for the rent, and that if he did so he would be
leniently dealt with. This, of course, left him admittedly
Davy's debtor, who moreover advanced other claims against
him. In the end he was forced or cajoled into assigning
the place to Forsyth in consideration of £12 a year during
his life and that of your sister. Your sister, an imbecile
and consumptive, died a month after leaving the Corner.
The allowance of £12 was not paid on some pretext or
other, and your father was on out-door relief when he
followed her eighteen months after."

"Do you think, doctor," Megillo asked, with judicial
gravity, "Davy Forsyth had a real claim on my father at
all equivalent to the value of the place?"

"I have given you only your father's statement. As for
the secrets of the office, they were as much known to us
here at the time as the secrets of the Russian Government.
To pry into its affairs, or question anything it did, few could
do and live in the country afterwards. But I credited what
your father told me, in the first place, because he was too
feeble in mind to be anything but literal; and, in the next
place, because what he said was consistent with Forsyth's
character, and with what was going on then under the rule
of the office."

Megillo kept like a man of business to his point.

" What would you say, doctor, was the market value of my father's interest at the time ? "

" A licensed house with forty-one acres of land, held under a for-ever lease, at a rent of £15, 15s., ought to have been value for from £800 to £1000, if it found a purchaser."

" Well, doctor, was Davy Forsyth able to lend my father, say, £500, or incur debt to that extent ? Three years' arrear of rent would have been only £47, 5s."

" Davy was called a full man in the country, but he had only twenty acres of land at will and his salary as a bailiff, and he was more given to scheming and intriguing than to working. I think he no more had £50 to lend than he had £500."

" That agrees with my information, doctor. But I am aware that you made some efforts on my father's behalf with unpleasant results for yourself."

" Oh ! what I did is hardly worth mention. I asked Lord Bosworth's then agent, Mr Moreton, to look into the matter himself, as I was afraid there was some mistake, of which he was ignorant. He was a polished gentleman, and although he let me see that I was meddling with what did not concern me, he admitted having heard nothing of the matter, and promised to make inquiries. So he did, from Forsyth and the clerk in the office, and when he met me again expressed surprise that I should take an interest in a man with the character of Leveson Megillo, said that Davy Forsyth was a decent and respectable man, on whose word he could rely, and as for those old leases, they were not worth the paper on which they were written. The fact is, Moreton had no mind of his own, had no business with such a thing. We had a passage at arms, in which he resented my indulgence in a luxury he could not allow to himself. I was a young man then, Mr Megillo, struggling for my living, and it was certainly inconvenient to be in the black books of the office, but I have never yet, I hope, had any true grounds for standing up for what was right only to regret it afterwards."

Mr Megillo shook his head, as men of action do at vague generalities, but Doctor John said, turning to me,—

"In those times, O'Gara, there was only one independent man in the country—the Roman Catholic clergyman. Everyone else—the agent, magistrate, poor-law guardian, Protestant clergyman, Member of Parliament, doctor, schoolmaster—was the nominee and creature of the office. Why, the farmers in whose interest I faced Lord Bosworth's agent were awestruck at my presumption, and took good care to stand aside and let me fight it out alone. But Moreton has had his revenge on me long ago. Now, I am a landlords' man, and in the farmers' black books because I object to them taking the landlords' place, and behaving exactly as the landlords did, setting up an office despotism of their own."

"It strikes me," I said, "that the farmers do not appear to lord it over you. You seem to be on the best of terms with them."

But Megillo allowed no digression.

"I told you, doctor," he said, "I would give you the reason my uncle and myself did nothing to help my father. My uncle, I believe, was aware of his habits, and looked on him as a lost sinner, but at the time of the Civil War he was not only a very poor man, but in a state of religious excitement, which made him pay little attention to family affairs ; he went about preaching a crusade against slavery. I, of course, a soldier, living on my pay, was unable to do anything, but, in fact, never thought of my people in Ireland, or supposed they needed the little help I could give them. When I came over here, by my uncle's direction, I learned something of my father's history, but it was only last spring I became fully informed about it. My uncle, who had been a poor man all his earlier life, became comparatively wealthy, not through any efforts of his own, but through increase in value of some plots of ground he owned beside Pittsburg, and which are now in the city. Two years after I sent over Forsyth to him he died, leaving his property to Belinda, his daughter. Last spring she died, and the house in which I had lived as a boy, with the rest of the property, passed to me, and, in going through my uncle's papers, I came across letters from my father, Davy Forsyth, the younger Forsyth, and some other persons which, for the first time in my life, made me aware of our family and its affairs. The earlier letters—those from old Davy—I may pass over, with the remark that they were evidently intended to prejudice my uncle against his brother, and had the effect, since, until my uncle was a very old man, and, as I said, had become well-to-do, he showed no desire to communicate with our people over here. About 1889, however, he appeared to have heard that my father had lost the old house, and was dead, and wrote, in consequence, to John Forsyth, Davy's grandson, for details. Forsyth's letters to him in answer were painful reading. You know, doctor, the Forsyths were unfortunate from the day they came into possession of our place."

"Unfortunate, Mr Megillo—the people here say that the Forsyths were under a curse. Old Davy died a drivelling sot ; his son, John's father, committed suicide in *delirium tremens*, and that is only part of the story. But luck had nothing to do with it. The Forsyths, or Foursides, as they were called, kept a low public-house, and their history is the common one of persons in that line."

"That's so, doctor, and the old Megillos appear to have been no better than the Forsyths. But John Forsyth simply attributed all the misfortunes of his family, not to the business nor to ill luck, but to the divine wrath, excited by the conduct of his grandfather, Davy, towards my father. He gave a description of this conduct, which was like the confession of a conscience-stricken penitent, and implored my uncle to relieve him from the heritage of sin and shame. Part of the land had been sold, and there was a debt of £300 on the place, which he was unable to pay. He would give it over to my uncle for the £300, and trust to God's mercy to find a living and peace of mind. In this way it came about that my uncle sent me over in 1890 to buy the place."

"What became of John Forsyth," Doctor John asked, " when he went to America ? "

"Forsyth and my uncle were kindred spirits, and they became as brothers. When my uncle died Forsyth became his successor as the leading minister of the Disciples of the Light, or Light-Tights, as our sect was called. I am, indeed, only a nominal adherent, but, although unable to agree with his religious opinions, I have a great respect and regard for Forsyth."

"When I knew him, Mr Megillo, he was in bad health in mind and body, just on the edge of religious monomania. But he did one good thing to my knowledge—he would not apply for a renewal of the licence for this house, though urged by the office to do so, under the impression that it was the interest of the estate to have it kept up."

"He is a strong man now, doctor, and particularly mentally. He knows that I cannot agree with his religious views, but he does not look on me as wrong because he believes himself right. Whatever evil his people did over here the good he has done, and is doing, goes far to atone for it. The old Megillos, by all accounts, left a long account behind them without leaving anyone to straighten it up. I have made pretty well, but only for myself."

"That is always, Mr Megillo, ruled by opportunity, and some would say you fought and lost your hand in a good cause."

"Yes, doctor, my uncle said so, but he was a strange man. When he sent me over here he commanded me strictly to acknowledge my lineage, and if it was in evil repute, to acknowledge that too and bear the burden of it. His doctrine was that we should confess, not hide away, the sins of our fathers, so that, knowing them, feeling them, suffering under them, we should know what beset us, what we should turn away from. You see I have done his bidding, but I cannot take credit for avoiding sins I have no inclination to."

Mr Megillo, with a faint smile, took up the box of cigars and held it open towards us. Visibly giving himself a dispensation in honour of our company he took one himself then.

"The O'Garas and O'Devines, Mr Megillo, do not go on the principle laid down for you by your uncle. We are proud of our ancestors, but it is because they were rascals. The fact is, they would never have figured in history if they were commonplace, decent people. Accepting an ancestry on such grounds, we really accept their title to fame. In a hundred years, when the Bosworths are reduced to poverty, their pride shall be that they are descended from the landlords of the Frayne estate—a pride tinged with regret that the estate system ruined not the people but the Bosworths."

This did not interest Megillo, who said, looking at me,—

"I knew your people in America, Doctor O'Gara, and have seen you once or twice in St Louis. Your family came from Georgia before the War and settled in Osage County in Missouri. You know my business brought me to know a great number of the farmers in Missouri and Kansas."

"I understand, Mr Megillo, your business was lending money to farmers, but I do not think my family ever found it necessary to borrow."

"Not on their land, doctor, and not from our firm, but your father and uncles did a good business, and, of course, needed advances from time to time."

I thought Mr Megillo said this to show that he not only knew my family but their affairs. He, however, went no farther, but said, turning to Doctor John,—

"Your trouble over here has been landlords; the trouble in America will be with money-lenders, but the fault will be none of the money-lenders'. Money on land should go to the land—improve it, enhance its value—but the farmers borrow to meet personal wants—borrow money to live on it. You have heard stories of railroad finance in the States, but the most rotten line that ever was put in the hands of a receiver was well managed compared with the farming business. I know that—it was my business to know how farms were financed. You are bursting up your landlords over here, but I expect when they go you shall have a new crop of difficulties to face."

"Yes, Mr Megillo, but the Britons would never have discarded paint and put on clothes if they had listened to the objections which could be made to clothes. When we have an evil straight before our eyes, we should go at it and not preserve it, because, indeed, we would have other evils to face afterwards. Territorial landlords like the Bosworths made owning land a means of obtaining political power, which simply meant keeping the masses in a servile state.

The title of the disabled, of the non-worker, to property and mastery over the means of existence is a just one, but they have abused and discredited it. Their system is the first evil in the way of progress—blocks the way to remedy for every other evil."

Mr Megillo let this position pass, and became discursive.

"I often, doctor, compared the farming business in my own mind with the business of a great railroad like the Pennsylvania, happening, you know, to have knowledge of both. In the farming business each farmer is his own financier, with the result that the finance of the whole business is simple lunacy. Then again, the organisation of labour is left to each farmer, with a waste of land and labour which would take more time to calculate than ever I had to spare. The whole business is just a big lot of family secrets that would ill bear the light. Your affair with the Bosworth office reminds me that I have brought down the house on me, when in the line of my business I had to go a little into dirty ground. Well, sir, take the Pennsylvania, the biggest railroad in the world; you have its capital, earnings, expenditure, and so on, before you in black and white, and if its finances are not the thing, there are men able and willing to lecture it. Then the man on the road, being able to work, is sure of his place and his wages, and what is more, in the big men over the concern he sees men who began as he did. He has his sick fund, his pension fund, often a free house, and, if he has a grievance, he has a mark to aim at. You know what the farm labourer is in this country, and I know what he is in America ; and though there is some difference we would agree that it is a bad business and badly managed, if only because it cannot afford to treat him better."

Doctor John rose to go, with the remark,—

"Yes, Mr Megillo, and the farmers, conducting their business in a secret hugger-mugger way, are always using their political power to raid on every interest which conducts its business in an open and intelligible way—banks, railroads and every form of organised industry. The merit of great trusts and combines is that, suppose they are robbing the public, the fact is ascertainable, or can easily be made ascertainable, and, therefore, open to correction, but a number of individual farmers and shopkeepers, acting individually, are not only beyond control, but can bring political power to bear against the collective forms of industry, even where these obviously best serve the community."

"In the course of my business, doctor, I was forced to see that. The farmer, to get a small and precarious income from a small turnover, must have big profits, and he can undertake nothing which to pay would need work on the large scale. What the public support in the farming system is a vast number of small, ill-managed concerns, which, just because they are small and ill-managed, need enormous profits. There is no real competition in the system; to barely live the farmer must make these profits, and so far from tolerating competition he is for ever casting about for means to increase them at the expense of competition."

"I might think, Mr Megillo," Doctor John said, bringing the conversation to a conclusion, "that your experience was formed in Ireland instead of America; what you say certainly applies here. But, may I ask, what induces you to stop in the Corner?"

"My health in part, doctor, and in part—I hardly know why. However, I found the voyage, and residing here when I came over first, was of service to me. At the time I thought I had not long to live, but I improved greatly, and, whether I am right or wrong, I believe living as quietly as a mouse here was the reason. I like now coming backwards and forwards. You know I got the habit of travelling in the course of my business, and it sticks to me. I came here only a week ago, and with your help I hope to be away in a month. But, doctor, as I said, it was only when I was in Pittsburg last that I came to know of your kindness to my poor father, and—"

"Now, Mr Megillo, do not say more about that, but when you are able come and see me in Frayne. I would like in particular to hear what you know about the O'Garas. The young doctor here interests himself about us, and when he is severe I would like to have a *tu quoque* for him."

"Now, Roddy," the doctor said, giving the youth a

shilling, "I hear the people of the Corner are not very kindly with Mr Megillo. Why is that?"

We were on the jaunting-car, and the reins in the doctor's hands before Master Roddy answered with a blank expression,—

"I never seed nothing of it. The mon is here and away, and no one knows no more nor me about him. He walks past them hisself as if he never seed one of them."

"Between ourselves, Roddy," Doctor John remarked in a careless tone, "he seems a quiet, decent man enough, and likely to serve one he might take a fancy to. He has plenty of money, the kind of man I like for a patient. Just you bear me in mind, and don't let the old women drive him out of the Corner with their fool stories."

The blank expression on Roddy's face disappeared, to be replaced by a highly intelligent and thoughtful look, which the doctor met with a significant nod.

"Roddy," he remarked to me as we drove away, "forms and leads public opinion in the Corner. As a boy, of course, a bit of persecution recommends itself to him, but once he gets it into his head that Megillo might possibly be of service to him he will put on innocent amiability towards him, and reserve the persecution for the lambs who are not trustfully innocent where he is. He is sure to make the Corner more agreeable for Megillo, and make a friend for himself who can serve him."

XIV

I was only two months and two weeks in South Tyrone, but the time was quite long enough to form a true judgment of the so-called land question.

To find any parallel to that question as it is presented to the popular mind, we would need to go back to the logomachies of the mediæval schoolmen, which endlessly and aimlessly dealt with words, not things which had no base in the observation of facts.

But the parallel would be an imperfect one and unfair to the schoolmen. These thinkers, it may be allowed, were honestly and sincerely in search of truth, and failed to find it through unconsciousness of the method whereby results could only be obtained, and not at all through personal interests determining them consciously or unconsciously to keep to the illusory forms of verbal disputation. In the agrarian question in its current presentation, on the other hand, there is nothing clearer than that personal interests, it does not matter whether consciously or unconsciously, determine the presentation to the form of an interminable and futile verbal disputation, to the form which allows arbitrary solution in favour of the disputant who may be able to get the upper hand by any and every means.

The *raison d'être* of the fairy tale is the intelligence of the child, that of the agrarian logomachy is the intelligence of the public mind. That intelligence stands ready to be trespassed on, and is inevitably trespassed on, played on, reduced to a condition of drivelling confusion and imbecility.

When we say this we enter on the region of observable facts, by the accumulation and comparison of which we may be enabled to form a correct judgment of the agrarian position.

Of the forty-one millions of persons in the British Islands, thirty-seven millions are non-agrarian, not owning, occupying, or living by land, entirely dissociated from possession of it. With the exception of a minute fraction this great non-agrarian majority lives by daily toil, and for each by specialised toil necessarily limiting mental scope. To appeal to the intelligence of this mass is an illicit mental operation, since each member of it, absorbed in his own special pursuit, has not time, means or opportunity to acquire the personal knowledge of facts without which its intelligence is certain to be abused. It trusts and has to trust clergymen for its religion, politicians for its politics, and so on, however much these counsellors by confusion and contradiction may land it in mental impotence. In the agrarian question it goes to the man interested or engaged in agriculture as the man who presumably best knows the business, with the result that its intelligence is not exercised but paralysed, or left merely sensible to flattery.

An attitude of indifference, of suspense of judgment, of muddleheadedness in the great non-agrarian majority, is a fundamental fact in the agrarian position. It is the condition of the position, the condition without which the position could not endure. In general the attitude is one not of downright ignorance, but of confusion of mind induced by conflict of opinion in quarters supposed best qualified to form authoritative judgments. The jury naturally cannot be of one mind when the bench and the lawyers are at variance. The knowledge of the agrarian situation is in the mind of the non-agrarian majority a mere sense of conflicting and contradictory opinions, reducing its intelligence to impotence.

With this fact in view we have to note another fact rapidly obtaining weight. So long as the agrarian minority apparently only trespassed on the intelligence of the non-agrarian majority, it might do so with comparative impunity, but the trespass, always in reality for a material object, is rapidly becoming, with that tangible end in view, calculated to evoke a revolt not to be met or moderated by the usual play on paralysed intelligence. The agrarian in traditional possession of inordinate political power is rapidly placing his conceived interest in mechanical antagonism to not merely the interest, but the vital necessities of the non-agrarian mass, measuring his demands by the tame submission and mental impotence of the last.

For a great many years a legislative experiment has been in process of being carried out in Ireland, which, according to those it was intended to benefit—the so-called agriculturists—has been a complete failure, a judgment corroborated by statistical evidence. The point for us here is that the experiment entails the use or abuse of a vast sum of public money in favour of the small number of occupiers who have an appreciable interest in the land. The use of £120,000,000 is taken from the mass barely above pauperism, and made over to a small body of persons already by virtual possession of valuable property far above the average level of circumstance. It is characteristic of the political juggle that this financial operation is disguised under the form of a loan.

More lately the agrarian has made another gross trespass on the non-agrarian majority by taxing it both in Great Britain and Ireland to pay his own taxes and rates. As a matter of course the majority in submitting to this invited the recent return to the principle of Protection in favour of the agrarian. This step, we may be certain, will be followed by others in exact proportion as the confusion of mind and tame submission of the mass can be reckoned on.

But can it be reckoned on, and to what extent? A conflict from which intelligence is banished can only take one form—the fraud and deception of the Green Republic must find its necessary complement in the untempered violence of the Red; the mass must retort on the agrarian, not in the light of reason, but under a sense of injury and under imperious necessity artificially induced by criminal legislation.

Our primary fact is that that legislation is possible only

as the mass is gulled and deceived, that it represents wilful blindness to the obvious and inevitable facts of human life—facts without due apprehension, due representation, of which its policy must necessarily be one of fraud and deception.

If one thing could be more criminal than this legislation, it would be conduct in a writer claiming clear perception of the facts, and using language calculated to relieve the legislator of responsibility, to allow him without rebuke to pose as the representative of the artificially induced mental impotence of the mass, only to betray it to its own ignorance. This is the only apology I can make for attaching the note of criminality to the long series of legislative measures in the conceived interest of the agrarian.

What is the one great fact of human life—the want of apprehension of which leaves the mass at the mercy of a small minority dominated by selfish interests ?

Averaged, in every hundred human beings only ten are really efficient labour machines—able-bodied men. Where universal military service obtains, it is found that only nine per cent. of the population can be reckoned on as efficient. For reasons well-known to medical men, a large percentage of apparently able-bodied men have to be rejected as inefficient.

The efficiency of this nine per cent. is not a constant quantity; a part is always under temporary disability. Even in peace times an army includes a number under temporary disability, and railroads and factories have the same experience.

Of course the ninety per cent. are not absolutely inefficient ; a large proportion are capable in degree of work, and, in point of fact, are self-supporting in part or whole, although under great liability to temporary total disability. But when this is allowed for, the fact remains that the vast majority of human beings is under complete disability, unable to support itself by its own exertions.

The primary fact of human society is that it is conformed to meet this condition of disability in the majority. This is done in two ways, both replete with glaring imperfection as observed in the actual field. By one way the element capable of labour in any degree is directly subordinated to meet the condition ; by the other, the condition is met by the institution of private property, giving those under disability command over their means of support.

In the first case the family is taken as the unit, and supposed, as a rule, to include a member or members capable by labour of meeting the wants of the members under disability. By going to the actual field and studying a large number of families, we find that the supposed typical case cannot be taken as the general concrete case. Disability, the lot of the majority of individuals, is, though in minor degree, the lot of the majority of families. In theory the head of the family is a worker ; in practice he is commonly aged, or a person otherwise under disability. He owes his position to status, not ability ; the form of the family, not being an industrial evolution, he is essentially a master or overseer of labour, and under no condition of fitness. The family, so far from being an industrial organisation, calculated to meet the general condition of disability, lessens the efficiency of the labour element by subordinating it to mere status, and bringing it under the control of an unnecessarily numerous body of masters under no guarantee of fitness. The failure of agriculture, as an industry, cannot be understood without a reference to the nature and conditions of family labour, to the inefficiency of the family institution as an industrial organisation.

In principle, individual ownership of property, particularly property in land, exists to meet the disability of the majority. By property, under no limitation as to personal ability, women and children, the aged and infirm, the insane even, find security and independence of their means of support. The principle of securing this position for the great majority of mankind is absolutely sound and desirable, and as far as the institution carries the principle into effect it cannot be objected to. The theories under which the majority under disability would be placed absolutely at the mercy of the small efficient element, left virtually dependent on its charity, when stripped of their pretentious disguises stand only for condemnation.

But the principle, as practically carried into effect, is abused rather than asserted, and particularly in respect of

land. Private property, not being designedly held to its
sanction, tends to accumulate in a few hands, and thus
loses its utility as a provision for disability. The opportunity for its accumulation being a function of time, it
tends to accumulate in the hands of the aged out of all
proportion to their numbers. In the hands of the disabled
it is strictly subordinated to the circumstances of disability, its potential application to industry involving
enterprise is limited; it is reduced to sterility and unpro-
ductiveness. From its very nature, again, it serves to
augment the naturally great element of disability by rendering voluntary and self-imposed disability easy and
practicable. The property-supported class, while composed in mass of women, children, the aged and infirm, as
the result of provision made for them by others, includes
men whose abilities are directed to accumulate wealth far
beyond the needs of disability, and use it for the purpose of
obtaining power over their fellow-men. Through that
power they are enabled to perpetuate and lock up by
legalised contrivances vast accumulations of property in
a few hands to the disadvantage of the mass under disability.

From this we can see that the great fallacy, which
vitiates and paralyses the popular mind, is the notion that
the owners and occupiers of land make up an industrial
class, that they carry on as their primary function a great
industry. This, like many notions of the kind, owes its
currency to being taken for granted—assumed as a matter
of course; the moment it is called in question, confronted
with facts, it disappears into the limbo of falsehoods. In
excess of even the average condition the owners and occupiers of land are persons under disability, including the
case of self-imposed disability, and their primary object
and interest is to make possession of the land meet the
case of disability in themselves. They do not carry on an
industry in any true sense; as far as they are concerned no
agricultural industry, speaking of Ireland, exists or can
exist since they are incapable of any industrial pursuit.

An industry exists relatively not to its instruments and
means, but to the extent to which these are worked. An
ironworks shut down for ten months out of twelve, a

factory worked quarter time, these could not be called with propriety industrial concerns; they would rather suggest some idea of loss, waste, or abuse of the means of industry.

In Ireland, of over 20,000,000 acres only 2,400,000 are tilled—under crops other than grass—and represent industrial effort spent on the soil. When we deduct from this worked area gardens, land sublet for cropping, the enforced tillage of small occupiers in barren and congested districts, and the tillage by villagers and others to meet mere personal wants, we are forced to the conclusion that in respect of the man who holds the bulk of the soil no agricultural industry exists; the land in his hands is in a state of nature unworked and waste.

Again the tillage area does not mean necessarily an area of *bona-fide* cultivation. One of the phrases of land agitation in Ireland is "prairie value" used in a wrong sense. When available the prairie value of land in general means the maximum value and productiveness of virgin soil. In Ireland the tillage area represents to a great extent land in process of being worn out, its store of fertility being exhausted by cropping for immediate results. If in one generation a farm by a rare chance is fairly worked, in the next it is certain to be worn out to meet the case of disability—necessarily the common circumstance of human life. Under the system of individual occupation cultivation of the soil is impossible, and much less possible is its sustained cultivation and improvement from generation to generation.

That the result of land legislation has been, not to promote agricultural industry, but to render it easier to the occupier to hold under the condition of disability, is shown by the fact that the worked area has decreased within the last twenty-five years from 3,000,000 to 2,400,000 acres, and is still contracting. Farther, the quality of the working of this area is notoriously deteriorating; its cultivation becoming more and more pinched, starved, and a trespass on the store of fertility in the soil.

Dismissing family labour as applicable to only a small fractional area, and inefficient on that, we find that the typical occupier, the man holding the bulk of the land, meets the condition of disability in himself by hired labour. The principle of landlordism is his principle too ; unable or unwilling to labour himself he uses his possession of the land to command labour. But in reality there are two ways in which he may maintain his position : by one he foregoes a share of the profits of cultivation in favour of the labourer, by the other he foregoes the potential capability of the soil, and reduces its working to a minimum, so as to barely support himself without regard to the capabilities of the soil.

In a not-distant past he had in Ireland at his beck a fiercely competitive labour supply — cheap, semi-servile, struggling to keep itself from starvation and extinction, and struggling in vain. One of the current delusions of our time is the reading of the agrarian position in the light of the interest of the owner and occupier of land. Like the majority of the whole community the majority of its agrarian section was, as it still is, at the mercy of the property-holding class, that is, the class peculiarly under disability. But the position of the agrarian majority, the agricultural labourer, was, as it is yet, far below the average level of the working class, and it was by command of this labour on his own terms that the occupier was able to maintain his position in the past.

But the terms allowed the labourer, the conditions of his existence were impossible, and with his disappearance the occupier has been forced to betake himself more and more to the expedient of minimising to the utmost the cultivation of the land. Given a sufficient area he can do so, and it is his interest to do so. Quite apart from the condition of personal disability which he has to meet, his interest is better served by holding 200 acres in a state of nature, as a cattle run, than by working twenty-five or fifty acres for an equal return. In general he is incapable of the latter task, while the vocation of a dealer or speculator in cattle, calling for little exertion in the way either of actual labour or of the employment and organisation of labour, is as a rule within his powers. But this is the business of the typical occupier, and the business is as much an industry as the business of a dealer on the Stock Exchange. With a difference, however. The occupier, in subordinating the possession of the land to the circumstances of his individual life, disadvantages to an incalculable extent the great non-agrarian majority, whose very existence is endangered by the non-cultivation of the soil and consequent dependence on foreign-raised food. Even setting aside the national peril implied by dependence on the foreigner for food, the vast sums paid away for such food represents so much money which should go to labour cultivating the land, and would if the land was not locked away out of the reach of capital and labour.

We are told that cultivation does not pay, that without protection, that is, the taxation of the community, it cannot pay. From what I have said it can be seen that the occupier, being in general a person under disability, protection, relief from local taxation and every other boon conferred on him at the expense of the community, only enables him the better to meet the condition of disability by still farther dispensing with the labour of cultivation. Under protection he would not raise two bullocks where he now raises one, but one where he now raises two.

It is evident that cultivation yields, and must yield, exorbitant profits. Such as it is, it is nearly altogether in the hands of small men carrying it on under the most disadvantageous circumstances. The tillage area is the very poorest part of the land, tilled because worthless as permanent pasture. A great part of it is land let year by year by auction at a rack-rent. The size of the patches, and the means and methods of the holders, show that its working is uneconomical in the extreme. This limited and ill-worked area of poor land supports certainly three-fourths of the agrarian population of Ireland, and obviously could not do so if the returns from it were not both large and certain. The small occupier tilling land is in no position to risk much ; his income is small indeed, but for that very reason, considering the size, working and tenure of his holding, must represent an enormous margin of profit. Like the petty trader and village shopkeeper because his turnover is small, to live at all, the profits of the small tillage farmer must be enormous. That his patch of ill-

worked land supports him from year to year is sufficient
proof of the fact.

We can have no more striking example of the mental
impotence to which the popular mind is reduced by the
agrarian logomachy than the assertion that cultivation
does not pay, and needs to be bolstered up by protection,
invidious differential taxation, loans of vast sums of public
money, and legislative juggles with property—juggles which
unsettle and disorder the whole social framework, and set
every principle of jurisprudence, every conclusion of common-sense, at defiance.

This is seen by the fact that politically this legislation
tends to the expropriation, not only of the landowner, but
of the large occupier, and the sub-division of the land
among a supposed working class of occupiers. A policy of
the kind is not an expression of principle or reason, but of
brute force actuated by immediate personal interest. Take
away the personal interest of the occupier of five acres to
increase his holding at the expense of his neighbour with a
hundred acres, take away his power of asserting that interest, and we would hear nothing of the policy. As matter
of reasoning from ascertainable facts, as an assertion of
principle, it would never occur to anyone.

The area in the hands of the large occupier—that is,
taking both quality and quantity into account, three-fourths
of the whole country—represents gross waste of the land to
the injury of the whole community. On this area it is scarcely
an exaggeration to say that there is one overseer of labour
to one labourer, and the overseer, being under disability,
there is virtually a loss of the whole area to efficient labour
and the purposes of the community. But though the community is deeply injured, the system does not directly produce a mass of misery; it produces paupers indeed out of
all proportion to the numbers employed, but it does not
and cannot produce them in such mass as to create a great
public danger.

In the case of the small and poor area on which the
agrarian mass is crowded it is different. Here there is
both waste of land and waste of labour. Broken up into
small patches in subordination to the personal conditions
of life of the occupiers, the land cannot possibly be economi-

cally worked; the work which one man could do is done by four or five, who, as labourers, are fitful, untrained, and, perforce, the greater part of their time in idleness. So far from being a school of industry, the small occupiers' system condemns even the efficient labourer to enforced idleness and all the evil habits engendered thereby. This, even more than limitation of area, accounts for the historical failure of the system, and condemns the attempts to turn the whole of Ireland into a congested district—a country in which the great natural majority under disability would be increased by the inefficiency and demoralisation of the labour element. Deeply prejudiced by the non-industrial form of land tenure the community would have, as in past times, to meet a horrible mass of human misery, famine and pauperism.

With the actual facts of the agrarian position, gathered in the field of observation, in view, it cannot be difficult to see the lines which reform of the agrarian system must take in the interest of the non-agrarian majority, imperatively demanding the cultivation of the land, and consequent freedom from dangerous and costly dependence on the foreigner for food; in the true interest also of the agrarian, whether a person under disability or an efficient labourer.

In the first place, the principle of preserving to the majority under disability independence of the means of support by means of ownership of property has to be firmly maintained. If the Irish farmer was a cultivator of the soil, which he is not, his claim on that ground to expropriate anyone—a landlord, a woman, child, lunatic— from their interest in the soil, to lessen that interest in any degree even, should be set aside as impolitic and unjust. In general, every claim made by the minority— the temporarily efficient labour element—to property in the hands of the disabled, on the ground that it is the actual producer, should be rejected as contrary to the general interest. The legislation which admits the claim of the Irish tenant to ownership of the soil on the ground that he labours it admits a false principle, and admits it under a false pretext.

But the title of the disabled to property in the soil must

be affirmed subject to the general interest; the waste and abuse of the land to meet the condition of disability invalidates the title, and the gross abuse of political power by the propertied agrarian class raises an issue which can only be ultimately settled in one way.

It is fully in the power of the class, the owners and occupiers of the land, not only to meet the general interest and so secure title under disability, their particular interest, but to increase enormously the return from their property. In the land they possess an unworked gold mine, the title to which is invalidated by its non-working, by trespass on the common interest, and by their own virulent and never-ending disputes. All that they can settle by working their property as a gold mine is worked, that is, by the methods of modern organised industry.

A gold mine, a railroad, a bank is worked not by its owners but for them by an efficient staff of workers under efficient managers, both in measured proportion to the work to be done. We can get an idea of what commercial and industrial enterprise would be if managed on the lines agriculture now is, since its development is a recent chapter in history.

A hundred years ago, like Irish agriculture now, the business of transportation was under the individualised system, in the hands of persons under or liable to disability. A country village for intercourse with market was dependent on a carrier, and when he or his horse fell ill its business was paralysed. Like the small farmer and petty shopkeeper, the carrier, to live at all, required to make relatively enormous profits; what would cost now £5 to transport would then for the same distance cost £100. But, virtually, the business as it exists now, with a vast number of persons finding constant and certain support by it, cannot be said to have existed. It was called into existence, not by depriving the disabled of their support, but by the elimination of their disability, with the result of not only vastly increasing the work done profitably, and the numbers employed, but of vastly increasing the fund available for the support of disability.

What is necessary, not to improve British agriculture, but to call it into existence as an industry in the proper sense, is not the destruction of the title of the owner and occupier to the land on the ground of disability to cultivate it, but the elimination of their disability from its management.   What stands to be swept away are not legal titles to property, but the crowd of useless overseers of labour with no labour to oversee, who call themselves farmers.   One efficient manager could do what a hundred of these men do, or rather pretend to do—he would, indeed, have his work almost entirely to create.   What goes now to this crowd as farmers, not as owners, would go to an efficient staff of actual labourers, but again, this staff in the main would create the fund which would support it as well as the dividends which would go to those having any legal title to ownership of the soil.   The crowd of small occupiers who are labourers with no scope for their labour, ever on the dangerous edge of things, would be equally bound to go as farmers, not as having any proprietary interests.   The principle to be affirmed is that if one skilled man can manage 20,000 acres he should do so in order that the margin for labour and the owner shall be as large as possible.   The self-evident vice of the present system is that a manager to every thirty acres under no condition of ability leaves no margin to figure as rent or wage fund.

It was not Free Trade in food, but the organisation of the business of transportation on the lines of joint-stock enterprise, rendering a great trade possible, which has left British agriculture a puzzle to those who, instead of studying it in the actual field, evolve conditions for it out of their own consciousness, and make them tolerate demoralising legislative expedients to bolster up what they do not understand, or take the proper means of understanding, the system of individual occupation in the actual field.

It may be said that it was the invention and application of machinery that created the business of transportation. Without the simultaneous development of joint-stock enterprise with the elimination of individual disability from management, its characteristic feature, the potentialities of machinery would have lain dormant and useless, as practically they do now in the case of the cultivation of the soil.

It is not only to be admitted, but to be borne constantly in mind for the sake of the lessons it conveys, that the history of that development is a long, chequered chapter of failures, gradually, and, even yet, only partially overcome. Most of the British railroad companies, and nearly all the American as they now exist, are built up of bankrupt concerns, representing gross mismanagement and loss of capital. The methods of collective industry were painfully blundered into as a matter of experience, but this is the strongest possible testimony to their vitality, and the record stands to guide us in the application of the principle to the cultivation of the land. In the light of experience it is not necessary to repeat obvious errors.

It is, of course, a gross mistake to speak of British agriculture as having been at any time a prosperous industry. The landowner confessedly was never an industrial; he devolved the actual task of cultivation on another to meet the case of disability, involuntary or voluntary, in himself. Under no test of ability, the occupier in the case of four-fifths of the area of the country did exactly the same thing, but was able to do so because the mass of the agrarian population, steeped in abject misery, was at his command to work for him on his own terms. It is characteristic of the trespass on the popular intelligence to ask us to measure agricultural prosperity by the rents and profits of the non-industrial owner and occupier, and not by the condition of the mass brutalised under perennial experience of famine.

What the owner and occupier complain of in common with other capitalists is an effect of the growth of wealth. With the growth of realised wealth the return from it tends to steady decrease. The man whose father got £500 from £10,000 in Consols gets now only £250 for the same investment, and the experience is general for capital not employed in progressive and developing business. I have said that the individualised system needs to maintain it enormous profits, but, restricting production, these profits are maintained with the increasing difficulty which returns from employment of capital and labour in every stationary and unprogressive business show. The condition of the agricultural labourer has improved, but that is due to the vast decrease in his numbers, the wage fund out of which he is paid being stationary or diminishing, but distributed among a greatly decreased number. Flow of new capital to the cultivation, reclamation and improvement of the land there is virtually none, and this means the amortisation of the capital already sunk in it. The industrial value of land, like that of railroads, to be kept up needs an incessant flow of new capital, but that is denied to it simply because the owners and occupiers, non-industrial and under disability, use it not as the means of industry but in subordination to the untoward fluctuating circumstances of individual life.

No legislation can recall to the service of the owner and occupier of land the famine-stricken mass of labour which made their system possible in past times. No measure of protection can meet the cheapening of food by the industrial organisation of the means of transport. No attempt in favour of the agrarian propertied interest to arrest the fall in the return from invested capital can be otherwise than mischievous and nugatory. That the propertied agrarian class demands and obtains compensation for the emancipation of labour from servile dependence on it, for the competition of the organised industry of transportation and for the fall in the return from capital is the clearest possible proof of the proposition from which I started, of the mental impotence of the British and Irish people to grasp the fact that their dangerous and wasteful dependence on foreign-raised food is due to the system which leaves their own land in the hands of the disabled.

To realise the folly of bolstering up that system at the expense of the community it so deeply injures should be the first task of awakened public intelligence. But that intelligence should go far beyond mere resistance to flagrant trespass on it. The necessity for doing away with the rude, antiquated and haphazard management of the land by the individual under the inevitable conditions of individual life, is such as calls for a new chapter in legislation. But the true interest of the agrarian is voluntarily to adopt the organisation on modern collective lines of agricultural industry, to create agriculture as an industry, what it never has been, never can be, under the system of individual management.

Under a system whereby the land would be worked by joint-stock companies, as the railroads are, the so-called landowner, the owner in reality of only a rent-charge visibly in process of being extinguished without compensation, would have an interest in the potential capabilities of the soil secured to him. The occupier, a man in general as much under disability as the landowner, incapable of labour and of organising labour, would equally find security for any interest he can justly claim. The agricultural labourer, representing the bulk of the agrarian population, would have the land opened up as a field for employment, without which "three acres and a cow," labourers' cottages and the rest, are but a play on his ignorance and childish cupidity. Put in the position of the workman on a railroad, old-age pensions, proper housing and chances of advancement in life would follow as a matter of course. The London and North-Western and the Pennsylvania railroad companies do not complain that their business is crippled for want of labour, as the farmers do, but that is because life is possible for labour under them, as it is not under the individual farmer. The greatest interest of all, that of the great non-agrarian majority, would be met by the sustained cultivation and improvement of the soil on the large scale which the collective organisation of agriculture only can effect. The maximum production effected by an efficient minimum of labour means not only a greatly increased agrarian population under secure conditions for life, but the relief of the whole population from dangerous and costly dependence on imported food. No one who realises the fact that little more than a tenth of the available area of the British Islands is under a pretence to cultivation can deny the potential capability of the whole area to support the whole population. It is for everyone to realise that that capability lies dormant through the utter disability of those who own and occupy the land to cultivate it under the system of management by the individual. Supposing the management capable, to force up the price of food would be impolitic and unjust, but to force it up only to enable the aged and incompetent the better to dispense with the labour of cultivation is the outrage which the community allows to be inflicted on its sense and interest. The cultivation of the land on the large scale as an organised industry could be reckoned on to increase the return to the propertied class from land, to increase the wage fund in the interest of the labourer, and to secure to the community a cheapened and abundant supply of home-raised food.

The steady decrease of the population of Ireland, ascribed to misgovernment, is the common case of all agrarian communities under the individual system. The agrarian population of Great Britain has decreased even more than that of Ireland ; the decrease being disguised in the larger island by a great increase in the non-agrarian element. Practically the same thing is taking place in America. Only a small part of the later settled areas in the United States is worked under exceptional conditions on the large scale so as to produce food for export. The long-settled parts under the inevitable operation of the individual system of occupation and management, under no guarantee of ability, physical or mental, are fast lapsing into the same condition as Ireland. The wearing-out, waste and abuse of the land to meet the circumstances of individual life, its general condition of disability, is just as apparent in America as in Ireland and Europe, and is rapidly becoming a menace to its future prosperity. The agrarian position in France, Germany, Russia and other countries is the same, due not to limitation of area and capability in the land, but to the disability of those who occupy and pretend to cultivate it. In Ireland, however, as a more purely agrarian country than any of these, the outcome of the incessant struggle of disability, the lot of the majority, to dispense with labour and live by rent, the revenue spontaneously offered by nature or accident, determines decrease of population, not only real but apparent. This decrease can only be arrested by organisation of agricultural labour ; unorganised labour, that is, making labourers small occupiers under the uncorrected conditions of individual life, would only add a mass of human misery to decay of population, turn a painless into a painful operation. As I said, agriculture has to be created in

Ireland; a waste and uncultivated country has to be brought under sustained and systematic cultivation. This would mean not only a vast increase in the mass employed, but an elevation of that mass to conditions of life unknown under the system of individual occupation and management. Under that system the agrarian mass has only given inefficient and uneconomical labour under famine-stricken and degraded conditions, has ever been, as it still is, a hopeless blot on humanity and civilisation.

This organisation of labour, depending on the elimination of disability in the actual management of the land can only be effected by replacing the crowd of incompetent farmers by great land cultivating associations, in which the cost of management would be, with due regard to efficiency, reduced to a minimum, leaving an adequate margin for effective labour. The present owners and occupiers would become shareholders in these associations, and, while foregoing the actual task of management, for which, from numbers and disability, they are unfit, retain the usual powers of control of shareholders in other industrial concerns. Setting aside the area necessary for residential and private purposes, the great area devoted to agriculture would be thrown into blocks allowing economical working and the application of machinery. The business of the association being purely industrial, speculative dealing in cattle, the true business of most of the large Irish farmers, would be swept away. The association would raise beef, mutton and bacon for sale, not drive cattle round country fairs on the chance of making a few pounds by buying and selling. It would cultivate grass and feeding-stuffs, and not depend on wild pasture, the poor yield of which is trampled and destroyed to a greater extent than eaten by the few wandering beasts it supports. It would raise cereals on the great scale, depending not on high prices for its profit, but on small returns from the largest possible yield, place the business on the sound basis of unrestricted production, not on the mischievous fallacy of high prices for a restricted production, the necessary principle of individual management. Instead of gambling and division of profits on no economical principle but to suit the circumstances of the individual, the association would aim at unifying the industry, so as to secure a small but adequate profit from a great whole, not large profits at the expense of the public from a great number of small parts. Thus it would revive the decayed milling industry of the country, because its policy would be to sell what it would raise in the form the immediate consumer buys.

The finance of the individual farmer is proverbial in spite of the fact that there is, and there cannot be, any accurate knowledge of it, and therefore no control whatever over it. The interest of a population of forty-one millions in the land is so great that what ought to be matter for strict public audit is beyond, not criticism, but guesswork, for its confusion, folly, and extravagance after all is only very imperfectly guessed at. The supreme merit of cultivating associations would be that their finance would be in the light, would and could be made to bear the light. For this reason they would and could command the capital necessary for the cultivation, improvement, and reclamation of the land. The command would follow on the open and intelligible dealings of a corporation giving the security depending on knowledge of its business, a security the individual system utterly fails to give.

The creation of agricultural industry under joint-stock enterprise would open a new chapter in the history of the British Islands, in the history of mankind.

" Of all possessions in a country, land is the most desirable. It is the most fixed. It yields its returns in the form of rent with the least amount of labour or forethought to the owner. But in addition to all these advantages, the possession of it confers such power that the balance of power in a State rests with the class that has the balance of land.

" The laws of most of the States of Europe since the Northern invasions have been made by the landowners. They represent the conquerors, and have been enabled to prescribe to the mass of the people on what conditions they shall live on the land, or whether indeed they shall live there at all.

" The term 'settlement,' of such great import in the history of Ireland in the seventeenth century, means nothing else than the settlement of the balance of the land according to the will of the strongest; for force, not reason, is the source of law."[1]

It is in these terms that the historian of the *Cromwellian Settlement of Ireland* introduces his subject. The terms apply with only verbal modification to what may be called the Gladstonian Settlement of the nineteenth century of the same unfortunate country.

Both these settlements are expressions of force, not reason, but the first was a natural common exhibition of force, while the last was non-natural and unprecedented. The first meant that the few strong should master the many weak, while the last means that the majority, irrespective of the fact that it is under disability, shall have the monopoly of force. Numbers acting as votes in the Parliamentary mechanism, the modern incarnation of force, decides that the possession of the land shall rest in the hands of the disabled, who have the majority of votes, and whose policy, dictated by the first rude mind of disability, is to use the possession, not as a means of industry, but as giving returns with the least amount of labour and forethought. It is a policy determined not by potential capabilities of the soil, not by the supreme interest of the community demanding the development of these capabilities, but by unreasoned subordination to the disability, which is the necessary lot of the majority of mankind.

But those who possess, or shall possess, the balance of the land under the Gladstonian Settlement of Ireland have neither force nor reason to rest on. The transfer of that balance from 2000 landowners to 50,000 tenants leaves force where it was—with agrarian disability—and the greater mass of non-agrarian disability armed with a precedent for its irrational employment. The power of the land in the hands of the disabled to support disability is extremely limited, but the possession in a form demanding neither labour nor forethought determines the mass under disability to a never-ending struggle for what meets its immediate necessities.

---

[1] *Cromwellian Settlement of Ireland.* J. P. Prendergast, 1875. Preface to First Edition.

Our position here throughout has been that the power of the land to meet the case of disability is wholly undeveloped, and that the propertied agrarian class misconceives and endangers its interest. This applies everywhere, not in Ireland alone. In the United Kingdom, however, the interest peculiarly representative of disability not only places the great non-agrarian majority under the disadvantage of being dependent on foreign-raised and therefore high-priced food, but makes incessant attacks on its interest, intelligence, and temper. It does so simply to meet the case of its own disability; it does so again because it is under mental disability; it is stupid, selfish, unintelligent, dominated by the immediate necessities of a false and uneconomical position. That position commits the agrarian,— landlord, tenant, labourer alike, to an interminable struggle one with the others, and to never-ending trespass on the industrial non-agrarian interest. It gives the country not only waste and abuse of the land and dependence on the foreigner for food, but distrust of government and legislation, not the less profound because vague, in the general mind. With the few who with clearer thought anticipate, and to some extent decide, future events, the feeling is one not of distrust but of bitter contempt for law, which, resting on no base in reason and conscience, can give no measure of finality, for anarchy under the form of law surely inviting the anarchy which sets the form aside as a mockery.

The creation of agriculture as an industry would indeed open a new chapter of human history. We can hardly realise what the United Kingdom would be, secure of its food supply, and employing on its own soil the vast sums it now pays to the foreigner for food. But this great benefit would not stand alone, the emancipation of the State from the pressure and undue influence of a system incurably distempered by its own internal economy, would clear out of the way the greatest obstacle to government rested on stable principles. Irish land legislation is only a passing expression of general agrarian action, the same always, differing only in using the forms of law instead of war to answer the arbitrary judgments of personal interests.

These judgments, once answered for the time being by open war, may now be answered by legislation for a time, but from their very nature only to serve personal ends, setting aside, prohibiting, or disadvantaging the principle of devoting the land to its industrial object by the best means possible. The Legislature, in committing itself to the struggle between landlords, occupiers, and agricultural labourers for the possession of the land, commits itself to what history shows is mere matter of what personal interest is uppermost. In the past it was subservient to the interest of the landlord, the charge against whom was that his interest was an incubus on industry. It has come to give weight now to the interest of the man who occupies but does not work the land, who is even more than the landlord an encumbrance on industry. As the agricultural labourer, through weight of numbers, is fast getting the upper hand, it is really committed to a policy of subdivision of the land in his personal interest, and to the protracted and mischievous struggle which the policy implies. But can it pretend to itself that this policy is determined by economic principle, or otherwise than as the policy in favour of the landlord and occupier was successively determined, that is, by the arbitrary judgment of the landlord and occupier in a position to assert itself?

The economic reasons against giving the land to the agricultural labourer, that is, indiscriminately to numbers, are far stronger than those against any other form of ownership, but how can we appeal to reasons which never had weight in the councils of the State? The labourer personally covets a patch of land, and how can we appeal against his arbitrary judgment in a position of power to principles the landlord and occupier ignored and violated? We need not tell him that he does not get what he really wants—security of his means of existence and under the condition of disability, since that requires not that he shall possess a patch, but that the land shall be worked under economic conditions for a maximum production. The possession of the patch meets his immediate necessity, and need we appeal to him in a position of power over the State to deny himself on the grounds that he would overload the land with disability and inefficient labour in perilous dependence on inflated returns from restricted production, that he would expose his class and the whole community to danger of famine and certainty of incalculable evils? We might, if ever we could point to peers and squires and farmers, who thought for themselves by thinking for others, and refrained from using their power over the State to meet their own personal ends.

We pass from landlord to occupier, from occupier to labourer, in a position of political power only the more clearly to bring into view the certain but incalculable evil of agrarian control of the State. The agrarian system is all of a piece, its power always the same, whether exerted by landlord, occupier or labourer; it is a mere delusion the idea now acted on, that the system by serving one of its factions at the expense of the others, or all of them at the expense of the community, can be endowed with the industrial ability it so conspicuously lacks. Retaining its present form, its essential evil, the mismanagement, paralysis and oppression of the capable industrial minority, must remain, and its disability exaggerated by standing in its own light remain a hopeless burden and insensate tyranny in the State.

Between an economic principle and its practical application there is, however, a vast difference. Principles sound in themselves receive effective application only as they overcome in practice the weakness of human nature, and the obstacle is one never to be completely overcome. The vital status of mankind allows only an imperfect development of industry; the general mind is not under the influence and guidance of industrial habits and aptitudes. I have not only pointed out but dwelt on the fact that the principle of working an industry for a maximum production by an organised minimum of efficient labour was only painfully and by gradual steps blundered into, and presents a long chapter of errors, contradictions and misfortunes. Not, indeed, until the principle was in actual operation did it receive recognition—a recognition even yet far from being logical or simply descriptive. But if anyone now would have modern industry discard the principle and return to ancient ways, he would express and illustrate, not imperfect apprehension of the principle, but true, though unconscious, apprehension of the fact that the general mind has no industrial objective, that though industry, and peculiarly its modern form, exists for the mass it exists in spite of it. But though the principle in operation may be obstructed by playing on this nature of the general mind, still the vitality it has shown in surmounting imperfection in the human agency and surviving embarrassment and disaster gives promise that its application to agriculture would be as successful as its application to the business of transportation, producing food as no unorganised crowd of individuals possibly can, just as it does what no unorganised crowd of individual carriers could do.

The proposal to work the land by joint-stock enterprise because constructive justifies destructive criticism of the existing agrarian system, but such criticism is able to stand on its own merits. Toleration of the system through inability to see anything to put in its place does not justify toleration of want of study of it as a form of human agency. Every day we hear the crowd of occupiers on the land described in endlessly varied terms of flattery, as an intelligent and industrious class of men, not as a mere crowd of average individuals. From the false assumption by reasoning equally in error, it is concluded that the class should have ownership of the land in contradiction to the fundamental principle that ownership of property should be the provision for the majority under disability. What the occupier really is in the concrete field is as obtrusive as the gorse thistles and rocks of the wasted land, but if he was fully competent as an industrial the fact would exclude his claim to ownership. His actual title is his personal disability, and the title to occupation and ownership on that base might be defended if it did not involve in waste and non-cultivation of the soil an intolerable injury to the community.

The indictment brought in these pages against the present agrarian system is that it inflicts such injury on the community, and again, under a disguise of transparent falsehood, makes government and legislation the mindless instrument of the most important and conspicuous failure of the human agency in its industrial capacity. The last point would stand for consideration even if reform of system on the lines of modern industry was not thought possible.

THE END